THE
HEALING
BEGINS
TODAY

A Memoir of
**Paralysis, Recovery and
Creating a New Life**

To Martha,

RANDY OATES

Randy Oates

ISBN: 1499705417
ISBN 13: 9781499705416
Library of Congress Control Number: 2014910135
CreateSpace Independent Publishing Platform
North Charleston, South Carolina
Printed by Createspace

For "Sam,"

whose unconditional love, support, and patience were critical to getting me back on my feet. She married a senior athlete and, seventeen months later, was the caretaker for a paraplegic. Without her, I wouldn't be putting one foot in front of the other today.

—Randy

Contents

Contents

Preface

This is a true, personal memoir about a life-changing paralysis that was the result of a common medical procedure gone tragically wrong, after one of my best triathlon finishes. There were many times I couldn't see any light at the end of a long, dark tunnel, as I was facing the prospect of living as a paraplegic for the rest of my life due to damage to the base of my spinal column. The doctors whom my wife and I consulted didn't have any good news, and most of them were unable to give us much, if any, hope of me being able to walk again. Consequently, we tried many different therapies to rebuild my body and create a new life.

Spinal column injuries have devastating consequences, and, as more than one doctor told us, no two injuries are the same. As a result, what worked for my recovery may not work for those with similar injuries. Even so, I found that with hope, perseverance, hard work, and the right therapists, it is possible to enjoy life and feel like a whole person.

We were fortunate to have the support of dear friends and capable and caring therapists, and we found some medical professionals who were very helpful. It's difficult to recall everyone who participated in my recovery, and I may have inadvertently left out a few names, which I regret. However, I have tried to mention by name the majority of the friends and therapists who were active participants in my recovery process. As I point out several times in this book, I couldn't have done this by myself. It took a village of dedicated people to help rebuild my broken body, and I am most grateful for their active participation in the process.

Please note that all of the doctors' names in this book have been changed to protect their privacy. However, I trust that Dr. Rehab and Dr. Hope will recognize themselves and their significant contributions to my recovery.

My goal in writing this memoir was twofold: first, to provide hope, encouragement, and guidance to anyone who experiences a tragic, life-changing injury; and second, to recognize the many people who made my recovery possible, especially my "Holy Trinity" of my wife, Sam; my son Greg; and my dear friend Mickey Freeman. I found no easy solutions or miracles; however, I have learned things over the last seven years that I believe will help anyone who is faced with obstacles that seem impossible to overcome.

Part I

One

The Summer of 2007

L iving in Little Rock, Arkansas, in the summer of 2007, I felt I had the world by the tail. One day a friend asked how I was enjoying my retirement, and I said, "I'm living the life I had only dreamed of." And I meant it.

While I was never a very good student in school, I surprised my father, and even myself at times, at how well I did in the business world. After graduating from the University of Arkansas in June 1965, I quickly found that the people I worked for didn't care about my grades in school or what organizations I belonged to. Common sense, the ability to learn the business, commitment to the job, and hustle were more important than academic background. I had worked at a local bank for a couple of summers during college, and after initially working for eighteen months with Foley's Department Store in Houston, Texas, I returned to First National Bank in Little Rock and found my career. At the university, I majored in marketing and really wasn't interested in being a traditional banker. What I wanted to do was advertising and marketing in the financial industry, which is where I spent most of my adult life. I was truly blessed to work for some very talented people and loved the challenge of bank marketing during the seventies and eighties, when the industry was changing and becoming much more competitive. Best of all, my last two jobs were my best two jobs, first as marketing director for a bank in Shreveport, Louisiana, and next creating a marketing department for

Bank of the Ozarks in Little Rock. I did have my share of stumbles in my career and made some mistakes, but I always recovered and was able to move forward.

As a child, I always wanted to be an athlete, but I was smaller than the other boys and was usually the last to be chosen for any pick-up game. As an adult, I realized that by working hard and learning quickly, one could enjoy most sports. I always loved the water and took up racing sailboats, and I was fortunate to win my share of regatta trophies. I also started running to stay in shape and started competing in some 5K and 10K races and eventually ran two marathons in under four hours. Then I added cycling, which I really enjoyed, and triathlons followed. As I look back, I can remember so many good times competing and having fun experiences in all of these sports. One of my biggest thrills was racing with Max Mehlburger on his thirty-eight-foot Swan sailboat to Bermuda. We finished first overall in our initial race and won our class in the second race two years later. That was quite an accomplishment for some small-boat sailors from Arkansas. I had done most of the things I wanted to do in life and was able to retire at sixty, in the spring of 2004. This gave me more time to indulge in my passion for running, biking, and triathlons. I also took time off every year to visit a sailing buddy in Apalachicola, Florida, for a couple of weeks. We had great fun together sailing in Apalachicola Bay and canoeing the Wakulla River, and we enjoyed the fresh seafood direct from the bay. Best of all, six months after my retirement, I met the love of my life. I had been divorced for many years and was determined that I was never, ever getting married again. But all that changed overnight when I met Hermine "Sam" Wellner. Eighteen months later, we were married, which was one of the smartest decisions of my life. The summer of 2007, we were having the time of our lives together. We hiked in Sedona, Arizona; rafted on the Colorado River; sailed in Florida; cruised in the Caribbean; and danced wherever we had the chance. On the dance floor, it seemed like we had been partners all our lives.

I originally met Pete and Sandy Heister at the sailing club in the 1970s and since they were also runners we started training and hanging out together at local races and became very good friends. They had already completed a couple of marathons and when I decided to attempt the 26.2-mile distance they helped me train for my first marathon. Twenty years later in 1996 they suggested we try a short-distance triathlon. They were both good swimmers, so they offered to help me learn to swim the distance, and I would help them with the biking. I was not a particularly fast cyclist, but I had good endurance, was a strong runner, and believed I could learn to swim up to a mile. With some training, I thought I could be competitive in this three-event sport.

While I was comfortable in the water, learning to efficiently swim anywhere from one-quarter to one-half of a mile in open water turned out to be more challenging than I expected. I could cover the distance well enough, but it wore me out, and I was anything but efficient in the water. Moreover, swimming in small and sometimes muddy lakes, surrounded by about a hundred or so other competitors all starting at the same time, can be a taxing experience. It's very difficult to swim efficiently while constantly avoiding other swimmers and trying to find the turn buoys, which look large from shore but can be hard to see at water level. Consequently, my first triathlons were, to say the least, not pretty. However, I did find that I had decent speed on the bike and was better on the run than many competitors in my age group.

The first part of a triathlon is usually the swim, and the organizers break the competitors up into age groups that start in "waves" about five minutes apart. Starting a race this way, especially on small lakes, keeps the congestion down on the swim course. All competitors' times are based on which swim wave they start in. I still have a fond memory of a very humbling experience in one of my early races at Beaver Lake in Conway, Arkansas. The legendary Arkansas Ironman, Kurt Truax, who was three years older than I was, started in a swim wave at least five minutes after my start and caught me on the run a half-mile from the finish line, wearing a neck brace from a bike accident several weeks before. Kurt was a very good competitor who always offered me helpful advice and encouragement. As he came up beside me in that crazy-looking neck brace, he congratulated me on a good race and said, "Come on; why don't you run in with me?" I appreciated the fact that he thought I still had enough speed left to run with him. While gasping for air, I told Kurt I was going about as fast as I could and advised him to go on ahead. Kurt was an amazing triathlete. He had done several Ironman Triathlons and finished on the podium in his age group a couple of times in Hawaii at the World Championships, yet he was always very humble and would congratulate other competitors on their finishes. He became a good friend, and I always hoped that someday I might be able to finish close to him, but it would have to be at a much shorter distance than Ironman.

The triathlons that I competed in were usually sprint distance races, which was something I could complete in around two hours or less, depending on the course. This was mostly a summer sport in Arkansas and surrounding states, so the lakes were warm enough for the swim. At a sprint triathlon, the swim courses were usually a quarter to a little over half a mile. The bike courses varied from thirteen to twenty miles, and the run was three to four miles, depending on the event. While none of these distances are very arduous on their own, when all three of them are put together, especially in the summer heat, even a sprint distance triathlon can be a tough test of one's endurance. One of the most critical components of having the endurance to finish a triathlon is proper diet and hydration. I was always careful about what I ate and drank in the thirty-six hours leading up to a race, and I tried to have a light dinner of mostly carbohydrates the night before. The morning of a race, I would eat a banana as soon as I got up, along with V8 juice, which helped my elimination process before leaving the hotel. I also made sure I drank plenty of fluids, mostly water with some sport drinks, for the three days leading up to a race. Drinking a lot of fluid twenty-four hours before a race won't do it. For a long, hot race of any kind, the body needs about three full days of hydrating before the event. I also did not drink any alcohol for a couple of days prior to a race. Many triathletes, including most of my friends, loved having a beer or two at dinner before a race, but I gave it up until after the race, and it paid off more than once in the heat at triathlons in July and August.

Most triathlons are on Sunday mornings to avoid traffic on the roads, so I would arrive at the race site on Saturday afternoon to preview the course. After checking in and picking up my race packet I would drive the bike course. Even if I had done this same race several times on the same course, I wanted to check out the sharp turns, the hills, and the condition of the pavement. There are times when race directors are forced to make changes in the course from year to year due to road construction or other issues. One year at Lake DeGray, Arkansas, the race directors modified the course and the new route had a steep downhill with a fairly sharp turn at the bottom. It surprised me while driving the new course and reminded me how important it was to check things out. Some of the young hotshots liked to ride their bikes over the course the day before a race, but my older body needed to save all its energy for the actual event. My final prep work before going to bed was making sure my bike tires were pumped up correctly. I didn't want to experience any last-minute problems.

On race mornings, I would get up a couple of hours before the start to do my bathroom business, put on plenty of sunscreen, and get to the race site early. Most races start and finish in the same place with one central transition area. This is where competitors would come in from the swim; put on their helmets, bike shoes, and race numbers; and run out with their bikes to the mounting spot. There was absolutely no riding in or out of transition, with painted lines marking where to mount the bike going out and where to dismount coming in. After the ride, the bike had to be racked in the same spot where it was picked up. Then it was time to drop the helmet, change to running shoes, and take off again. Competitors' individual times start when the gun goes off for their respective swim waves and doesn't stop until they cross the finish line on the run; therefore, having a quick transition is very important. To have a quick transition I always made sure I could find my bike in a transition area with anywhere from a couple hundred to over a thousand bicycles. In races with a large number of competitors, the bike racks in the transition area are numbered to match competitors' race numbers, and this is where all competitors' bikes must be placed. However, in most of the races I did, competitors were allowed to pick their own spots. Getting there early usually gave me time to select a good spot where it was easy to find my bike. I also bought a bright red bath mat to put on the ground next to my bike, which helped in finding the bike. Bikes come in many different colors, styles and sizes, so it can be difficult for competitors to swim a quarter to half a mile in a muddy lake, wade out of the water surrounded by other competitors, run fifty to a hundred yards to transition, and then remember exactly where they left their bike. It is especially trying if it was a rough swim.

In spite of the challenges involved, I enjoyed the sport and believed if I devoted more time to training for the swim and working on fast fifteen- to eighteen-mile bike rides, I could be competitive in my age group. I found the training was actually easier on my body when I focused on a different discipline in each training session, rather than just running to train for 5K races.

In the older age groups of fifty- and sixty-year-olds at triathlons, there was always a feeling of camaraderie. We all congratulated each other after races and hung out together. Frankly, on a really hot day over a long course, just finishing the race was its own reward. I especially relished the pleasure of passing some of the younger competitors midway through the run, even though their swim wave usually started ten or fifteen minutes ahead of mine. Many of the youngsters spent too much energy in the early part of the race and struggled to finish.

One of the challenges for beginning triathletes is the physical transition of going from the bike to the run. For almost everyone, it is very difficult to start running immediately after a hard bike ride. It's a completely different dynamic, and without proper training for the transition, it can be a humbling experience. As a result, there are frequently several competitors walking or just trying to jog a little after getting off the bike. I learned early on the benefit of practicing going from the bike to running just a quarter to half a mile, which is about the distance it took me to get my rhythm. Even after years of training, I found the transition to the run to be a challenge. However, I knew from experience that if I just kept going at an easy pace, within a quarter of a mile or so, I would be able to get into a comfortable rhythm and could begin to pick up the pace. The good news was that, by the halfway point, I usually felt pretty good and was able to maintain a good pace to the finish. I can still remember passing a lot of competitors of all ages on the run who were dehydrated, worn down, and walking the hills, or were just spent and barely had the energy to finish. Competing in triathlons, I learned a lot about being patient, holding back some on the bike to conserve energy for the run, and hydrating on the bike.

Since the races I competed in were in several states, I only saw some of my triathlon friends at certain races. It was great to visit again and talk about what we had been doing over the last year. In some cases, we would make plans to get together for dinner the night before. Triathlon is a very friendly and inclusive sport. I remember more than once giving someone a spare tire or tube, and at one race I even lent a guy a spare wheel I carried with me. Triathletes were always helpful with training advice and nutrition tips, and before the race, if any competitor ever had a mechanical problem with their bike, there was always someone around to help.

I had three objectives for every triathlon: first, to cover the distance comfortably; second, to finish strong; and finally, to enjoy the sights, sounds, and feelings of the event. Sure, I wanted to be competitive, but at the end of the race, regardless of where I placed, if I fulfilled those three objectives, I had accomplished my goal. It was difficult for me to think about these objectives during the swim. I just wanted to get through the swim with as little difficulty as I could. However, on the bike, I always found time to think about how much I enjoyed the sport and how fortunate I was to be competing at my age in such a rigorous activity. Like most things in life, it wasn't easy. It took a lot of practice and hard work, but I enjoyed the training, and then the race itself became the fun part. After every race, no matter how tired I was, I felt proud and satisfied that I finished the course.

The Final Season

In the summer of 2007, Sam was my faithful support team and companion on the triathlon circuit, and we were having a great time. Over the previous ten years, I had become good enough at the sport to usually finish in the trophies for my age group. In 2003, when I turned sixty, I was very proud of the fact I earned an Honorable Mention on USA Triathlon's All American list in my age group. That means I was ranked among the top ten percent of triathletes in the nation, aged sixty to sixty-four. Frankly, I was stunned when a fellow competitor sent me an email with the 2003 rankings, and my name was on the list. I felt ten feet tall that day.

My first race of 2007 was the Dragonfly Triathlon at Sardis Lake, Mississippi. I always enjoyed this race, as it was in a lovely state park, and both registration and the trophy presentations were in a nice, grassy area full of beautiful, old oak trees. Dragonfly was one of the longer events I competed in with a half-mile swim, a seventeen-mile bike ride, and a tough four-mile run. My best of the three disciplines was the run, and this one was mostly on trails in the park, with plenty of short but steep hills. At this race, the organizers went out the day before and spray-painted all the big roots and rocks on the narrow running trail so the competitors wouldn't trip and fall. I loved running in the woods and was always able to catch a couple of fellow age-group competitors on the run. In 2007 I had a very good race, catching two guys in my age group on the run in the last two miles, and was thrilled to win the sixty-plus age group for the second year in a row. After the race, Sam and I drove over to Oxford, only twenty-five minutes from the race site, to eat lunch at the legendary Acme Café on the town square. Oxford is a beautiful college town, home to William Faulkner, John Grisham, and Ole Miss. Strolling through the town square and having a burger and beer after a tough race was a great way to celebrate.

A few weeks after Dragonfly, I competed in the Mighty Mite Triathlon in Forrest City, Arkansas. Mighty Mite was the shortest event of my season, and it was an unusual course, with a point-to-point race. This meant we had a transition area near the lake between the swim and the bike ride, and then another transition area thirteen miles down the road, where the three-mile run to the finish started. The good news was that after competitors rode out of the park, which had some tough hills, it was mostly downhill to the bike-to-run transition area. I finished the race strong and was second in my age group to a competitor I had beaten at Dragonfly.

I decided not to race at the Four States Triathlon in Texarkana, Texas, that summer because I was having some minor pain in my back after mowing the yard and decided not to push it. This was always a fun race, but I thought it was prudent to pass on it in 2007. My next race was the Big Dam Bridge Duathlon, which was a run-bike-run event at home in Pulaski County, Arkansas. The race was supposed to start at Burns Park in North Little Rock and go over the new pedestrian/bike bridge that had been built over a dam on the Arkansas River. The course would cover a few miles on the Little Rock side of the river and return to the park. However, the Arkansas River was up above flood stage, and access to the bridge was closed off, so we did several run and bike loops in Burns Park. Two of my friends who were very good competitors were on hand, and it made for a great competition. Wilburn Powell frequently beat me at most triathlons because he was a better swimmer and biker. I could usually beat Bill Crow at a triathlon because he was, by his own admission, a terrible swimmer. However, he was an excellent runner, and I was never close to him at the finish of a 5K run. Fortunately I was able to stay close to Bill on the first run and was about a minute ahead of Wilburn. Wilburn passed me on the bike, but the bike course had an extremely steep hill where most people, including Wilburn, had to walk their bikes. Knowing how tough the hill might be, I used my road bike, which had a much lower gear than my race bike and was able to pass Wilburn both times we climbed the hill. Of course he was strong enough to pass me back, but it kept me in the mix, and I thought I might just catch him on the run. Bill and I were closer on the bike than I expected, but I had some speed left in my legs and was ahead of him. Part of the way into the run, I spotted Wilburn ahead of me and I was gaining on him. I caught him with less than a mile to go, and as I went by he told me with a smile, that he knew I was coming. It was a small field of competitors, but it was still a very satisfying finish and I won my age group. It was also one of the very few times I remember passing Wilburn Powell.

At this point I was having the time of my life racing triathlons and an occasional duathlon. Sam was a good supporter and having her travel with me to these events made the races much more fun. She got to know the other competitors and enjoyed visiting with everyone. She and I were having a great time and looking forward to making some fun trips to interesting places and enjoying our new life together. Little did we know at the time how soon that would all change.

Two

The Last Race

One of the oldest and biggest triathlons in the four-state area is the River Cities Triathlon in Shreveport, Louisiana. This race was usually the first Sunday in August and attracted a very talented field, especially from Arkansas, Louisiana, and Texas. For most of the serious triathletes in the area, this was a "don't miss" event to test themselves against the best of the best. Registration for the race was only available through the race website, which opened at 6:00 a.m. on June 1, and all 1,300 entries would be sold out before noon. It was also a very professionally organized race, and every competitor received a full bag of athletic gear. Most races gave out a t-shirt and maybe a running cap, but not River Cities. At check-in on Saturday before the race on Sunday, race organizers usually handed out custom race duffel bags or backpacks, and each was filled up with a custom race t-shirt, one or two running shirts, a race cap, a water bottle, a small towel, one or two pairs of running socks, a pair of running shorts, and an event poster—all of which was top-quality gear from athletic sportswear companies supporting the event.

Since I had worked for a bank in Shreveport for several years before returning to Little Rock, I had many friends there, and going to this race was like a reunion of fellow cyclists and aging triathletes. For this race, Sam and I stayed with my cycling buddy, Pierre Rousset. The previous year, Pierre, who grew up in the Normandy region of France, led us on a weeklong bike tour of the Loire Valley, along with our friends Craig and Liz Rambin. This was also a honeymoon for Sam and me and was a delightful trip, especially with someone who spoke the local language.

August in Shreveport is always hot, and Sunday, August 5, 2007, was no exception, with a high of ninety-four degrees. With 1,300 competitors, the organizers divided us by age groups into nine different swim waves starting in five-minute intervals, which helped keep the field spread out over the entire course. This was especially helpful for the swim and bike portions of the race. River Cities was a major race, and to accurately record finishes at each leg of the race, organizers assigned all competitors individual computer chips embedded on straps that we wore on our ankles. These chips would record competitors' times when they started and when they ran or biked over one of the special electronic mats placed at strategic spots next to the transition area and at the finish line. With this system, which has become common at all major races around the country, the results were readily available at the finish, along with split times for each leg of the race for every competitor. This was very helpful, as all competitors could look at their times for every leg of the race and see where they were gaining or losing time on their competition. For me it was always a reminder of how weak I was in the water but also how well I did on the run.

The course at River Cities was challenging with a thousand-meter swim, a nineteen-mile bike ride on county roads, and a three-mile run to the finish. The swim course was a clockwise triangular course with buoys at the outside corners and the start and finish areas close to each other on the shore. Being in an older age group, I was in one of the later swim waves with about 130 other competitors—males age forty-five and up. This is a large group to start all at once, so I lined up on the far outside of the group in chest deep water. The swim was the toughest part of the race for me, and I didn't want to be banging bodies with a lot of other competitors. I found that getting into a rhythm early in the swim was critical, and if I could keep my composure, I would usually pass some people on the last leg back to the beach. Of course, with nine separate groups starting only five minutes apart, there were always large groups of swimmers within a few feet of each other; and rounding a buoy was always challenging. Overall I had one of my better swims and finished the course in good shape, ready to get on my bike.

The bike course, which goes around the lake with some rolling hills, was on very good pavement, which was helpful. In a race like this, there wasn't much time to look around, but it was a pretty course, and I did my best to enjoy it and turned in a good time for a sixty-three-year-old. With 1,300 bikes in the transition area, it was crowded going in and out. I dismounted in good shape, ran with the bike to my assigned spot, and racked my bike. I then dropped my helmet, changed from bike shoes to running shoes, grabbed my cap, and was off.

In transition from bike to run at last triathlon

The run had a slight uphill grade on the one-lane road leading away from the lake until it turned onto a main park road and then flattened out with a long, slight downhill to a U-turn. I got into a good rhythm on the run and believed I was ready for a strong finish. After the U-turn, the course leaves the pavement for a trail through the woods and then up a steep hill back to the main road. As I started down the path into the woods, I looked ahead and couldn't believe my eyes. There in front of me was the legendary Ironman Kurt Truax, whom I had never beaten. He was about thirty yards ahead, and I was gaining on him. I was so surprised that I wasn't even sure it was he, but as I got closer I could tell I was going to pass Kurt and might be able to beat him to the finish. I could feel an adrenaline rush as I got close, and when I went by him, he offered a word of encouragement to finish strong. What a nice gesture.

As I turned onto the steep hill, which was basically a dirt slope used for drainage, I glanced back and saw that I had opened the gap on Kurt, and then I focused on keeping my head down and running up the hill comfortably with short, choppy steps. Since this was a very steep hill in the last mile of the race, there were a lot of competitors walking, but I was determined not to walk and continued running. At the top of the hill, the course turned back onto the park road and a slight downhill run to the finish. I felt good on the last half mile, and with about fifty yards to go, the course turned down a slight grassy slope with lots of banners marking the course to the finish line on the beach. In the last stretch of the run to the finish, the public address announcer calls out the name and hometown of each runner coming in, which alerts the spectators who are looking for friends at the finish line. It was at this point that I felt a slight pain in my right thigh. It didn't slow me down much, and I finished in one of my best times for this event at 1:43:58. This placed me third in my age group, which was only my second time at this race to pick up a trophy. Kurt was a couple of years older and won his age group by a big margin of about ten minutes. I was pleased to finish ahead of this great competitor and friend by a whole minute and twenty seconds after a hard hour and forty-four minutes of racing.

Problems after the Race

After the race, I felt like I had a slight cramp in my right leg, so while waiting for the trophy presentation, I went to the medical tent, got some ice for my leg, and relaxed with my friends. Unfortunately, the pain in my leg got worse, and I had to hobble over to pick up my medal. While the pain initially appeared to be a cramp, I was pretty sure this was not due to dehydration and realized this was more than just a muscle cramp. Then, on the walk to the transition area to pick up my bike and all my gear, I felt a sharp pain shoot down my right leg with every step. Sam walked the quarter mile to the parking lot and drove back to pick me up for the trip home. The pain was so great that I was barely able to get in the car. On the way back to Little Rock, we stopped at a rest stop, and it was all I could do to get out of the car and walk to the bathroom. The pain was intense, almost to the point of tears, and it was then I suspected that a pinched nerve might be causing the pain. That night I could barely sleep because every time I moved, I felt a shooting pain from my back down into my leg.

I set up an appointment for the following day with a physical therapist I occasionally used to loosen up any sore muscles and keep me in good shape. She worked on me twice but was unable to give me much relief, and the clinic where she worked referred me to a well-known orthopedic group in Little Rock. At this point, we believed that my problem was a pinched nerve in my back and that I would need a fairly routine procedure to relieve the pressure.

Three

A "Routine Procedure"

A few years before the pain in my leg began, my regular doctor had recommended the same orthopedic group for some minor knee issues, and I assumed it would be a good choice. The doctor I met with was an orthopedic surgeon who now specialized in back problems. After a brief exam and discussion, he believed I had a slight bulging disc that was putting pressure on a nerve and said I needed to get an MRI, which he had his office schedule for that day. In discussing treatment, he first suggested an oral medication, which would take some time, possibly a week or more, to be effective. I told him I was in intense pain and unable to sleep, and he then suggested a steroid injection, which was a common procedure for this problem. He indicated that this would give me immediate relief and said, "You'll be able to walk out the door in an hour without any pain." That seemed to be an easy choice. When I inquired about when we could do this, he said I had to get an MRI first and then he could do it right away, maybe even that afternoon. He also added that he did this all the time and performed twenty or more of these a week. That seemed like a very high number to me, and it should have prompted me to ask more questions, but I was anxious for some relief.

Sam and I then left for the surgical center to get an MRI of the injury, which we brought back to the doctor that day. On the way to get the MRI, Sam made the point that this was happening awfully quickly and we should take time to think about the procedure before going ahead with it. Unfortunately, I was eager for some relief from the intense pain and failed to take her concerns seriously. That turned out to be the biggest mistake of my entire life.

I was always eager to accomplish a given task quickly and tended to act first and ask questions later, which was frequently a mistake. It is always helpful to take a deep breath and think before acting, but unfortunately that wasn't how I usually did things. The quick decisions I made on Thursday, August 9, 2007, proved to be a life-changing disaster. We did the MRI and delivered the results to the doctor. The MRI confirmed the diagnosis, and the doctor set up a time for an injection at a local surgery center. He also indicated that the problem was a very slight bulging disc, which was impinging on the nerve. Frankly, he was surprised that it was causing so much pain because it didn't appear to be that big of a problem. He reiterated that I would be able to walk out in an hour or so after the procedure without any pain, and I wouldn't need surgery or even any therapy, just some rest.

At this point, I had not asked many questions because I knew several people who had undergone this procedure, and the doctor was confident it would relieve the pain. Of course I should have asked about potential complications or problems, but I didn't. At the time, it seemed like a routine procedure, and neither he nor his nurse gave us any verbal or written information about any potential risks or problems. They didn't even ask me to sign a waiver or disclosure.

The Injury
A few hours later, Sam and I met the doctor at the surgery center. His nurse asked me whether I wanted a Valium or a sedative. I opted for sedation since I was in so much pain. Next I undressed and put on a hospital gown; I then laid down on a gurney, the nurse sedated me, and I was out.

Thirty minutes later I woke up, and while I was a little groggy, I was pleasantly surprised to find that I was not in any pain. I also found that

I didn't have much, if any, feeling in my right leg. The doctor, whom I will refer to as Dr. X, stopped by to check on me and said they used medication in the epidural injection to relieve pain along with the steroid, and it might take a little time for it to wear off. "Wear off" was an expression Dr. X would frequently use over the next week, and it became quite annoying. After about an hour, Dr. X returned again to see how I was doing and asked if I was "ready to walk out" of the surgery center. I informed him that I had no feeling in either of my legs and was unable to move them. Again he was confident this would "wear off" and said he needed to go to his office and would come back later. In the meantime, Sam and a nurse helped me get dressed and moved me to a chair in the waiting area.

Since Dr. X was convinced that the numbness would "wear off," we assumed that everything would be OK. Four hours later, when feeling still had not returned, Dr. X said I could either go home or go to a local hospital. He was confident I would be on my feet in the middle of the night, and it was my call whether to go home or go to a hospital. Thirty minutes before he showed up, I discovered that I had wet my pants and didn't even know it until I put my hand down on the chair to change positions and found I was soaking wet from my own urine. Since I had urinated all over myself and didn't feel anything, I realized that I had lost not only the use of my legs, but also the use of my entire body from the navel down. Consequently, I told Dr. X I needed to go the hospital, even though he was confident I would be on my feet in the middle of the night and ready to go home.

Sam brought the car around, and Dr. X and a nurse helped load me into the car for the ride to St. Vincent's Hospital. He got me checked in and Sam went home to pick up some things I might need and brought them back. We thought, based on the doctor's comments, that this might be a one- or two-night stay at worst, until I got feeling back in my legs.

After I was wheeled into a room at the hospital, the lead nurse on the floor asked if I wanted to have a catheter tube connected to a bag or wear a diaper. I told her I had already wet my pants once and thought a diaper would be more comfortable. That turned out to be another mistake, and I had a horrible night. Sam returned with some fresh clothes for me, and I encouraged her to go home and get some rest, and hopefully I would be ready to go home in the morning.

During the night, nurses came in every two hours to check my vital signs, and I noticed that my heart rate, blood pressure, and temperature were rapidly rising. As an athlete, I knew what my vitals should have been, and while they were rising into the normal range for most patients, I suspected there was something wrong. Then I started feeling some pain in my abdomen. Finally, in the middle of the night, the pain got much worse, and I told the nurse (who didn't speak English well) that I was in terrible pain and needed to see the head nurse immediately. The head nurse was there right away and said that since my diaper was dry, my bladder was probably backing up. Apparently my urethra would not naturally release, so the head nurse put in a catheter tube and drew off more than 1,300 cc of urine. I only knew something was wrong because I felt so much pain in my gut, but the nurse realized the problem immediately and indicated that the urine in my bladder was about to back up into my kidneys. At this point, I realized I had lost complete feeling and use of my bladder and bowel. After draining the urine and leaving a catheter tube in place connected to a bag, the pain slowly subsided and I was able to get some much-needed rest. At the time, I thought this was the worst day of my life. However, there was more bad news to come.

Bright and early the next morning, Dr. X showed up and asked in a cheerful manner, "Are you ready to walk out of here?" I forcefully told him that I still had absolutely no feeling in the lower half of my body and described the potentially dangerous bladder problem that had occurred five hours earlier. He did a quick examination to confirm my lack of sensation and then said he would order another MRI to find out what the problem was. This was the first time I saw any concern from him indicating that there might be a real problem. To this day, I don't know whether he was completely unaware of the severity of the damage caused by the procedure he performed or whether he was just hoping that it would, as he said, "wear off."

Sam showed up that morning before they wheeled me off for a new MRI. I told her about my bladder problems and said that Dr. X was calling in two experts, who would see us later that afternoon, to review the new MRI. The first expert to visit us was a well-known neurosurgeon whom we would soon refer to as "Dr. Doom." He was very blunt and told me I had suffered a stroke to the conus of the spinal column. When I asked about the prognosis, he said that most of the recovery that I would get, if any, would be in the next six months. Sam and I were dumbfounded! I then forcefully asked, "Six months until I can walk?" He replied, as if he was just stating a fact in a classroom, "Oh, I don't think you'll ever walk again." We were both in a state of shock. I didn't know what to say next. Sam and I had only been married for seventeen months. We had moved into a house that we loved and were having the time of our lives together. We both started to cry, and the doctor turned to us and asked if he had been too frank. All I could think of to say was, we wanted to know the truth. I couldn't believe what I had just heard and asked several other questions, looking for a ray of hope, but there was none. When I asked how this could have happened, he asked me whether I had been in a car accident. I told him about the procedure Dr. X performed the previous day, and he could only conclude that the paralysis must have been caused by the steroid injection. He also added that he had never heard of this happening from that type of procedure—a comment we would hear again and again and again from several other experts. Finally, I told him that Dr. X was confident this would "wear off." His blunt and confident reply was, "Anyone that says this will wear off is sadly mistaken!" When I asked him about my bowel and bladder, he explained to us that I would need to learn to either catheterize myself regularly or wear a leg bag connected to an internal catheter. For the bowel, I would need to explore options for manual evacuation. After he left, we were devastated. We knew immediately that my care and rehabilitation, if rehab were even a possibility, would be extremely expensive. We didn't know what, if anything, to do at that point. Lots of questions ran through our minds. Sam even asked me something I had already thought about but wouldn't say: "Can we afford to keep the house?" My initial thought was that we would need to find some sort of nursing facility for me. This was the absolutely worst moment of my entire life, and I wondered whether life as a paraplegic would be worth living.

At this point, our only hope for better news was when the neurologist, Dr. Hope (not his real name), came to see us later that day. But there was no good news. He confirmed the previous doctor's diagnosis. However, he did offer some encouragement and a little hope. He said, "We don't see patients like you." He talked about my vital signs, which were back to their normal levels and in his opinion were excellent. The numbers were so low that on my first night in the hospital, the nurses called the doctor on duty because they thought there was something wrong. The on-call doctor, whom I met later, told the nurses that I was an athlete and my vital signs were very positive and it's what he would like to see in more patients. Dr. Hope had a nice, comforting manner and always wore brightly colored shirts and ties, which was different from the antiseptic hospital look of most doctors and nurses. He asked me about my athletic background and talked to us about how beneficial my fitness, training regimen, and determination to work hard would be to the recovery process. He thought that with my history of training and maintaining a high level of fitness, I might be able to achieve some limited recovery. This gave us a little bit of hope, which we desperately needed. He also said he would like to come back to check on me, and we told him that would be very helpful.

Frustration, Depression, and Anxiety
That first full day in a hospital bed in a small, crowded room, completely paralyzed from the navel down and connected to a urine bag, I genuinely wished I had died during the procedure. After getting two expert opinions on my condition, it was impossible for me to see any way out of this devastating situation. I am not a very religious person, but for the

next several nights, I prayed to God to take me in my sleep. I hoped I would never wake up again. I hated to do that to Sam, but I believed in time she would be able to get on with her life and be better off without the burden of caring for a paraplegic who would need twenty-four-hour care. I did not want to live the rest of my life as a paraplegic!

Being in the hospital on that Saturday and Sunday, only a week after one of my best triathlon finishes ever, was a surreal experience. We still didn't know what to do next, but at least I was starting to consider setting some goals for my recovery. The hospital food and the small room didn't help my outlook much. My view from the window was of the side of another hospital building and the roof of a smaller building below. Hospital food is not exactly fine cuisine, but I had no appetite anyway, so it didn't make much difference. Sam wanted to stay with me as much as possible, but I knew she needed to get some rest, and there wasn't any need for her to be at the hospital all day and night. I strongly encouraged her to go home before dark, but it was hard to get her to leave. As I told her, there was no sense in both of us being miserable, and I knew she was as fearful and scared as I was.

On Monday, Dr. X had me wheeled downstairs for another MRI. He was still deluded with the thought that "this will wear off." The new MRI showed no change and confirmed the original disastrous diagnosis: I had experienced a stroke to the conus of the spinal column with no expectation of recovery. Dr. X, hoping for some improvement, requested another MRI a day to two later, but again, there was no change. By now it was becoming painfully obvious that my paralysis was real and most likely permanent, and that it was never going to "wear off." With one wrong, fateful turn, one mistake, one questionable doctor, I had become a classic paraplegic.

That first week in the hospital, it was extremely difficult to find any hope. I had continuing doubts about whether life was worth living as a paraplegic. I even told Sam she hadn't bargained for this. We could find a place for me, and she could have the house and our investments, get a divorce, and move on with her life. Of course, she told me to quit talking foolishly because she loved me and wasn't going anywhere, and then we both cried.

While biking, running, swimming, and sailing, I was always aware there was some risk involved, but I never imagined losing the use of the entire lower half of my body. I knew a few cyclists who had cracked a collarbone or broken a wrist, but nothing like paralysis had ever crossed my mind. I kept thinking, "How could this happen to me?" I tended to blame myself and rethink everything about going to this doctor and not asking enough questions. What if I had gone to a different doctor? What if I went to the same doctor but on a different day? What if I had done this or that differently? Obviously, at this point, none of this kind of thinking was helpful. I knew that beating myself up for something in the past was wasted energy. However, with all that time in the hospital, unable to do anything, my mind continued to wander back again and again to what ifs. Most nights I would go to sleep and pray I would never, ever wake up again. But I did wake up, and there I was, without any feeling or movement below my navel.

For me as an athlete, losing the ability to stand on my own two feet and run, walk, hike, bicycle, or do practically anything outside, was like losing my reason for living. I imagined that artists who lost their sight or musicians who lost their hearing must feel much the same way. I had so many questions: How does one cope with such loss? What is left to life? Is there any reason to continue going forward? Is there any hope at all?

While Dr. Hope was only called in to read the MRI of the injury and give us a prognosis, he did come back to check on me almost every day during that first week in the hospital. His bright pastel shirts and colorful ties seemed to match his positive attitude. Again, he told me that doctors and hospitals generally didn't see patients at my age in such good physical condition. My resting heart rate, blood pressure, and every other vital sign were those of someone much younger. He further said that anyone who trained as hard as I did at my age—sixty-three at the time—must have the determination to accomplish amazing things. Since I had exercised most of my adult life, he believed there should be some strong muscle memory in my body and maybe, just maybe, I might be able to recover some partial feeling and use of my legs. He indicated that my body had been trained to be active and it knew this current condition was not how I was supposed to be. Maybe my body could find some way to partially recover. He cautioned me that it was not likely I would get much back, but I might get something. For Sam and me, that was at least a tiny glimmer of hope.

Four

Trying to Find a Way Out

That first week in the hospital was a horrible, gut-wrenching blur of despair, frustration, anger, and confusion. It's amazing how we never know when a single wrong turn—one missed step, one fatal encounter—can change our lives forever. The questions then become: Can I survive? Do I want to survive? What is my quality of life going to be? Can I heal myself? Is there really any hope for recovery? Am I going to be confined to a wheelchair for the rest of my life? However, I knew in my heart that no matter how bad things were, if I didn't believe I would walk again, then I would spend the rest of my life in a wheelchair. So on the second full day in the hospital—Saturday, August 11, 2007—I decided this would be the first day of the rest of my life. I committed myself to finding some way to fight my way back. Fear, hate, and anger would only drag me down, so I set about trying to have hope and find something positive to focus on. I asked Sam to bring my autographed copy of *"It's Not About the Bike"* by Lance Armstrong. I wanted to read again the story of his fight back from cancer to win the Tour de France (note that this was before the news of Armstrong's doping issues during the Tour). If he could do that, then surely I could somehow, someway get back on my feet again. I also had Sam bring me my journal that I hadn't used in a year or two. I thought writing about my situation might help me deal with it better. Throughout my business career, I found that writing things down helped me deal with difficult situations in a more positive way. Getting negative thoughts out of my head and onto paper seemed to help me face difficult problems in a more rational way.

I also knew it was important to have a visual reminder to help keep my mind focused on healing and recovery. So I called my friend and former partner in the advertising business, Joe Dempsey, in Pine Bluff, Arkansas. I told Joe what had happened and asked for him to work up something with the words "The Healing Begins Today," with the date and "Randy & Sam" underneath the title. I told Joe just to make up something on a standard sheet of paper and fax it to the nurse's station at the hospital. Then I would put it on the wall where I would see it every morning when I woke up.

Having been raised by an extraordinary mother, I was always taught that there was hope and that if I wanted something badly enough, I could get it. She was the embodiment of a positive thinker. When I was a child, she would wake me up every morning for school with the same words: "Another day, another picnic." She was a one-of-a-kind mom. While I had lots of doubts and questions, and I didn't know what to think or whom to believe, I knew a positive attitude would be critically important if I was ever going to recover.

Good Friends

Over the weekend, word had spread about my injury, and I was beginning to get lots of phone calls and cards, as well as some visitors. One of the biggest surprises came on Tuesday when I got a call from Craig Rambin, my cycling buddy in Monroe, Louisiana. We talked for a minute or two, and then he said he had to go and hung up. I was disappointed that he didn't have more time to chat and that he kind of cut me off on the phone. Moments later, much to my surprise, Craig and Liz Rambin, along with Pierre from Shreveport, walked into my room. I was stunned! These were three of my dearest friends and cycling buddies who had driven two hundred miles from north Louisiana just to visit me in the hospital. I couldn't believe it. The four of us had ridden well over two thousand miles together in Mississippi, Louisiana, Texas, Arkansas, and the Loire

Valley in France, and suddenly on Tuesday morning, they appeared at my hospital door. Pierre had driven up from Shreveport, while Craig and Liz drove up separately from Monroe, and they met in the hospital parking garage. Sam had called to tell them what had happened to me, and they worked out the surprise visit with her. What an enormous lift it was to see them. We laughed about old times, especially the trip in the Loire Valley. Visiting with the three of them took my mind off my physical condition and gave me hope. Seeing their smiling faces in that small hospital room was an immediate boost to my morale. It filled my heart with joy and my mind with expectations and hope of better days to come. They sincerely believed I would and could get better. For the first time, I began to believe that maybe, just maybe, I might be able to recover. The warmth and feeling of support in that bleak hospital room was so strong that day; it took me back to better times and reminded me of how much fun we all had together over the years. Their visit was a wonderful gift at a time when both Sam and I desperately needed it.

Over the next few days, the support from many friends was overwhelming, and I needed the support more than I realized at the time. In my condition, it was hard to recall everyone who stopped by in the first few days, but I did recall some of the encounters. Patti Freeman stopped by to visit and told me her husband Mickey was out of town but would be back soon. He and I had been friends for over thirty years. We worked together in marketing for a couple of banks, and we loved discussing marketing, politics, and new business ideas. After Mickey returned home from a business trip, he came to the hospital every day to check on me until I ultimately went home. Steve Barnes who was a news broadcaster, writer and friend came by several times and was a great listener.

Henry Noor, my local cycling buddy, came by, and his visit reminded me of how much I missed riding a bike. Henry was a good cyclist, and we had such fun riding anywhere from fifteen to twenty-five miles together a couple of mornings every week, plus longer rides on the weekends. Henry also rode alongside Sam and me on our new tandem bike in the worst rainstorm I had ever seen on a bike ride. The Ferndale route, which was regularly used by cyclists, was on a county road through pretty farmland out to a highway junction and back for a total of twenty-five miles. It was one of those days when the weather looked fine as we started out, even though there was a chance of showers. At the turnaround point, we took a break, and Sam was concerned about some clouds rolling in, but Henry and I thought the rain would miss us. Then, five miles down the road, with about eight miles left to ride, the storm hit with lots of wind, rain, and lightning, and even some hail. Unfortunately, there was absolutely no shelter anywhere along the road, so we just kept pedaling. We finally did find a small church near the road and stopped there as the rain eased up. We were wet but otherwise OK, and after a few minutes, the rain quit and we rode back to our cars. In the hospital that day, we talked and laughed a lot about that crazy ride. Sam and I had scheduled a big trip in October with the Noor's for a riverboat cruise in Europe. We were really excited about it and now didn't believe it would happen. Talk about bad timing: in addition to the riverboat cruise, my niece Somerset was getting married in three weeks in Sedona, Arizona, and we knew that was out of the question. The devastating injury was bad enough, but it also meant the end of some wonderful plans we had made. Sam and I loved Sedona and had been there a couple of times to go hiking in the beautiful red rock country. We had booked ten days at a resort in Sedona for this trip so we would have a full week of hiking after the wedding festivities. We hated missing those trips, but now our lives had changed forever, and fun vacations were the least of our concerns.

On Tuesday, August 14, I suddenly remembered the next day was Sam's birthday. Unfortunately, we had previously experienced some difficult times on her birthday. The previous two years, we celebrated her birthday in the hospital with my mother after she had a bad fall, and had another birthday with Sam's arm in a sling from a bike accident. Now it appeared we were going to have her third consecutive birthday dinner in a hospital. What rotten luck! However, Fran Holmes and her daughter Anna came to the rescue. Fran is my sister's oldest friend, dating back to when they were five years old, and Fran and her husband Joe were good friends. So Fran, Joe, and Anna offered to bring in a birthday dinner from one of Sam's favorite restaurants. That was an incredibly kind offer, and we greatly appreciated the catered dinner in the middle of the worst week of our lives together.

Looking back, it was interesting how crowded it became in that small room at St. Vincent's Hospital with just a couple of people in the room. It certainly wasn't much of a place to have visitors, but then that's true of most hospital rooms. Frankly, it was just where the hospital could put me at the last minute, until we decided what to do and where to go for my rehabilitation, if that was even an option. There was barely enough room for Fran and Anna to bring in the food for Sam's dinner, and Joe had to stand in the doorway. At the time, nothing tasted good to me, so even this wonderful meal wasn't very appealing, but Sam enjoyed it. Initially, I thought I didn't like the hospital food, but it was more than that. I didn't want to eat much of anything. I had no appetite, which was probably a result of my depression and frustration. It got to the point that the man who delivered the evening meals would just step in the door and show me the dinner tray. I would usually shake my head no, and he would move on to the next room.

The hospital staff did try to give me some mobility. They would help me into a wheelchair and let me wheel myself out of the room and down the hallways, which helped my attitude. The hospital also set up a meeting with a staff member who provided a wealth of information about spinal column injuries and gave us contact information for the Arkansas Spinal Column Commission, which turned out to be an extremely valuable resource. Two days later, Jon Breen from the Spinal Column Commission stopped by for a brief visit to introduce himself and offer help. At the time, we didn't know what we were going to do or where we might go for recovery, but we appreciated his offer to help and assured him we would be back in touch as soon as we settled on a plan of action. Jon was a delightful young man who was eager to do whatever he could to help us, and he turned out to be very helpful.

31

As bad as things were that first week, there were some bright spots. My son Greg arrived from Plano, Texas, early in the week, and my sister Debbie flew in from Buffalo, New York, a few days later. They both provided much-needed support and help for both Sam and me. Greg was great at taking care of things around the house and running errands for Sam, while Debbie, who holds a PhD and has over twenty years' experience in cancer research, provided valuable insight from a medical standpoint.

Toward the end of the first week, I remembered that my "The Healing Begins Today" poster had not arrived from my former partner, Joe Dempsey. I called Joe on my cell phone and asked why he hadn't faxed something to the nurse's station. As usual, Joe thought he could come up with something better than what I requested. He told me there was already a poster waiting for me at Kinko's. On Greg's next trip to the hospital, he stopped by Kinko's and picked up two beautiful, twenty-two by twenty-eight-inch color posters. One was for my hospital room, and the other one was for Sam to put on the refrigerator at home. The posters each had a photo of a rising sun in the background with the words, "The Healing Begins Today," along with the words "Randy & Sam" and the date, August 11, 2007, which I had decided was the first day of the rest of my life. Having that poster on the wall of my hospital room, where I would see it when I woke up every morning, helped focus my concentration each day on the task at hand.

After a grueling first week, I knew Sam was wearing herself out getting up first thing every morning and coming immediately to the hospital. I begged her to wait until later in the morning and tried to get her to leave the hospital and go home by nine o'clock or so in the evenings. But she was so concerned about me that it was hard to get her to do so. Fortunately, having Greg and Debbie on hand helped, and I finally was able to get her to cut back some on her time at the hospital.

My sister Debbie had worked at the University of Arkansas Medical Center in Little Rock for twenty years; she had lots of contacts and reached out to several for information and advice about dealing with my injury. One of those contacts was a back surgeon whom she asked to visit me. He showed up on Wednesday before Deb arrived and was extremely helpful. After a brief discussion about what had happened and the various negative prognoses we had received, he gave us some excellent advice. He said in a very forceful manner to Sam and me, "Hospitals are for sick people, and you will not recover from paralysis staying in a hospital. Yes, they will take care of you. However, a rehab facility is for injured people, and that is where you need to be." We then asked him about various spinal column injury facilities around the country that we were considering based on Deb's recommendation. He told us that they were all good facilities and a couple of them were in some beautiful places. However, he strongly suggested we consider Dr. Rehab (not his real name), who specialized in spinal column injuries right here in Little Rock.

I vividly remember him telling us that he thought Dr. Rehab was as good as we would find anywhere, and he was just three miles down the road from where I was at that very moment. When I asked when we should make the move, he said "as soon as possible." I told him that Dr. X had recommended some oxygen therapy in a decompression tube, which I had started, and I wondered whether I should continue. He reiterated the importance of starting some sort of rehabilitation as soon as possible, plus he confirmed what we had heard from our insurance company: that there was absolutely no evidence that oxygen therapy was helpful for a spinal column injury. It seemed to us that Dr. X was just searching for anything he could find that might help until this condition, "wore off." As it happens, Dr. Rehab accepts only a limited number of patients in order to continue his research on spinal column injuries. Later that same day, when we saw Dr. Hope again, we asked him about Dr. Rehab and he agreed it was a good choice. We called Dr. Rehab's office that day and found that Dr. X had already sent him my information to see if he could help. The following day, one of Dr. Rehab's assistants stopped by to give us some paperwork to fill out and told us that Dr. Rehab would work with me and had made arrangements for me to move to the spinal column wing at the Baptist Health Rehabilitation Institute. Two days later, on Friday, August 17, 2007, we made the move and immediately knew it was the right place to start my recovery.

Moving Forward

After a grueling week of frustration and anxiety, Sam and I were excited to be moving to a rehabilitation facility. On Friday, a nurse came to my room at St. Vincent's with a wheelchair and, with some help from another nurse, got me into the wheelchair and ready to go. Sam was busy packing up all my accumulated belongings, including cards, flowers, books, and my stash of Clif Bars and other snacks. The nurse wheeled me down to the ground floor where the van driver would load me in with a lift on the back of the van. It was the first time I had been outside since I was paralyzed, and while everyone was complaining about the intense one hundred degree August heat, it felt terrific just to be outside again. In the past, I enjoyed running and biking outside, regardless of the weather. There was something about feeling the breeze and the warmth of the sun that always made me feel good. Leaving the hermetically sealed environment of a hospital was a good feeling, even if it was only for a brief period. Riding in the van was a break from my routine, and it was nice to see something other than the inside of a hospital room. When we got to Baptist Rehab the driver opened the ramp, lowered me to the pavement, and offered to move me into the air-conditioned lobby while he moved the van out of the loading zone. However, I insisted on staying outside. I told him I would have plenty of time in air conditioning over the next several weeks, and for now I wanted to enjoy the air and the sunshine. I continued to see that nice man on a fairly regular basis as he delivered patients to Baptist Rehab. Unfortunately I can't recall his name, but I do remember his kind, caring manner and positive outlook. I saw him for over a year as I continued therapy at Baptist Rehab as an outpatient, and he would always compliment me on how much progress I had made since we first met. The last time I saw him, he told me he was being shipped off to Iraq with the National Guard. I didn't think they took people at his age, but he was being called up. Hopefully this kind and caring soul made it back home safely.

Paraphrasing Charles Dickens, the first afternoon and night at Baptist Rehab was the best of times and the worst of times. We met with Dr. Rehab briefly around five o'clock in the afternoon, and he said that he had some family plans that evening but could come back later or first thing next morning and spend whatever time we needed with him. I was most anxious to get his input and told him that if he was willing, we would like to see him whenever he could return, no matter how late. My family support team—Sam, Greg, and Debbie—were all with me, and it felt great to be in a nice, new place, on the spinal column wing of Baptist Rehabilitation Institute. The room was on the second floor and was big enough for two beds, but they usually had only one patient to a room, so there was plenty of room for visitors. The room also had a big window next to my bed, looking out over a garden with lots of trees and part of the parking lot. The view enabled me to see friends coming to visit when they got out of their cars. Things were looking up.

Having a large window right next to my bed was wonderful. Looking outside, I longed to be able to walk again. Even though many visitors talked about how hot it was outside, I would have given anything to be out on my bike again, even in the heat. While the doctors we had seen so far didn't think I would ever walk again, much less ride a bike, looking out my window encouraged me to work hard in the hopes of once again being able to stand on my own two feet, feel the sun on my face, smell the air, and watch the breeze move through the trees. Ever since I was a child, I loved playing outside. There was something special about running, biking, and playing in a natural environment, and I sorely missed that feeling.

That first evening at Baptist Rehab, Greg smuggled in some beer, and we popped popcorn in a microwave at the nurse's station, told family stories, and laughed a lot. It was an enormous relief to move to a rehab facility and start focusing on recovery. Dr. Rehab returned at 10:00 p.m., did a complete pinprick test on my lower body, and found significant nerve damage throughout the lower half of my body. He spent almost two hours with us and answered everyone's questions. With Debbie's background in medicine for twenty-plus years, she had a lot of questions and grilled Dr. Rehab about every possible treatment option. The bottom line was that any recovery would be extremely slow and very difficult, without any guarantees of positive results. Overall, it was not a promising outlook. None of the experts who had examined me gave us much hope of any sort of recovery. However, as I noted in my journal after Dr. Rehab's visit:

We start again tomorrow.

I frequently say "we" because I quickly learned that I couldn't do this by myself. It takes a tremendous amount of support from family, friends, doctors, therapists, and especially from my best friend and soul mate. Sam was amazing. As I look back, I sometimes wonder how she was able to do everything she did for me. The truth is that I would not have survived without her.

The morning after our visit with Dr. Rehab I wrote in my journal the following comments:

My previous life is now nothing but memories. I can still see it and almost touch it, but I know it is gone. Things I knew before seem less familiar somehow. I lay here with a broken body and don't know where to go. Perhaps I will find a new way. I will try to be open and available to what may come my way.

I was terribly frustrated and depressed, but at least I had reached the point where I felt like I needed to focus on moving ahead. Later that same evening, I wrote these words:

It is easy to see the darkness, but I shall strive to focus on the light. The light, not the dark, will free me to grow, heal, and recover. Belief in the light will save me. In time, it will reveal to me how to redefine my life. This is a new starting point, a new beginning, a new way of life. With Sam as my rock, I cannot fail. There are lessons to be learned. Is the lesson patience, understanding, or the distinction between "human doing" and human being? I do not know, but there are lessons to be learned, and I will be open to learning.

Debbie and I had frequently talked about mom and how she tended to frequently be as busy as possible and was sometimes more a "human doing" than a human being. I knew a lot of that rubbed off on both of us. We loved mom and learned much from her but sometimes she didn't take the time to stop and smell the roses.

And then I wrote the following questions to ponder as I approached my new life:

Who am I? What is left for me? How do I redefine myself? Where do I begin? How do I participate in life again? Where will I find joy and pleasure? What are my alternatives? How do I keep focused on the positives? I have been a "human doing"; now how do I become a human being?

I also came across a helpful quote from Mary Waters, a local poet I admired. Sam had brought me a couple of Mary's books and in "Sandpaper Blankets," I found the following: "The wish must become a clear intention." It was a reminder to me that it was not enough to hope, pray, and wish for recovery. I must take the wish and make it a clear intention. Instead of saying, I hope to recover; I needed to say I will find a way to recover some use of my legs. I will focus positively on getting back on my feet.

Love and Support

Still, even now, several years later, I remember so many people who cared about both Sam and me and wanted to help in any way possible. The outpouring of love and concern in those first days in the hospital was a wonderful blessing. Pete and Sandy Heister, my regular running buddies, were among some of the first to hear about my injury and came to visit several times at St. Vincents and also at Baptist Rehab. Pete had been through a difficult cancer surgery and treatment, and they could certainly appreciate the situation we were in, which was helpful. Pete and Sandy also lent me Sandy's iPod and earbuds, which became a wonderful companion in the rehab facility. I don't think the Heisters realized how much the iPod helped me. At times, by myself, I would turn it on and play some of their Yo-Yo Ma's music, and it helped me to relax and do some writing in my journals. Sandy also brought me a new journal to use and suggested I might think about a book, which was the farthest thing from my mind at the time. At that time the journaling was just another way to help me cope with my situation.

Sandy knew Sam probably needed a break and talked her into going out for a meal. They went to Cheers in the Heights, which had a tasty menu, including an outstanding burger, which was one of my favorite indulgences. They brought me back the best-looking cheeseburger I had ever seen, but unfortunately, I could barely eat half of it. I had very little appetite for anything. Normally I would have eaten the whole burger plus fries, washed it all down with a cold beer, and maybe even split a dessert. Not being able to enjoy the burger was disappointing. I knew I was losing weight too, but I just didn't have the energy or desire to eat.

Frankly, I couldn't have cared less about food, and during my time at St. Vincent's and Baptist Rehab, I lost about fourteen pounds. While some of the loss may be related to institutional food, most of it was because of depression and lack of appetite. I could have gone all day without a meal, but I knew I needed something in my system to fuel my body for therapy. During my first week in the hospital, I got most of my calories from energy bars. I always kept a supply on hand for long bike rides, so I asked Sam to bring a small supply to the hospital, along with a bottle or two of Powerade. I could always eat one bar and drink a glass of Powerade every day.

There were so many kind people that's it's hard to mention them all. They brought food, gifts, and special mementos. At one time or another, all the key people I worked with at Bank of the Ozarks came and took a lot of time to visit and offer encouragement. Darrell and Julie Russell brought me an Arkansas Razorbacks blanket. Melvin Edwards and I ran together some, and he knew I was careful about what I ate while I was training, so he and his wife, Phyllis, put together some foods into a "healthy goodie basket" for me. George and Linda Gleason stopped by one evening for a nice visit. George is the CEO of the bank and had built it from a very small bank to the second largest financial institution headquartered in Arkansas at the time. He and Linda stayed for over an hour and told me to call if I needed anything. Paul Moore, CFO of the bank, and his wife Linda had been close friends for many years, and it was great to see them. Mark Ross, the president of the bank, and his wife Diane stopped by for a nice visit. Mark knew Russ Harrington, the CEO of Baptist Hospital, and called him to tell him what had happened and to let him know I was in his rehab facility. Sure enough, a day or two later, Mr. Harrington stopped by to check on me. Then the next day, his assistant came by, left me his card, and told me to call him if I needed anything. It's always nice to have friends in high places.

I received many flowers, cards, foods, and offers of assistance. Henry Noor, my cycling buddy, even offered to mow our yard. He thought it would be an easier job than it turned out to be. His yard is flat, but our yard had a steep slope in front and in back. He told me later that the first time he mowed the yard in the August heat, he had to go home afterward and take a nap. I was surprised when he was still up for it again a couple of weeks later. That was going above and beyond the call of duty. About a week into my stay at Baptist Rehab Larry and Kris Mougeot brought me some of Kris's delicious chocolate chunk cookies, which I loved and kept hidden away so no one else would eat them. Even though I didn't have much of an appetite for real food I could always eat a few of Kris's cookies. I enjoyed having one or two of those a day as a special treat, and I spread them out over several days to maximize the experience. Over the next few weeks, it boosted my spirits to visit with friends that came by and called on the phone. Sometimes it got so busy that we had to put a note on the door about limiting the time of a visit so I could get some rest. But I knew in my heart that the visits and support were more important to my well-being than anything else. As I wrote in my journal:

There is much love for me, and I will honor that love and support and try to prove worthy of it.

Five

Rehabilitation Begins

On Saturday, my first full day at Baptist Rehab, I met briefly in the morning with an occupational therapist who said she would work with me the next morning about dressing, bathing, and other issues. I thought I would have Sunday off, but if the therapist was ready to work with me, I was ready to get started. Saturday afternoon, one of the nurses on my floor removed my internal catheter and urine bag and taught me how to catheterize myself. I thought I would only need to go through that process every six hours or so but found that wasn't nearly often enough. I also tried to have a normal bowel movement and spent an hour on the commode without anything happening. At this point I was beginning to realize that emptying my bowel would also be a manual process. With all that was going on—my bowel and bladder issues and the challenges that come along with settling into a new environment—I didn't sleep much Saturday night and, at five o'clock on Sunday morning, drained my bladder of over 1,000 cc of urine, which was entirely too much. Managing my bodily functions was obviously going to be a challenge, especially since I had lost all sensation below my navel and couldn't tell when I needed to empty my bowel or bladder.

The first week in rehab, I started learning how to adapt to life without the use of the lower half of my body. I was amazed at just how many things we take for granted. On Sunday morning, the occupational therapist arrived as scheduled and told me that her job was to teach me how to do as much as I could for myself. We started with learning how to put my clothes out for the next day and place them by the bed every evening. Next I worked with her learning how to get dressed in my bed. Initially it was very difficult for me to put on a diaper, shorts, and shirt, and putting on support hose was the toughest job of all. The therapist reminded me that if I forgot to lay out my clothes the night before, I would have to call a nurse in the morning to help me transfer from the bed to the wheelchair, roll over to the closet and get the clothes I needed, and then get a nurse to come back to help me transfer back into the bed to get dressed. The critical component here was getting me used to doing things for myself instead of asking a nurse to do it all for me. More than once, the therapist pointed out that there will be times when there may not be anyone around to help me, so I must learn to do as much as possible for myself. Just transferring from the bed to the wheelchair and back turned out to be a big deal. For my own safety, I was not allowed to transfer without a nurse to help me. As Dr. Rehab reminded me again and again, if I fell and broke an elbow, wrist, or anything else, I would be finished working on my rehabilitation for six weeks or more until things healed. It was a sobering thought. The therapist also showed me how to get down to the rehab gym in my wheelchair and talked to me about using a catheter on a regular basis; we also discussed alternatives to help manage my bowel issues. It turned out to be a very educational Sunday morning. While I thought I was in rehabilitation primarily to work on physical rehab, an important part of my rehabilitation was to prepare me to go home and be able to function as well as possible in a wheelchair.

Now that I had landed in a place where we knew I would be for several weeks, we had a lot of visitors and phone calls. While it was great to see friends and visit over the phone, it sometimes wore me out. I was still adjusting to the new surroundings and discussing issues with the family about the major changes going forward with me as a paraplegic. Debbie was stressed over my situation; in addition, she was in the midst of planning her daughter's wedding in Sedona in a couple of weeks. She obviously had too much on her plate, but she was a big help in dealing with medical issues and doctors.

Monday, August 20, 2007, was my first full day in rehab, and I woke up feeling frustrated with myself and wrote the following in my journal:

Impatience is my worst fault! That's what got me here. I need to take my time, slow myself down, and focus more on the task at hand. If I had gone to one of my two family doctors first, I wouldn't be here today. But I can't look back. I must take what has happened and move forward. I must!

Doctors H and M were friends and had been my primary doctors for many years. Frequently I would catch myself looking back at what got me to this point and blame myself. As hard as I tried to focus on my recovery, early on it was very difficult not to second-guess my decision to go forward with the procedure. The pain I was in for the three days before I met Dr. X was terrible, but I still should have thought through alternative solutions and asked more questions. However, I grew up with a father who was a doctor, and my sister is a physician/researcher at Roswell Cancer Institute. All my life I had trusted doctors and the medical profession, so I naturally assumed I was in good hands. What a terrible, life-altering mistake.

Later that first week at Baptist Rehab, I spent an hour and a half with a different occupational therapist, learning to bathe in a chair that rolled into the shower. It was an exhausting experience, as was most everything I did in those first few weeks. And then there was the continuing process of learning to manage bathroom issues, which was not a pleasant experience. Managing my bowel and bladder issues was somewhat degrading, and those issues limited what I could and could not do. Again with a therapist, I spent more time learning to catheterize myself on a regular basis using a sterile kit with all the supplies I needed. It was an involved process that initially took at least twenty to thirty minutes each time, including cleaning myself up afterward. I still had to wear a diaper to take care of accidents. However, if I wanted to get away from having a bag with me all the time, it was something I had to learn to do. One of the therapists told me that if one asks paraplegics first coming into the hospital what they miss the most, they will usually say it's the ability to walk. However, after a few weeks, most paraplegics, including myself, would give anything to be able to have use of both bowel and bladder. Taking care of my bowel and bladder manually was very difficult, and there was always a risk of urinary tract infection, which is fairly common for anyone who uses a catheter tube every few hours.

Initially, I held onto the hope that I still might have the ability to have some sort of bowel movement. Unfortunately, that was not possible. My choices were either to take a quick-acting laxative and go to the commode to wait for the laxative to work or to learn to manually evacuate the bowel. Since I tended to have an irritable bowel anyway, a laxative wouldn't work very well for me. When I had used laxatives in the past, I found that once things started moving, my body would continue flushing for a couple of days. Consequently, I chose to have a therapist teach me how to digitally evacuate my bowel. Without going into the gory details, let me just say that it involves double-gloving your dominant hand and using your longest finger, usually the middle digit, to evacuate the bowel. It is a nasty, miserable process, but one that many paraplegics have to learn to live with, and one that I initially did three times a day after each meal to avoid accidents. Not being able to walk is restricting enough as it is, but early on, managing my bowel and bladder was the most humiliating process for me. Over time, I found I could learn to live with some frustrating issues, especially when I didn't have much of a choice.

The most positive thing about moving to Baptist Rehabilitation Institute was starting the recovery process. Being able to focus on something other than my paralysis was most helpful. In this new place, I believed I could learn to function again at some level. The move definitely brightened my spirits. I didn't know what to expect but was very impressed with the quality of the nursing staff for spinal injury patients and with the dedicated therapists I worked with for an hour twice a day, five days a week. There wasn't much we could do with my lower body other than stretch my muscles, so most of the therapy was teaching me how to transfer from a wheelchair to a bed or mat and back to the wheelchair using my arms and a slide board. The board was a beautiful piece of laminated wood with a cutout at each end for a handle, and I carried it in a bag on the back of the wheelchair everywhere I went. I still had good strength in my upper body from swimming, but I needed to develop the proper techniques to move around.

The in-patient therapists I worked with while at Baptist Rehab were extremely helpful both physically and mentally. Randy Hayden and Lisa Anderson were very patient and sympathetic, and they always had a positive attitude. They were also excellent teachers. Every therapy session started and ended with me working on transfers until it became second nature. This was critical to give me some mobility and to make sure I didn't fall and hurt myself in the process. As a result, my arms and shoulders got more of a workout than anything else. As an athlete who regularly exercised, I found that while an hour of therapy was exhausting, I still wanted more of a workout. I asked and got permission to use the rehab gym on weekends or evenings if I had the energy for more work. It felt strange to me that in a matter of weeks I could go from being able to win my age group at a regional triathlon to being exhausted from a very light sixty-to-ninety-minute workout lying on a mat. The rapid decline was surprising and frustrating. But I knew when I moved to Baptist Rehab that this was going to be a very long process. I remembered thinking about the training I did for almost three years to run a marathon in under four hours. When I started competing in triathlons, I was already a strong runner and a good cyclist, but it took me almost three years to get to the point where I could complete a half-mile open water swim in a decent time. So if it took three years or more to learn to stand up and walk, then I would treat it just like training for any kind of athletic competition. I never had much patience, but I was determined, and I believed that if I worked hard enough and long enough, I might be able to recover some use of the lower part of my body. It wouldn't be easy, but with enough hard work and support from family, friends, and a variety of therapists, maybe, just maybe, I could fight my way out of the wheelchair.

Good News

In spite of all my efforts with the therapists to make something happen with my legs, there were no signs of any feeling or movement. On Tuesday, August 21, twelve days after I was paralyzed, two residents who worked with Dr. Rehab came by to check on me. They did a brief exam of my legs and asked if I had gained any feeling or movement in them, and I told them no. Next, they had me sit on the edge of the bed with my lifeless legs hanging down and asked me to try to move my legs. I told them I regularly tried to move my legs with absolutely no result. Apparently, my mind either didn't have a connection with my legs or didn't know which muscles to activate. I asked one of the residents to put his hand on the muscle he wanted me to activate and I would see if I could move the foot. He put his hand on my left thigh while I focused as hard as I could on activating that muscle. Much to my surprise, I looked down at my foot and wow, it moved! I couldn't feel it move, but I could see it. It wasn't much, only a fraction of an inch, but there was movement. There was hope. There was a chance my legs might come back. There was a glimmer of light at the end of my tunnel of despair. I could only kick the foot forward ever so slightly, and I could only do it two or three times before it quit. Apparently there was some slight connection from my brain to my left leg, which was all that mattered. We tried the same thing on my right leg but there was no response. But still, I thought if I had a connection in the left leg, maybe over time, I would get other connections. Hope can be a wonderful thing.

While there was finally some good news, I still struggled with depression in spite of Dr. Rehab putting me on antidepressants. Suddenly losing the use of my legs was devastating and I still couldn't imagine living my life as a paraplegic. There were many, many times in the dark of night, lying in my bed at the rehab center with a complete absence of feeling below my navel, when I wished I had died during the procedure. But every morning when I woke up, the first thing I would see on the wall opposite my bed was Joe's poster, which read, "The Healing Begins Today." At that moment I knew I had to get my mind right to start a new day. The truth is, healing my mind was every bit as hard as healing my body.

I was told there were lots of people praying for me, and I appreciated their support. I also ran into some people who gave me the standard line that "this was all part of God's plan," which I do not believe and frankly didn't want to hear. I do not believe in some master plan that controls our lives. We make our own destiny by the decisions we make. If this was all part of some plan, then what did I do in my life to deserve this? The truth is, things happen that we can't explain or control. Was the death of more than three thousand innocent victims in the twin towers on September 11, 2001, part of God's plan? Was the Holocaust part of God's plan? Was the tsunami that hit Japan in 2011 part of God's plan? Bad things do happen to good people.

I knew in my heart that if I were ever going to recover, I would have to work harder at this than anything I had ever done in my life. In the first week at Baptist Rehab, I decided I would not allow myself to live in a wheelchair. The wheelchair was a wonderful tool, but I considered it to be a temporary tool, not a permanent one. It was obvious to me that I couldn't sit back and say, "Well if it's God's plan for me to walk, then I will walk; if not, then I won't." The truth, I understood, was that I needed to put forth the effort to recover. I firmly believed that my future was in my hands, not someone else's. Yes, I needed a professional support team of doctors, nurses, therapists, and friends to help me do the work, but I alone had to make the effort to do the difficult and challenging work. When I did pray, I decided, rather than asking for things, it would be a prayer of gratitude for what I accomplished.

At the end of my first week of therapy I had a good day working with Lisa, my inpatient physical therapist. I asked her about my chances of walking, and she thought that with my determination and work ethic, I should regain the ability to walk again. This was the first time in the fourteen days since the injury that any doctor, nurse, or therapist said, in a positive manner that I "should" regain the ability to walk. I also told Lisa how badly I wanted to just stand up again, so she offered to put me in a hydraulic standing frame. It was a very strange-looking contraption, but I was game for anything to get me on my feet, if even for just a minute or two. Using the frame starts out with the patient sitting down with legs and chest blocked with pads from the front. The therapist pumps a hydraulic cylinder, and the back of the seat presses against the patient's back as the seat raises the patient, and on the way up, the seat moves to the back of the butt. The patient slowly becomes vertical with full support in both front and back. It was so wonderful being vertical again that I cried. However, there are some issues with a patient who hasn't been vertical in a couple of weeks. When a paraplegic tries to stand, blood tends to pool in the lower part of the body and the patient can quickly become dizzy or lightheaded. As a result, Lisa brought me back down pretty quickly, but it was still a wonderful feeling. After that, Lisa and another therapist helped me get into a three-wheel handcycle and let me ride around the gym while there were no other patients for me to run into. Talk about fun! I went up and down the halls on the bottom floor of the rehab area and rode around for about fifteen minutes. This was my best day since the injury, and it really felt like the first day of the rest of my life.

On Wednesday morning I wrote the following in my journal:

My wishes and hopes are becoming clear intentions. I will not let this injury defeat me. I am so lucky in many ways. There is love, hope, and faith all around me. I could not find a better life's partner than Sam. In spite of my injured physical body, I can still grow, learn, and live a rich, full life that is rewarding. We have tried to find the best solutions, doctors, rehab place, etc. The silver bullet we are trying to find is within me. I am starting to smile and chuckle at my little problems getting dressed. I am seeing lots of beauty all around me. Sometimes I am even able to laugh at myself. Who knows, this could be a meaningful growth experience.

After a full week of therapy at the rehab center it was not uncommon for me to wake up with a positive attitude and try and do my best to focus on a positive start to the day. However, many times during the day, dealing with my inability to do ordinary things would really frustrate me.

Fortunately, I was starting to get into a regular routine at Baptist Rehab, which was comforting. I was getting used to showering and dressing. Even using a catheter to empty my bladder was becoming more of a routine procedure. However, the bowel process three times a day was a constant and humiliating reminder of my disabled condition. My workouts with Lisa and Randy were hard but felt good, and again I got to stand up in the frame after my workout. Of course, we always worked first on transferring from the wheelchair to the mat and back. We would repeat the transfers again and again and again until I did it just right, both to start the workout and to end it. This was a constant reminder of how careful I needed to be when transferring, especially from my bed.

As I got into a regular routine, I had a talk with Sam about changing her routine. There was no reason for her to show up at rehab before noon. I was working with the therapists, and I asked her to sleep in, relax, and not come in until noon or later. She was pushing herself too hard on my behalf, and she needed time away from the hospital. They had me on a fairly full schedule each morning, so there was no need for her to come in early. It was a bit of a struggle to convince her, but she finally relented.

Thursday, I was looking forward to more therapy, but Dr. Rehab strongly encouraged me to participate in a group therapy session in the morning. I had already bailed out on having breakfast with the group on the spinal column wing, because some of them had such negative attitudes. I didn't want to start my day by comparing stories about how bad things were or hearing about how they didn't like this nurse or that doctor or the food. So, after a couple of days, I started taking breakfast in my room, which was great. It gave me time to work on my journal, listen to music on the Heisters' borrowed iPod, and most important, focus on my therapy for the day. So I took Dr. Rehab's advice and did the group therapy thing, which was usually a trip somewhere in the hospital van. Dr. Rehab thought it was helpful to get patients outside of the hospital in a small group, which sounds like a good thing; however, this trip was to an auto conversion place that installed wheelchair lifts and controls in vehicles for paraplegics like myself. I found it terribly depressing. I wanted so badly to walk again, and just thinking about spending the rest of my life in a wheelchair and using a lift to get in a van was more than I could deal with at the time. I felt nauseated and couldn't wait to get back to my room. As I found out later, I was coming down with a urinary tract infection, which really set me back more than the trip to the conversion place.

Fortunately, I ended up having a very good therapy session that afternoon and was able to put the car conversion business behind me. I got to ride the handcycle again, and Randy talked to me about having an occupational therapist come to our house once I went home to help Sam and me on issues around the house.

Six

Progress in Therapy

Friday at the end of the second week since my injury, and after only one week at Baptist Rehab, things were looking a little better. Randy Hayden worked with me again teaching me how to manage my toilet duties, and we had another session on bathing. It seemed crazy for a sixty-three-year-old man to need someone to teach him how to bathe, but that was an important part of my therapy. As Randy pointed out numerous times, bathing is an extremely risky task for a paraplegic. Being in an environment with lots of soap and water, which makes everything slippery even when sitting on a shower seat, can be treacherous. Since I had no feeling or muscle response in my feet to help me balance, I could easily fall and do serious damage to my shoulders, arms, wrists, etc. Consequently, all of my showers were with a nurse or therapist. As far as modesty went, I lost that early on after having nurses clean me up after accidents and teaching me how to manage my bowel and bladder. In a very short time, it all became a purely clinical activity. My pride was the least of my concerns.

I did some good work with Lisa Anderson on Friday, and she had me try out a seated elliptical trainer for a short period without much success. Meanwhile, my technique with making transfers was improving enough that we worked on doing a few without using the board. Since my wheelchair was the same height as the mats in the gym, it was much easier to transfer to a mat than transferring in and out of the higher hospital bed. Experimenting without the board worked just fine.

The day after I moved into the spinal column wing of Baptist Rehab, they had a specialist on staff who spent an hour with Sam and me discussing issues regarding spinal column injuries. She gave us some helpful brochures, books, and other information on coping with this type of injury. We had previously met Jon Breen from the Spinal Column Commission, and he showed up at Baptist Rehab on a regular basis to provide services for all the patients on that wing of the hospital. He always wore a smile and had a cordial manner, and we enjoyed his visits. One of the things he suggested on his first visit at Baptist was doing an assessment of our home to see what modifications we would have to make to accommodate me, especially in a wheelchair. On Friday, he met with Sam, and they did a complete evaluation throughout our home. Fortunately, our house, which we bought only eighteen month before this, had a master suite on the ground floor. While we liked having our bedroom on the main floor and the other bedrooms upstairs, we had no idea at the time how important it would be. It also helped that while there were steps from the garage up into the house, the driveway at the side of the house was connected to a level sidewalk that led to the front of the house with only one step to the porch and one more to enter the house. If this had happened while we were still living at my previous house, we would have had some significant problems. That house had a very steep driveway that was difficult to walk up, as well as several steep steps into the house without room for a ramp. Fortunately, our new house had plenty of room for a ramp, and so we figured that it should work out quite well. While I believed we would need a ramp to get me in the house, I thought that was about all in terms of modifications. The reality was that we were going to have to make many other modifications to accommodate me as a paraplegic in a wheelchair.

Dr. Rehab received regular reports from my therapists and personally met with them at least once a week to keep up with my progress. In addition, he came to the gym on a regular basis to see for himself how his patients were doing. Friday evening, prior to his leaving for several days to attend a spinal column conference in

Florida, he stopped by my room to visit. He told Sam and me that he was pleased with the progress I was making in therapy, which boosted our spirits. While it didn't seem like much progress to me, he thought it was significant. However, he was still hoping for some sensation in my feet, which wasn't there yet. Once again, he reminded us that this would be a very long, slow process, but if I could get some feeling or sensation in my feet, we could get really excited about that. He also scolded me about doing transfers from the bed to the wheelchair without a nurse present. My transfers were going well, and I didn't think I needed to wait for a nurse. He told me he had gotten reports about me not calling the nurse when I was getting out of bed, and he once again described the dangers and risks involved if I were to fall. So I promised him I would be a good patient while he was gone and have someone present when I needed to get out of bed.

After only two weeks of therapy at Baptist Rehabilitation under Dr. Rehab's care, we knew we had made the right decision. He was very open and honest about my situation, which we appreciated. He was also receptive to our questions and suggestions about possible alternative therapies after I left the hospital. While he appreciated my aggressive approach to therapy, he reminded me about how careful I needed to be and warned me not to push things beyond reasonable limits. Sam and I both liked him and felt very fortunate to have him on our side in this ordeal.

After our positive discussion with Dr. Rehab on Friday night, I woke up Saturday morning feeling good and wrote the following in my journal:

I genuinely believe I can walk again, but it is going to be a long and difficult journey to get there. With Sam at my side, I can do this. I know I can. It will take all the determination I can muster, as well as great patience. This is going to be the hardest challenge of my life.

I was determined to focus my therapy and my recovery on the following goals, which I wrote down in my journal:

First, build the strength in my upper body necessary to support me until my legs start to return.

Develop range of motion in my legs.

Work on the use of more muscles in the lower body than just my legs.

Remember the wheelchair is merely a temporary device. I will accept it as a friend to get me to the next step.

I had a real treat that weekend. My good friend, Fred McClanahan, from Shreveport, Louisiana, came to visit and set up my new MacBook computer. This would enable me to stay in touch with friends by e-mail and continue to do some marketing consulting work from my bed. Fred is a Macintosh wizard and was an invaluable resource for me when I was marketing director at Commercial National Bank in Shreveport, Louisiana. I called him a few days after the injury to tell him what had happened and asked for his advice on purchasing an Apple laptop that I could use during my hospital stay, which I thought could last a couple of months. He not only told me what to buy, but also offered to come to Little Rock and set everything up. On Saturday morning, August 25, 2007, he and his teenage son Kyle made the three-and-a-half-hour drive to Little Rock and showed up at my hospital room. It was terrific to see them and really brightened my spirits. After we had a nice visit, they went to the house to meet with Sam and set up the MacBook. He synced everything together between the MacBook and our larger iMac computer in the upstairs office, plus he installed some upgrades for both and did some much-needed cleanup work on the iMac. He also tested our wireless capability at home and then brought the new MacBook to me, and we tested the wireless capability in the hospital room. What a wonderful friend. Sam then took Fred and Kyle out for a late lunch at the Buffalo Grill before they left to go back home. I was concerned that Kyle might be bored devoting his Saturday to this project, but he seemed to have a good time, and it appeared to be a fun father and son outing. At the time, I sure wished I could have joined them at the grill for a cheeseburger, skins-on fries, and Fat Tire Amber Ale on tap. Oh well, that too shall come in time, I reminded myself.

Having access to e-mail and the Internet was a wonderful treat. I could stay in touch with friends and family and give everyone updates on my progress. In addition, I could stay in touch with my beloved Razorbacks, as they were about to start the football season under a new coach. Like most Arkansas fans, I was excited about the new coach; however, the arrival of football season was bittersweet. For many years, my family had season tickets for the same seats in both Fayetteville and Little Rock, but I knew I wouldn't be going to any games any time soon. Sam and I loved our trips to Fayetteville, where we would eat lunch before the game at one of the many bars and restaurants on Dickson Street. The town would be full of Razorback fans in their red and white gear going up and down the street, and it was always a festive atmosphere. After lunch, we would stroll across the campus and look for the three generations of Oates family names engraved on Senior Walk. Then we would follow the growing crowd down the hill to the stadium. Fayetteville in the fall, with the leaves turning, was a beautiful place to be, especially on a football weekend. I could feel the energy and excitement as soon as I saw Old Main and the stadium from the highway. Old Main is the original school building on a hill, and it is visible for miles around. It was a great place to go to college for my parents, my sister Debbie, my son Greg, and myself. Today the family seats are still being well used by Greg, Debbie, and her daughter, Somerset.

My training and competing over many years of racing sailboats, running, biking, and competing in triathlons left me with a strong work ethic. I wanted to work on my therapy as much as I could, so I tried to schedule therapy on the weekend, but I could only get a thirty-minute session. So I did some work on my own Saturday morning in the gym with push-up bars, elastic bands, and some stretching. Even though my body was unable to do much, it felt good to try to push myself. Anything, absolutely anything, was better than just lying in bed. In the afternoon, I worked with a new therapist since my regular therapists had weekends off. She helped me get in the standing elliptical machine for a little bit and also helped me transfer to the handcycle for some riding in the gym and empty halls. This did as much for my mental state as it did for my physical condition. Afterward, I took an hour's nap, which felt great. After the nap, I sat up on the side of the bed and tested my legs for movement. Much to my surprise, I found I could move my right foot ever so slightly, just as I had moved my left foot, and I found I could now actually kick my left foot. It was only once or twice, and then the muscles gave out, but at least there was some connection in the upper part of both legs, and the muscle in the left leg was getting a little stronger. This was an exciting development and I couldn't wait to tell Sam about it.

Seven

The Strange Case of Dr. X

A few days after I had checked into Baptist Rehabilitation, Dr. Rehab told me that Dr. X was concerned about me and wanted to have regular medical updates on my progress. Dr. Rehab said the doctor was really upset about my situation and just wanted to know how I was doing. Because Dr. X was no longer my doctor and I was under Dr. Rehab's care, I would have to give my permission to share any information about my condition. Sam and I discussed this and decided that at this point we didn't need or want Dr. X to be involved. However, during my time in the hospital, Dr. X continued to regularly check up on me. He seemed genuinely concerned about me but didn't seem to grasp the severity of the injury he caused. I believe he was just hoping that I would get better quickly. He continued to tell me, "This will wear off," even though the experts he called in to review the MRIs before and after the injection were confident this was not the case. He even asked his wife, who was a nurse, to conduct a search on the Internet, and she found a doctor in New York who had something similar happen to a patient as a result of an epidural injection. He called this doctor and reported back to me that this patient was recovering and was walking in about six weeks. I assumed he wouldn't lie about this, but I suspected the severity of the injury to the patient in New York was not anything like mine.

Dr. X came to see me almost every day, either before he went to his office or on his way home. And each time, he acted like he expected some sort of significant improvement from the previous visit. At first I almost felt sorry for him. There was no question he was upset about what had happened. He even said to Sam how disappointed his late father, who was also a doctor, would be with him. However, after a while, I wished he would move on and stop visiting me. Seeing him on a daily basis was a constant reminder of what a mistake I made in trusting him in the first place. I tried my best to not let anger and frustration cloud my mind, but seeing him didn't help.

One day, while I was in the Baptist Rehab gym, Dr. X showed up to watch me work with a therapist and stayed for about an hour, through most of my afternoon therapy session. The session included having Sam work with the therapist to learn how to help me when I went home with exercises and work on the flexibility in my legs. Dr. X wanted to do whatever he could to help, but sometimes in very strange ways. He knew I generally ate a healthy diet, including fresh fruit most mornings, so on my first day at Baptist Rehab, he sent a fruit bouquet shaped like a floral arrangement. It was beautiful, and when it arrived, it created quite a stir with the nurses. The fruit was tasty, and there was plenty to share with visitors. He also found out I was a big Razorback football fan, so while he was there in the gym that day, he told Sam he would like to take us to the opening game in Fayetteville, which was only ten days away. When Sam told me, I didn't know what to make of such a bizarre invitation. There was no way in hell I could ride for four hours, one way, in a car to Fayetteville, much less manage my bowel and bladder on a trip with him and his wife. I don't think he really understood how difficult my situation was, or maybe he just didn't want to face what had happened. Except for two trips in a handicap-equipped van, with me seated in a wheelchair, I had not been out of a hospital or rehab environment since the injury. Getting in and out of a car was something I hadn't even attempted yet, plus I had to drain my bladder every two hours or so and evacuate my bowel three times a day, after every meal. Plus I was still peeing on myself from time to time. Going on a trip anywhere at this point was definitely out of the question. When I told him I couldn't do it, he tried his best to explain how he had a great parking spot right next to the stadium and could get me in a wheelchair and into an accessible seat. At this point, I told him it would be too difficult, and I declined his offer as politely as I could. I was sure Dr. Rehab wouldn't allow me to go anyway, but regardless of that, I didn't want to go anywhere with Dr. and Mrs. X.

The next day, Dr. X showed up again, this time at my room, and wanted to know how I was doing and whether I would like to "escape" for a couple of hours that weekend and go for a ride in his convertible. What was he thinking? Frankly, I couldn't have cared less about a ride in his BMW convertible. First of all, I wasn't prepared and didn't have permission to leave Baptist Rehab, and second, I thought it was more important to work on my recovery and get some much-needed rest. He acted like he wanted to be my buddy, but I wasn't interested. At this point, Sam and I agreed that we needed to distance ourselves from him.

The following Saturday, Dr. X showed up as usual, this time with his young daughter, while I was doing therapy on my own in the gym. At this point, I told him that I was taking Sunday off and he should too. He didn't seem to get the message and still said he wanted to stop by. This time I bluntly told him, "Don't come by; I need a day off." Apparently he thought he could ingratiate himself with me, in spite of the fact that he virtually destroyed one half of my strong, healthy body.

Legal Issues

By now, Sam and I were coming to grips with the fact that my recovery was going to be very long and expensive. We were already talking about modifications to our house and long-term professional therapy. We both agreed we would spend whatever it took and seek out any source that might help me recover. However, we were fearful that this would quickly drain the assets we had put away for our retirement.

Frankly, I hate the fact that our society has become so litigious. However, it was becoming obvious to us, from the many comments and opinions we received from several medical professionals, that I should not have been paralyzed from this procedure and that something must have gone terribly wrong. Seeking a legal resolution was an especially tough decision for me, since my father was a doctor and I had been raised in an environment in which I completely trusted the medical establishment. However, in this case, I was given no disclosure or explanation about the risks involved. I wasn't even told how the injection process worked. If I had known that the injection was going to be directly into the spinal cord, that certainly would have raised my level of concern and caused me to seek out other opinions. Sam and I were beginning to believe that somebody should be held accountable. This was supposed to be a routine procedure, and yet every doctor we talked to had never heard of or seen this type of serious damage from an epidural injection. So it was becoming obvious that Dr. X had made a horrible mistake.

I had a long talk with Debbie about medical and legal issues. She was back in Buffalo, working at the Roswell Cancer Institute, and contacted some doctors at the hospital there about my condition. She also asked about legal issues related to this sort of paralysis. As a result, she came to the same conclusion we did. It was time to seek out legal counsel. Henry Noor also supplied some helpful information. Henry spent most of his life in the insurance business and sold coverage to the medical community. He told me that the legal process would be long, exhausting, and very involved, much like my therapy. According to Henry's experience, it usually took three to five years from the time of the injury until the resolution of a medical malpractice lawsuit. While I continued to have mixed feelings, I thought it was time to talk to a couple of my attorney friends about recommending a firm that handled medical malpractice. There was no rush, but we decided it was time for me to make some phone calls and start exploring our options. Even if we didn't get a settlement, I wanted to tell my story in a public forum. People with back pain need to be aware of the dangers of such a procedure, and as I learned from several doctors we talked to, this procedure was not a long-term solution to the back pain that had initially brought me to Dr. X's office anyway.

Eight

Introspection

Sunday, August 26, was a relaxed day, which I desperately needed. I slept in until seven o'clock and spent the morning updating my journal and getting familiar with my new MacBook computer. This was my first truly relaxed day since the injury, and it gave me some time to reflect.

First of all, my entire world was my room in the rehab facility, where I spent about twenty hours a day, only leaving in a wheelchair for a few hours of therapy. I didn't know or care much about what was going on outside of my room and the gym downstairs. To me, there was no season or time or weather, just my hermetically sealed environment. My entire focus was on my body and trying to get it to work again, even though the experts we had seen didn't give us much hope. My world was built around getting the hang of bladder and bowel function, fighting for recovery in my legs, and building strength in my upper body to support myself. My total focus was on my body, and even very minor changes were a big deal. I believed that if I could find a way to stand and walk again with a walker and braces, I might still have a real life again. And if I was somehow able to walk, who knows what I was capable of doing? My discipline was strong, and I was singularly focused on recovery. As a result, I had become extremely self-absorbed. In talking with some of my closest friends, they pointed out that I could sometimes be this way even before the injury. I noted in my journal that I needed to be careful to not be so absorbed in my recovery, thinking only about myself. There were others intimately involved in my recovery, especially Sam. The recovery process can frequently be more difficult for the caregiver than for the patient, and this was especially true with a paraplegic like me.

It was nice not to have anything scheduled until the afternoon, and I had asked Sam to sleep in and get some rest. We both were exhausted, and I'm afraid I wasn't being very supportive of her. As I wrote in my journal that morning:

She is amazing—patient, kind, and very loving.

It reminded me once again that I couldn't get through something like this on my own. As we said more than once, it takes a village to help anyone recover from such a devastating injury. In spite of what I wrote in my journal, in the heat of the moment, I tended to forget, and Sunday was one of those moments. I don't know why, but I was a little cross with Sam that evening, and I could tell I had hurt her feelings. As I noted in my journal the following day:

I have not been sensitive to Sam's needs. I have corrected her and told her what to do instead of asking. At times, I have acted like I am in this by myself when I know it is a joint effort. I will become more sensitive to her needs.

Sometimes I could be so damn pushy about some things and thought I knew better than anyone else. I hated that, but it happened. So, Monday morning, I called Henry Noor and asked him to please deliver some flowers to Sam for me. He took care of it, and he let me know that he told the lady where he bought the flowers that he wasn't the one in trouble; it was a good friend of his.

I had good workouts on Monday, and my new therapist, Lou Tretter who worked mostly with out patients, encouraged me to try an electrical stimulator on my legs. There have been a lot of advances in technology for paraplegics, and this was one that stimulates the leg muscles to help a patient walk. Unfortunately, the damage to my spinal cord was too great, and we could find absolutely no response to the electrical stimulation. It was a nice try, and we planned to do it again in a week or so.

Once again, the support I received from my many friends was incredibly helpful in my recovery. Kurt Truax, my triathlon buddy, stopped by to visit and brought me my race packet from the Lake DeGray Triathlon I had signed up for at the beginning of the summer. He also passed along comments of support from fellow competitors at the race. He usually won his age group at the races in the surrounding area, and yet he was always so humble. There in my room that afternoon, he told me that after the Shreveport and Lake DeGray triathlons, he just couldn't beat me anymore. He had checked my finish time for the Lake DeGray race the previous year and said it was faster than his time this year. I told him that every race is different, even on the same course, but he was confident that I was faster than he was. It was good to see him, and we had a delightful visit. I still have a get-well card he gave me months afterward with a wonderful personal note inside. The front of the card read, "Strength, Hope, Courage," and inside he wrote, "I am so amazed at the outstanding progress you have made and continue to make. We are all in awe of your indomitable spirit, courage and determination, and you serve as a wonderful inspiration to everyone around you." For many years, he was the best and most gracious competitor I ever met at any race. He knew how hard I had worked to get proficient in the sport of triathlon, and he said if anybody would be able to walk after what had happened, it would be me. That was a wonderful compliment, and I knew it came from the heart.

Late in the day, I had another big group of visitors, including Bill Miller, an old friend I had known since grade school; Don Renshaw, a former sailing buddy; and Dudley Rodgers, a fellow sailor I had raced against and crewed with on a sailboat we chartered in Honduras. We had a great time and a lot of laughs on that trip. It was fun to see everyone, but it was also a little tiring. It was amazing how little energy I had and how I could only work on my therapy for a limited time before feeling exhausted. Before the injury, I was proud of my endurance and found I could push as hard as anyone in my age group for two hours or more at a race without slowing down. And now a one-hour visit with friends or a forty-five-minute therapy session absolutely wore me out. The decline in only a couple of weeks, from competitive triathlete to being worn out from a forty-five-minute therapy session, was dramatic.

Modifications to the House

That evening, Sam and I went over the results from the spinal commission's assessment of the house again and discussed some key issues. Dr. Rehab had indicated before he left for the weekend that he wanted to send me home as soon as possible and would talk to us when he got back, so we knew we needed to move ahead quickly on modifications to our home. A crew was already scheduled to install the wheelchair ramp on Tuesday before the Labor Day weekend, and other modifications inside the house were to follow. We were so very fortunate to have a first-class aluminum ramp donated to us by our friend and real estate agent, Dorothy Willoughby. She called shortly after she heard about my injury and offered to help in any way she could. A couple of years prior, she had purchased a fourteen-foot ramp for her father to use, and over time, he had gotten better and didn't need the ramp, so she had it removed and put in storage. When she first offered it to us, I was confident we wouldn't need anything that long and thanked her for her kindness. However, when Jon Breen calculated the distance and height for a wheelchair ramp, he told us we would need a fourteen-foot ramp. I thought a ramp that long would ruin the beautiful front entrance to our house, but we had no other alternatives. Immediately after getting the news from Jon, we called Dorothy and told her we would take her up on the offer but wanted to pay for the ramp. She not only refused any payment but also told me she knew a contractor, Jonathan Rogers, and would call him right away about installing the ramp and making any other modifications to the house that we needed. Jonathan and his crew did a terrific job for us on short notice, and at a very reasonable cost. I don't know what we would have done without Dorothy's generosity and Jonathan's help. They both were there for us in our hour of need and continued to stay in touch on a regular basis in case there was anything else they could do for us. This would turn out to be just the first of many times when we needed special resources and were fortunate to find the right solutions.

Our next step involved resolving some wheelchair issues. In the hospital, I started out using a heavy-duty hospital wheelchair, which was made out of tubular steel and was quite heavy. Of course, these chairs get a lot of use, so they have to be durable and stable, and they are designed to support considerably more weight than my 170 pounds. Also, most of them are designed to fold up to be put in a car. Chairs of this type are cumbersome and, weighing sixty to seventy pounds, would be very difficult for my petite bride to put in our car. Fortunately, Baptist Rehabilitation had a very lightweight chair in the gym to use as a demo. After a week or so, they let me use it full-time while working out at rehab. The chair was small but fit me just fine. It weighed about twenty-five pounds, was extremely maneuverable, and the back folded down easily so it could fit in the back of our Toyota Highlander. Frankly, putting the chair in the car turned out to be much easier than getting me inside. This type of lightweight chair costs about two thousand dollars, but with my therapist's help, we started exploring ways to get something similar for me through the Spinal Column Commission.

Getting the right chair was only the first step. Next was completing modifications to the house. In addition to installing Dorothy's ramp, Jonathan's crew did the following in a couple of days: removed the door from the master bedroom to the bathroom; took out the sliding shower doors and all the tracks holding the doors; installed a handheld showerhead and a set of grab bars in the shower; installed wedge-type ramps to get me over the front doorsill; and put in small wedge ramps from the kitchen to the deck. Our house had a nice-sized wooden deck that overlooked a beautiful greenbelt behind our back fence. This area was full of trees, birds, and squirrels, and a whole family of raccoons.

Before my paralysis, we frequently sat out there, and I wanted to be able to enjoy it again when I returned home. When I did get to go home, we still found some minor things that needed to be done around the house, but the major issues were resolved.

Tough Days

Starting what turned out to be my last week in a room at Baptist Rehab was a difficult time for me. I wasn't sleeping well, partially because Sam and I were wrestling with a lot of issues on the house and concerns about the future. Dr. Rehab told us he hoped to send me home the following Friday, which was the beginning of Labor Day weekend. I was concerned that it was too soon and was very apprehensive about leaving the rehab center where I had round-the-clock medical support. However, if I did go home, that meant Sam and I had a lot to accomplish—especially Sam, since she needed to be at the house while the crew was finishing up modifications to the house. In the meantime, we had received several recommendations on possible law firms, and I started making some exploratory calls. We also discussed revising our wills, and I called the attorney who drafted our initial wills when we got married. And there was still the issue of getting me a lightweight wheelchair, because Baptist Rehab couldn't give me the chair I was using since it was on loan to them as a demo. In addition, we had some substantial bills coming due and other expenses we needed to take care of. With everything that was going on, I was down emotionally and still grieving over the loss of my legs. I would see people walking around the gym and hated the fact that I couldn't stand up, much less walk.

As it turns out, I was physically coming down with what I thought was a cold. During therapy on Tuesday morning, I told one of my therapists, Lisa Anderson, that I felt weak, had a headache, and felt like I might be getting sick. She thought it might be a urinary tract infection, which was common for patients like me who were using a catheter tube every couple of hours to empty the bladder. As she said, that orifice is designed to excrete waste and not to have something regularly put inside it. That night was horrific for me, with intense chills and fever, which kept me awake most of the night. I asked one of the nurses to get the on-call doctor, who was one of Dr. Rehab's residents. I hadn't met the doctor I will call Dr. Y, but found out later that she was disliked by most of the patients and all of the staff on the spinal column wing. In fact, there was one story of a patient yelling at her, in a voice that could be heard down the hall, to "get the f—— out of my room." I told her my symptoms and asked her to please run a urine test for a possible bladder infection. The nurses had already taken a sample and had it ready to send to the lab. Dr. Y listened and seemed very skeptical while standing at the foot of my bed, leaning against the wall with her arms crossed. Having spent some time in sales, I could see this was a classic defensive stance. She asked me whether I had ever had a bladder infection before. When I said I didn't think so, she then asked in a voice like a teacher scolding a student, "How would you know if you had a bladder infection if you've never had one before?" I asked her to please go ahead and run the test and told her I had already given a sample to the nurse. She said she would "think about it" and walked out. She treated me like a damn child and had this arrogant manner about her that indicated that, as far as she was concerned, I didn't know squat and she was the expert. As an athlete, I knew my body pretty well and could tell I was in real trouble. At eight o'clock that night, as my condition was getting worse, I called for Melissa, the registered nurse on the floor, who informed me the test was not ordered. She and Bud, the licensed practical nurse, could tell that I was in a great deal of pain; all my vital signs were negative, and my urine was a dark orange color and had an intense odor. They really went to bat for me. The two of them called Dr. Y to report my symptoms and made every effort to get her to order a urine test. She finally relented and agreed to order the test.

The chills and fever continued throughout the night, and I struggled to get any sleep at all. Both nurses continued to check on me, and while my initial urine volumes were small, in the middle of the night, they drew off 1,200 cc of urine, which was way too much. I was in a great deal of pain, and the nurses were confident that my body was withdrawing fluid from my body to try to flush away the infection, and as a result, I was becoming dehydrated.

Wednesday morning, I was very weak and dehydrated, but the nurses wanted me to hold back on the fluids so I didn't overload my bladder. This was particularly critical since I had no feeling down there. I still tried to do some therapy that morning but couldn't do much. I went back upstairs to get some rest and found Dr. Caring (not her real name), another of Dr. Rehab's residents, at the nurses' station looking at my chart. Apparently, she had heard about my urinary tract infection, and I asked her to track down the results from the urinalysis. I went back to my room to rest while she called the lab, only to find out that the lab had lost the urine sample. Unbelievable! Fortunately, Dr. Caring took immediate action and told the lab to track down the sample, have it tested, and then call the nurses' station with the results as soon as possible. As the nursing staff and I expected, the test was positive and I did have a bladder infection. Dr. Caring contacted Dr. Y and got antibiotics ordered for me, which started to work within a few hours. Dr. Caring was a caring, gentle lady, and while I wasn't technically her patient, she was concerned about my condition and wanted to help. She was the antithesis of Dr. Y. The symptoms were so obvious to the nursing staff and others, and yet the arrogant Dr. Y thought she knew better. I don't know where that woman is now, but I hope she is in some area of medicine where she doesn't have to personally deal with patients on a regular basis.

Later that Wednesday, Dr. Rehab called and said he was sending me home on Friday. And fortunately, that day Jon Breen found a lightweight wheelchair for me to take home and use for a while. The chair was practically new and had only been used in a wheelchair basketball tournament the previous weekend. Now we had to get the measurements for the bathroom door and see whether the wheelchair would fit. As it turned out, it was going to be a very, very tight fit. Most wheelchairs have their big wheels angled in at the top and out and the bottom to add stability and to make it easier to push with the hands. My therapists were confident they could realign the wheels to a more vertical position so it would fit. They worked on the wheels and adjusted them to where we thought it would just barely fit in the doorway. However, the proof would be when I went home. In all other respects, the chair was great. It was very maneuverable, weighed only twenty-one pounds, and was easy for Sam to fold down the back and lift into the car. I liked the way it felt even better than the other lightweight chair I had been using.

After three very tough days both emotionally and physically, I was exhausted. It was so difficult for me to keep my mental composure when I was sick with a bladder infection. This limited my ability to do much, if any, therapy, which added to my frustrations. Combine that with little sleep over the previous two nights, and I desperately needed some rest. Fortunately, the medication was beginning to work, so I fell asleep quickly on Wednesday night and didn't stir until the next morning.

Thursday morning, I was groggy but could sense there was someone standing by my bed holding my hand. I felt the touch on my hand first and then thought I could hear my name. I slowly opened my eyes and saw Dr. Caring gently holding my hand and asking how I felt. It was so comforting to wake up and feel the touch of someone who cared and was expressing her concern about my condition. For just a moment, I felt like a child, and she seemed like a mother figure to me. Her touch and her presence gave me comfort, and I knew then that I would be OK. With her there, I relaxed and felt safe. She understood what I had been through over the last few days, and she wanted to check on me and make sure I was recovering. It may have been only a few minutes, but her touch and soothing voice had a powerful impact on me, which I will never forget. I realized after she left the room how rare human touch is in a hospital environment, which is most unfortunate. To prevent infection, almost every member of the hospital staff puts on rubber gloves immediately upon walking into a patient's room. I understand the need for this in many cases, but in the spinal column wing of Baptist Rehab, most of the patients have problems other than infections. It appeared to me that the rubber gloves were a habit, but patients also need human touch. I know how much it meant to me when Dr. Caring held my hand that morning, and also how wonderful it felt when Sam came in the room, hugged me, and held my hand.

After Dr. Caring's visit, I felt like this was going to be a very good day, and it was. I knew that if I was going to be discharged on Friday, I had to get my mind focused and my body working in the right direction. While I was still very weak, I was able to do some work in the gym with my therapists. That afternoon, I made some exciting new discoveries on my own. Sitting on the bed with my legs hanging down, I was able to flex my left thigh muscle enough to raise the lower part of my leg and hold it for just a second or two. I also found I could slightly move both of my big toes. This was one of those aha moments. If I could move my leg even slightly, then my left leg might recover. By moving both toes, I knew there was some limited nerve connection. When I discussed these developments with Dr. Rehab, he was pleased but also cautioned me about reading too much into these movements. He told me that when I gained some dorsiflexion, which is the ability to raise my toes upward, that's when we could really get excited.

The good news continued on Thursday. That afternoon, Sam told me that all the modifications to allow me to get around the house in a wheelchair were completed. We both were so thankful for Dorothy Willoughby's donation of the wheelchair ramp and for Jonathan Rogers's crew who installed the ramp and did all the modifications to the house on very short notice.

Nine

Going Home

On Friday, August 31, 2007, it was time for me to leave Baptist Rehab and go home. Dr. Rehab wanted his patients to spend as little time in the rehab facility as possible. He encouraged his patients to move back into society as soon as was reasonably possible, in order for them to get on with their lives. He believed I was at a point where I could manage in a wheelchair around the house. Of course, I would continue my therapy as an outpatient at Baptist Rehab while living at home. I hated to admit it, but I was afraid to leave rehab. I didn't know whether I could adapt to living at home without nurses on call twenty-four hours a day. I didn't know whether I would be able to get in a car or how I would move around our house. I was apprehensive about other unknowns, which would not be apparent until I was home and then didn't have the resources of a hospital. It was a little overwhelming and frightening. Moving me from my room at Baptist Rehab to our house was very involved, and Sam had to do it all. She enlisted our good friends, Mickey Freeman and Larry Mougeot to help with the move, and they were lifesavers.

Hospitals require a doctor to officially discharge a patient, and I couldn't believe who showed up for my official discharge. The evil Dr. Y came waltzing into my room with a nurse in tow and said in a cheerful voice like she was giving a child a surprise, "Are you ready to go home?" I didn't know what to say to her. This was the first time I had seen her since we first met on Tuesday and I had asked her to run a urine test, which she didn't think was needed. I wanted to tell her what I really thought of her, but instead I paused for just a moment and gathered my thoughts. Bud had helped me into the wheelchair and was standing beside me when Dr. Y entered the room. He, like many of the nurses, had previously had a confrontation with her and didn't want to be in the same room with the woman. He stood there stoically as I gathered my thoughts and said, "Doctor, I just can't deal with you today." She smiled, turned around, and left. I looked up at Bud, who knew how I felt about the damn woman, and he nodded his approval and told me I did just fine. A nurse gave me the paperwork to sign, and Bud wheeled me out.

Sam had been working diligently getting all my belongings together for the move, and she tried to move as much as she could on Thursday. It's amazing how much I had accumulated over three and a half weeks, first in a hospital and then at Baptist Rehab. In the first couple of weeks, Greg and Sam brought me several pairs of loose shorts, shirts, and underwear. Then there were all the hospital supplies I was paying for and wanted to take home, especially the diapers and bed shields. Added to that were flowers, cards, and many gifts from friends, and it made for quite a load. The staff on the floor brought a couple of carts into the room to stack everything on, and over a couple of trips, Sam, Mougeot, and Freeman moved it all down to their cars. Sam brought her car for the move, which was easier for me to get into than our SUV, but it wouldn't hold the wheelchair, so the guys loaded the chair and some of the other stuff in their two cars for the trip home.

The nurses on the floor for spinal column injury patients at Baptist Rehabilitation Center were always very helpful to us. I was impressed with their professionalism and concern for their patients. They did an excellent job with patients who had suffered devastating injuries and were having a hard time dealing with their situations. Some of the stories about patients on that floor were frightening. In spite of my injury, I could always look around the rehab gym and see people significantly worse off than I was. I felt fortunate to find an accomplished doctor and be treated in a facility with well-trained nurses and skilled therapists. I got to know my two inpatient therapists pretty well and was concerned about leaving them and starting therapy as an outpatient with a new therapist. However, my fears quickly disappeared as soon as I started working regularly with Lou Tretter. Over the next two years, we would become a great team and good friends. Early on, as an inpatient at Baptist Rehab, I quickly found that most therapists enjoy working with someone who is dedicated to his therapy and is willing to do whatever it takes to get better. I did see some patients who appeared to just be going through the motions and not making the effort necessary for recovery. While everyone wants to get better, some patients expect the therapist to make them better, when in truth it's up to the patient to work hard enough to make a difference. I believe therapists are much like teachers or coaches: they appreciate those who listen, pay attention, and do whatever it takes to gain some use of their damaged body.

The ride home was a little scary. It was the first time in almost a month I had been in a car, and it felt strange. A wheelchair doesn't go very fast, but with its big wheels and armrests, it is very stable. In the car, I felt very unstable. I didn't realize how much I used my feet for balance, and since I had no feeling in my feet, I had to hold on with my hands on the car door and armrest to balance. Sam is a very careful driver, but even at only thirty miles per hour, it felt like we were flying, and every time we turned a corner, I thought I might fall over in the seat. Fortunately, we lived only a few miles from the rehab center, and it was a short trip. Arriving at our house was wonderful. It felt so good to be back in familiar surroundings, and immediately all my fears about going home disappeared. Surprisingly, it seemed like I had been gone for a very, very long time. So much had happened since the last time I was able to walk into our home.

While in the hospital, I was concerned about the wheelchair ramp ruining the appearance of our beautiful house. Much to my surprise, it looked just fine. It was bright, shiny aluminum, and the handrails were very helpful. Over time, I found I could use the rails to pull myself up the ramp and into the house. After I went inside, I could see that all the modifications Sam had orchestrated with the construction crew were quite functional and looked good. It all seemed to work, and since the first floor of the house had an open floor plan, I could get around better than I expected. It also helped that the doorway to the master bedroom off the entry hallway was wide enough that I could go in and out fairly easily. Getting into the bathroom was a little bit tricky because it was a tight fit. However, if I lined up properly, I could squeeze through in the small wheelchair, but I had to be careful to keep from banging my knuckles. Sam had picked up a shower bench for me to use to bathe in the shower and also to do my bowel procedure. The bench had a flat space that allowed me to transfer from the wheelchair to the bench, as well as a section cut out like a toilet seat. After checking it out, we realized that a standard, small water bucket wouldn't work for my toilet issues, so we asked Mickey to run over to Home Depot and get us one of their large orange buckets, which was a perfect fit. This was all necessary since our commode was in a tight space with three walls, and I couldn't get close enough to transfer from the wheelchair to the commode. Initially, I had to do my bowel procedure three times a day, which meant Sam had to come in and empty out the bucket into the commode three times a day. In the process of manually evacuating the bowel, the waste tends to come out in large clumps like sausage balls. As a result, when the bucket was dumped into the commode, it frequently would not flush properly. At least once every day or two, Sam would have to work with a plunger to flush everything. I don't know how she put up with all this. Plus, I had to get up several times at night and transfer from the bed to my wheelchair and catheterize myself into a urinal jug. This meant Sam would get up and go empty the jug into the commode. In retrospect, I don't know why we didn't think of just buying several jugs and dumping then in the morning, but we had so many other issues to contend with at the time that we didn't think about it.

After we arrived home, I was checking out the house while Sam, Mougeot, and Mickey were busy hauling stuff in. During this process, I noticed there was a guy mowing a neighbor's yard and asked Mickey to see what he would charge to mow ours. I figured that since the lawn guy could do two lawns across the street from each other with only one trip, he might make me a deal, and he did. More important, I didn't want to ask Henry to mow the yard again. I knew he would be glad to do it, but I thought I might be taking away the opportunity for him to go out for a bike ride, and that was something I would never ask him to do.

It was so nice to be back home that when I woke up Saturday morning, I wrote the following in my journal:

Being at home is very therapeutic! Sleeping in my own bed, eating breakfast on the deck, and watching the birds and squirrels with Sam are wonderful. They give me a feeling of normalcy. I no longer feel like a patient.

Learning to Live at Home as a Paraplegic

Coming home meant adapting to challenges I didn't have in the hospital. While it was great to be home with Sam, I had to learn how to do things differently. Getting around the house in a wheelchair was a challenge, and learning to use the shower area for all my bathroom procedures was difficult. Plus, transferring from the wheelchair to the couch, the bed, and the seat in the shower took some time. Using the bucket under the U-shaped shower seat for all my bodily waste was a mess. In order to hopefully prevent me from wetting the bed, I set the alarm clock to go off every two hours for me to drain my bladder. That made it tough for both of us to get a good night's sleep, but it was what I had to do for the first few weeks. While things were challenging, it was delightful being back in our house. Hospitals are notoriously noisy places with lots of people coming and going at all hours. Going home made me feel like I was making some progress.

In spite of emptying my bladder every two hours, I slept very well lying next to Sam in our bed. However, I could tell the bladder issue was something I would have to get used to, maybe for the rest of my life. Sam helped me figure out how to work around the lavatory from my wheelchair and transfer into and out of the shower, which was a big challenge. Since this was Labor Day weekend, I planned to watch some college football and just relax and enjoy being back home.

One of the law firms we had called about helping us was the McMath firm, led by Bruce and Phillip McMath, whom I had known for years through my family. I wasn't aware they handled medical malpractice cases, but a sailing buddy and good friend, Max Mehlburger, who was also a lawyer, recommended them to me. I knew Bruce from the sailing club, so I called him from the hospital, and we scheduled a meeting at our house after I returned home. However, before I left the hospital, Bruce called and said he and Phillip had worked on some lawsuits with a retired anesthesiologist whom he would like us to meet. He told us the doctor who was from Colorado would be in town for a few days over the holiday weekend. Bruce thought it would be helpful regardless of whether we selected their firm or someone else to represent us. On Saturday afternoon, the doctor stopped by and it was a very informative visit. We told him all the details about the injection and the resulting paralysis, and I could tell he was surprised about several issues. Like the other doctors we met, he had never heard of this happening from this procedure. He was surprised we received no warning or disclosure about potential risks involved. This is something Dr. X should have done when he first discussed the steroid injection. He also wondered why the doctor hadn't pushed harder for me to initially try some oral medication for the pain, since the bulging disc issue appeared to be a minor problem. The bottom line from our discussion was that it sounded like Dr. X followed accepted procedures, but if the injection had been done properly, there was virtually no chance of paralysis. In telling our story, it was obvious that this doctor was as stunned as we were by my paralysis. He wished us his best and said he would follow up with Phillip and Bruce.

I had told my story about the injury to enough doctors and other medical professionals that I was used to seeing the look of surprise on their faces when they heard what happened. At first it felt like I was reliving the whole thing over and over again, but after almost a month, it was what it was, and I needed to get beyond worrying about how it all happened. There were still many times when I would relive the whole thing in my mind and I would blame myself for going to the wrong doctor and ask, "Why me?" This mostly occurred when I went to bed at night or first thing in the morning. Sometimes at night, I would dream I was walking around our yard or riding my bike on one of my favorite routes, and then wake up and realize I was paralyzed and might never be able to do any of those things again. That was devastating. And some days, I couldn't even bring myself to get out of bed to go to therapy, but I knew I would never get any better lying in bed.

Sunday of Labor Day weekend, I slept in until nine o'clock and felt very relaxed for a change. Sam and I had breakfast on the deck and took our time reading the newspaper. It was so nice being outside on our deck with my soul mate. It almost seemed like we were on vacation. Later in the day, with Sam's help I did some Thera-Band exercises on the bed, mostly for my upper body. I also had a good visit by phone with my two sons, Greg in Sedona, Arizona, and Matt in Houston, Texas. This was the weekend of my niece's wedding in Sedona, and Greg called back later to give me all the latest information about the family and the wedding. Sam and I loved hiking in Sedona. We so wanted to be there for the wedding with the whole family, but it wasn't possible.

Sunday night, we had a great time. Sam picked up a pizza, and the Freemans and Mougeots joined us for dinner on the deck. We talked about previous adventures and laughed about old times, and it was a marvelous time together. The Freemans and Mougeots had been so supportive of us, and we needed all the support we could get. What a great weekend it was, leaving the hospital on Friday and coming home. These were truly my best two days since the injury. For a change, while I knew my body was broken, I felt like a whole person. My mind was still working reasonably well, my spirits were good, and there was hope in my heart. In my condition, I couldn't have asked for much more than that.

While Sam and I had a fun weekend and I got some excellent rest, we knew there was a lot to be done that first week at home. For starters, we needed to plan my therapy going forward. Initially, I planned to go to Baptist Rehab three days a week, but I knew I needed to do more if I was ever going to recover. We also scheduled a home health nurse to visit several times during the first couple of weeks to teach me how to do things around the house. Finally, we planned to start going to the Little Rock Athletic Club a couple of days a week to work out. Before the injury, I had gone there regularly for several years; I liked the environment and thought it would be a good place to work on my rehabilitation.

One of the key things I learned in this process is that if I only did what insurance paid for, it would be difficult to make much progress. If I was ever going to walk again, I knew I would have to push myself and do much, much more than just the limited therapy covered by insurance. Yes, physical therapy is expensive, but I asked myself, "How badly do I want to get better?" I was determined not to live the rest of my life in a wheelchair. As I said repeatedly, mostly as an affirmation, "This wheelchair is a temporary device, and I will use it as a tool to help me get better." Because my complete paralysis was such a rare occurrence from an epidural injection, most doctors were reluctant to give any kind of a positive prognosis. However, a couple of the therapists I saw at Baptist Rehab thought there might be some chance for limited recovery, and I was going to do everything I could to recover at least some of the function in the lower half of my broken, paralyzed body. I told myself I would look at this like another form of training. I didn't run a marathon in three hours and thirty-eight minutes without training hard for almost three years. When I first started racing sailboats, it took me four years to beat the local fleet champion in a single race. When I took up racing triathlons, it took me three years to get to the point where I wouldn't be completely exhausted after a half-mile open water swim. So if it took me one year, two years, three years, or more, whatever it took to be able to get out of a wheelchair and walk with a walker, I would do it. And regardless of the cost, I knew it would be worth whatever it took in terms of money and effort.

On Monday of our first week home, Henry Noor stopped by to bring us a board he had cut to fit underneath the cushions on our couch for more support. The couch was a large sectional I'd had for several years, and with Sam's strong encouragement, we planned to replace it at some point. When I got home, I found that without the use of my legs, it was almost impossible for me to get off of the couch and into my wheelchair by pushing myself up with my arms. Henry was a lifesaver, and the board made a significant difference. I knew I could call on him for anything. I also informed him that we had made other arrangements for the yard work, and while he didn't say so, I believe he was quite relieved.

Tuesday turned into a very busy day. Henry showed up with another board to put under the cushions on the other half of the couch, which I much appreciated. Then our home health nurse arrived and was very helpful. She worked diligently with both Sam and me on exercises to do at home for my legs to help develop a good range of motion. In the afternoon, Phillip and Bruce McMath drove out to our house for a meeting on our potential lawsuit. I had known the McMath brothers casually for most of my life. Our parents were good friends, and my sister Debbie was about the age of the McMath twin sisters, and they played together as kids. Their father, who had died a few years before, was a general in the Marine Corps and a successful attorney who had also served as governor of our state. I trusted Phillip and Bruce, and we believed they would be a good choice to represent us. They listened patiently, were very sympathetic to our situation, and took the time to explain that this would be a long and arduous process. However, they believed we had been wronged and should seek a legal resolution.

The following day, Wednesday, September 5, we met with another well-known attorney who was strongly recommended by my friend Pete Heister. This attorney had a lot of experience with malpractice and is considered to be one of the best litigators in a courtroom. Sam and I agreed this would be a tough decision, but as my friend Mickey Freeman said, we couldn't go wrong with either choice. We ended up hiring the McMath law firm because I knew them personally and believed I would be much more than just a client they were representing. I was a friend. That proved to be the case, and they did an outstanding job for us.

On Thursday of my first week out of the hospital, Dr. Rehab scheduled a meeting with Lou Tretter at Baptist Rehab for outpatient therapy. Dr. Rehab wanted to make sure I didn't miss a beat on my therapy. That outpatient session was scheduled for 8:00 a.m., which meant I had to wake up at 6:00 a.m. to have a small breakfast, do my bathroom routine, and get dressed. All of that took well over an hour, and getting me out of the house and into the car was not an easy task.

It's amazing how much we take for granted. Having lost the use of the lower half of my body, doing ordinary things became very difficult and time consuming. Before the injury I showered every morning in less than fifteen minutes, but after my paralysis I moved taking showers to later in the day because it took so much time, usually an hour or more from start to finish. My daily routine during the week started with transferring from the bed to the wheelchair, and then wheeling myself into the bathroom to do my bowel and bladder routine, and if had a full bowel this could take twenty to thirty minutes or more. Then I had to shave which took some practice. Since I couldn't stand and the sink had cabinets underneath, I shaved while sitting in the wheelchair sideways next to the sink so I could get close enough to lean over and shave. Then it was time to get dressed which meant laying out the clothes on the bed and transferring from the wheelchair back to the bed. I couldn't hang my legs off the side of the bed to put on my shorts or pants because I would fall off the bed if I leaned forward. So I would lay on the bed and first change my diaper and then pull on my shorts, which was much easier than pulling on long pants. Over the next six months I was able to sometimes give up the diaper and wear underwear with a urinary shield. To pull my shorts on I had to roll back and forth on the bed and then put on a shirt and finally shoes. This process would take fifteen to twenty minutes. Then I would transfer back to the wheel chair and go to the kitchen for a light breakfast of cereal, juice and fresh fruit. And before we left the house I would brush my teeth and catherize myself again to make sure my bladder was empty. Several months later when I was starting to get on my feet for a limited time in therapy, I had to put on braces, which added more time to the process. Overall it would usually take from and an hour and fifteen to thirty minutes for me to be ready to leave the house. And after I was done Sam had to roll me down the ramp and over to the car, help me get into the car and then fold up the wheelchair, put it in the back and drive me to therapy. When we arrived at Baptist Rehab, the athletic club, or a doctor's office for an appointment, she had to unload the chair and me, park the car and then help me into the building. Going through this process, five days a week for two to three different appointments a day, was exhausting for Sam and a significant change in the lives of a couple who had been married for less than two years. Frankly, I don't know how Sam managed all that plus the cooking, shopping, cleaning and everything else that had to be done.

At Baptist Rehab Lou did a thorough assessment, and he was pleased to find some limited firing in the muscles in my legs. It wasn't strong enough for me to feel it, but Lou could feel it, which gave us hope that there was a chance of recovery. Lou and I agreed to a goal of getting me up and standing in the next four weeks, which, based on the nature of my injury, was unrealistic, but at least it was something to shoot for. I knew it was a stretch to accomplish that in only four weeks, but if I couldn't do it in four weeks, maybe I could in four months. I was retired, and recovery was beginning to look like it would be my lifelong career. Loss of my bowel and bladder was devastating, and as I quickly learned, it was much more of a limiting factor on my activities than going around in a wheelchair was. Unfortunately, as more than one doctor had explained to me, the bowel and bladder are right next to the base of the spinal cord and would be the last thing to recover, if they recovered at all. Also there wasn't much in the way of therapy I could do on that, so we focused on trying to get my legs working again.

I really liked Lou Tretter and found him to be extremely helpful and encouraging in my rehabilitation over the next two years. Lou appreciated my situation of going from an athlete to a paraplegic, and he understood that I wanted to work as hard as I could and that I would do anything to improve my condition and get more mobility. As a result, he was always coming up with new things to try out on me, because he knew I was willing to explore different techniques, exercises, or anything that might help.

Ten

Therapy -- The Hard Work Begins

After the first session with Lou, which was just over an hour, Sam drove me back home, and we both laid down for a nap. I was exhausted after not sleeping well and getting up early, and Sam was worn-out taking care of me. In spite of antidepressant medication, I was still struggling with frustration and depression, especially at night. However, I was looking forward to seeing Greg, who was flying in late that night for the weekend, and the Heisters were bringing dinner to the house for us. Pete, Sandy, and I had run a lot of miles together over many years, and their company was always a treat.

Dr. Rehab assigning Lou Tretter to work with me was a blessing for us. Once again, we were fortunate in this process to find the right resource at the right time. Over time as we explored new treatments, doctors and therapists, we found some who were not a good match. However, we would work at finding the right person, and we were always able to find someone who was a good fit for my rehabilitation, both mentally and physically. Lou was one of the best, and we started seeing him three days a week and working hard on getting some movement in my legs any way we could. I frequently refer to "we," since Sam had to drive me everywhere and then would stay for the hour of therapy and drive me back home. This was a team effort for us and was frequently more demanding on her than me.

The same week I started working with Lou, I also set up a schedule to work with a craniosacral therapist, Anne Miskin, and a personal trainer, Carla Branch, both at the Little Rock Athletic Club. Working with Lou, Carla, and Anne quickly became the foundation of my recovery. Craniosacral therapy, which was developed by a doctor in the late 1970's, uses light touch to enhance nervous system functioning and release deep musculoskeletal restrictions. My treatment included traction of my legs, coccyx (tailbone) and spine along with using pressure points at the base of the skull to promote mobility and restore the neural pathways, which were blocked by the stroke to the conus of my spinal column. By doing this Anne hoped it would enable my brain to connect with the lower half of my body. Carla's primary goal was to help me exercise the few muscles that were barely working in my legs. We also included some upper-body work to keep my arms and shoulders strong because they had to lift my body to make transfers to and from the wheelchair.

Friday morning, September 7, 2007, was the end of my first week at home, and I had my first therapy session with Anne Miskin. The following week, I started working with Carla. She and Anne would visit each week to discuss my situation and plan my workouts. Just being back at the athletic club felt great. Even though I was in a wheelchair, I knew it was a start in the right direction. I was a regular at the club for several years and knew many members who offered their encouragement and hope for my recovery. The athletic club was always a very positive environment for me, and I was glad to be back.

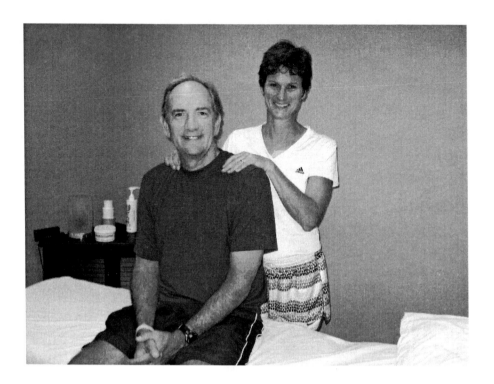

Anne with me

Having Greg with us again for the weekend was wonderful. It was now thirty days after the injury, and we believed it was time to get out of the house and see if I could do something besides just therapy. So, for my first meal out in the "real world," we went to one of our favorite spots, the Pizza Café. It was a picture perfect day to sit outside, so Sam and Greg wheeled me onto the deck, and we had a great time with beer and pizza. It was a struggle for both Sam and me, but it was nice being in a familiar place again, and a week after that, Sam took me to a movie in the wheelchair. I was beginning to believe there was some light at the end of the tunnel, and those outings helped relieve some of the frustration from having to cancel our Sedona trip.

My first week at home was a big change from the Baptist Rehab environment, and I made the following thoughtful entry in my journal about this process:

I am learning to be patient and take my time, especially on my transfers. I need to think things out before I act. At this point in recovery, if I make a mistake, it could be disastrous. Thinking before I act is crucial to my survival. It is hard to imagine how I got to this point and what it will take to recover. But I can't look back. I must look forward and focus on recovery. I am finding tiny victories in my progress, so I will continue to enjoy those victories and work to achieve more. It is slow, small, hard progress. There are no easy answers or sudden revelations. There are only long days, restless nights, and hard work toward some sort of recovery. Keeping my mind focused is critical. With Sam's help and full support, plus the love and support of many friends and family, I will recover. I cannot let them down. They believe in me, and I will not let them down. This is a very self-absorbing, narcissistic process, but that's how it works for now. I am going to owe Sam more than I can ever repay when I get better.

While that was a positive entry in my journal, the following day's entry showed the terrible mood swings that I couldn't seem to control:

Today I am angry, frustrated, and grateful, all at the same time. I am angry with the doctor who did this to me, and I am frustrated with many of the doctors we have seen who have no explanation and no prognosis and offer so little help. It makes me mad as hell! I want more information, and I get so little. Very frustrating! But, at the same time, I am grateful for Sam, Greg, and the dear friends who have been so supportive and who believe in me. They believe in me more than the doctors.

There was also some good news those first two weeks at home. I was very proud of the fact that I was able to move my toes ever so slightly. I e-mailed an update to some of my close friends, and Pierre Rousset sent me a response about a neurosurgeon in Shreveport whom he had talked to about my condition. This doctor, who only knew what Pierre had told him, thought that if I could move my toes, I should be able to walk again. While this doctor had not examined me or seen the MRIs of the injury, it was a relief to finally have a medical professional who thought maybe I might be able to walk!

In my first couple of weeks at home, we had several visitors come by the house, which was always a boost. Mickey came by a few times and called on a regular basis. Bob and Jane Goff, whom I was in school with from first grade through high school, came by for a delightful visit. Bob had come to the hospital shortly before I left for home and was very patient and concerned. We had such a nice, long visit on our deck when they showed up at the house. The Mougeots stopped by for another visit and brought some of Kris's homemade chocolate chunk cookies, which are divine. They were always interested in my progress from the very beginning, and I showed them how I could move my left leg and some toes, along with a little foot movement. They were impressed, compared to where I was when they first visited me in the hospital. Since I was living with this on a daily basis, I rarely saw much change, but those who were not around me all the time could see noticeable improvements. That was always a boost for my morale.

But in spite of all the support I had, I still struggled mentally. Sam and I finally made the decision to cancel our European riverboat trip with the Noor's and called to tell them. I had hoped Sam could go, but it was obvious to both of us that I needed full-time care and transportation to therapy. Of course, this frustrated me, and that Friday morning, I wrote the following in my journal:

In spite of a good day yesterday and my efforts to focus on the light, I still find the darkness creeping in on me, particularly in bed at night. I frequently think of death as an option. While it would initially hurt Sam, my family, and my close friends, it would lift a terrible burden from Sam and Greg. It would also end my own mental frustration and suffering. But then, I do hold out hope to be able to walk again, and my progress continues at a very slow pace. So I shall try to focus on the light and continue to have hope. Maybe I will be able to keep the darkness away for another day. But it is so difficult at times.

Toward the end of September, I could push down slightly with my right foot and found I was getting a little bit more feeling in random places in my legs. In rehab, Lou tried to get me up in parallel bars with a fixed full-leg brace on my right leg and a partial brace on my left leg. It was extremely difficult. I was pushing as hard as I could in therapy and wanted to try this, even though I knew it was probably too soon. My legs wouldn't support me at all, in spite of lifting myself up with my arms. It was then that I fully realized how far away I was from ever walking again. As I wrote in my journal at the end of the day:

This is going to be a real challenge.

That week, I also met with Dr. Rehab, and while he was pleased with my limited recovery, there still was no prognosis of what I might be able to do, partially because not a single doctor I talked to had ever heard of this kind of injury from the epidural injection that Dr. X administered. Dr. Rehab also sent me to a wound clinic to try to heal the bedsore on my bottom from the time I spent in the hospital and rehab facility. That's just what we needed; another physical problem to deal with.

Sam and I were settling into a regular therapy routine, which was helpful. It gave me something to focus on and kept me from feeling sorry for myself. I loved being back at the athletic club, and Sam could also get in a good workout while I spent time with Carla and Anne. Sam needed the break, and this was very helpful for her. Many people at the club, some I didn't even know, would take time to wish me well and offer encouragement. Robin Hanley, who worked the membership desk at the club, made a point to tell me that a lot of people were supporting me and expecting me to recover. With all these people counting on me, I felt I could not let them down. My recovery affected more than just me. There were many people who believed in the human spirit's ability to succeed and expressed their faith in my recovery. This abundant outpouring of encouragement had a very positive affect. Over time, their expectations supported my hope that somehow, someway, I might be able to make some sort of recovery. My hope was slowly becoming a belief in my ability to recover.

We finished my first month at home with a fun weekend. Our dear friends from Louisiana, Pierre, Craig, and Liz, came up for the Big Dam Bridge 100 bike ride and stayed with us for the whole weekend. Back in the spring, we had planned for all of us to ride in this event, which had become the biggest bike tour in the state. I obviously couldn't ride a bike, but I still wanted to attend the event. Sam drove me over to the finish line and helped me into the wheelchair, and we had the opportunity to visit with people I had ridden with over the years and to meet up with our Louisiana friends. After the ride, the five of us went to the Buffalo Grill for burgers and beer. What a fun time we had, and while I didn't feel like I was making much progress, Pierre, Craig, and Liz were quite impressed with my improvement since they visited me that first week in the hospital. Being with them and talking about our riding adventures together was a big boost to my morale. They continued to stay in touch with me throughout the entire ordeal, and I appreciated that. I'd had some memorable bike trips with this group. They were the best of companions.

My heavy therapy schedule continued with as many as six or more therapy visits per week, including three with Carla, one with Anne, two or three with Lou, and a visit to a wound clinic for treatment of a bedsore Sam discovered before I left the rehab center. Some weeks there were also regular doctor visits added to the schedule. Anne was doing hands-on work trying to open up my spine and limber up my legs. She was particularly pleased with the reduced swelling at the base of my spinal cord and thought the muscle tone in my legs was getting better. With Carla, I started out working from my wheelchair doing exercises to strengthen my core and upper body. Initially, Carla would help me line up my wheelchair next to a machine where she could give me handles attached to pulleys and weights for strengthening exercises. Lou and I would usually work on an elevated mat, trying to get movement in my legs along with some stretching. He also started teaching me to balance on my knees by kneeling on a mat, which was extremely difficult in the beginning.

The support from friends and therapists was critical to both my physical and my mental condition. I had always believed I could do almost anything on my own, but this experience completely changed that. Never before had I been so grateful for the support and help of so many people who cared so much about both Sam and me. We had only been married seventeen months when this happened, and not only had my life completely changed, but so had hers. A lot of marriages would not have been strong enough to survive this, but Sam was determined to do everything humanly possible to help me recover, regardless of how long it took. In addition to the physical problems she had to help with, she also had to deal with someone who was not a fun person to be around a good deal of the time. There were many days when depression just overwhelmed me and I didn't want to get out of bed, go to therapy, or eat. Sam found that if she couldn't get me out of bed, then she would threaten to call either Mickey Freeman or Greg and get them to straighten me out. In several cases, she did call them, and it usually worked. They both offered meaningful physical and mental support to Sam throughout this whole ordeal.

Eleven

A New Start

October 2007 was the real beginning of my recovery. Up until then, most of what Sam and I were doing was figuring out what kind of therapy to focus on, learning how to get around the house in a wheelchair, venturing out into public for the first time, and adapting to living with a severe handicap. Things that used to seem so easy and simple were now major undertakings. Obviously, I was unable to drive a car, so this meant that Sam had to take me everywhere I went, and that involved a whole lot more effort on Sam's part than just driving the car. She had to help me bathe and dress each morning, then wheel me out the front door, down a fourteen-foot aluminum ramp, and around the house to the garage. There she helped me transfer into the car, folded the back of the wheelchair, lifted it into the back of our SUV, and drove me to therapy. Once we got there, she had to repeat the whole process to unload the chair, fold up the back, bring it into position by the passenger door, and help me transfer from the car to the chair. In some cases, if there was ramp with even a slight upgrade at the entrance, she had to push me into the building and help wheel me into therapy. An hour later, she would repeat the process to go home. Frankly, I don't know how she did it all, plus she had to put up with me giving her directions while she was driving. Not many people would have survived living with me at that time.

I still had good days and bad days, but at least now I felt like I was making some progress and wished my doctors would be more reassuring.

However, as Anne Miskin reminded me, all they could do was tell me about my condition at the time and what they thought I should do for rehabilitation. Anne and Carla were the ones giving me the most encouragement, as they could see tangible signs of small changes Sam and I didn't see. The truth was, it was virtually impossible for anyone to predict how much recovery I might get over the next month, next year, or next five years. All we knew for sure at the time was that it would be a long, slow process with no promise of positive results. Consequently, at times, my mind would wander off to doubts about ever walking again, riding a bike, and regaining use my bowel and bladder. It was hard not to think about the quality of life I might have long-term. All of our friends were very encouraging, but I wondered whether they were just trying to be supportive and really didn't know what else to say. None of the doctors we saw had ever seen anything like this from an epidural injection, so they couldn't predict anything. While the future was unknown, all I could do was work hard and hope for positive developments. As Pierre said to me when he called, "Randy, this will be your greatest race." Anne Miskin told me I should look at this as an opportunity to rebuild my life. It was hard to think of rebuilding my life at sixty-three years old, but the thought did make some sense. Reflecting on her comment, I wrote the following in my journal that evening:

I have been pretty self-centered for the last fifteen years or so, and now is the opportunity to rebuild my life with my partner, Sam, as a couple. That would be a good thing. This whole process is not just about me. It is about us.

The first week of October was busy with regular therapy, a check-up with the dentist, and the first visit to see my mother since the injury. Mom was an amazing woman who had been active all her life, but she was now eighty-nine years old and had declined to the point that, several months before my injury, we had moved her to a nursing home. She had fallen twice in the last couple of years, causing a concussion the first time and then breaking her hip the second time, which was devastating. So we knew she had to have full-time care. Even prior to the nursing home, we already had an in-home nurse visiting her every day. The doctor who fixed her hip was very straightforward with Debbie and me. He said mom was already losing some cognitive ability, and the best he could hope for, after a three- to four-hour operation, was to get her back to where she was before she fell. Even though mom was declining, she still knew who I was, called me by name, and was always glad to see me. In spite of not knowing where she was most of the time, she had a positive attitude, and the staff at the nursing home enjoyed taking care of her. While she knew who I was before I was paralyzed, she didn't recognize me in a wheelchair. Over a couple of our visits, she made comments to Sam that indicated that she thought I was a close relative and she appreciated Sam looking after me. But, in a wheelchair, I wasn't the son she remembered. The son she knew was fit and strong, and she frequently commented about how good I looked. Prior to my paralysis, she would frequently tell me how proud she was that I stayed in such good physical shape. In her mind, she really didn't know who the person in the wheelchair was, and sometimes neither did I.

That same week, I made good progress at rehab. Lou suggested trying something new, and I was thrilled to find I had enough strength to get up on all fours and crawl a little on the workout mat. Maintaining my balance was difficult, but both Lou and I were pleased with my ability to get up on my hands and knees. However, my shoulders were a little sore the next morning from the effort. Anne was pleased with my continuing improvements in muscle tone in both legs, and at the end of the week, I also noted some slight tingling in my right leg. It seemed to me that various places in my legs were trying to wake up. It wasn't true touch sensation, but it did appear there were some neural connections that might be waking up.

The second week of October 2007 marked day sixty of my fight to recover some use of the lower half of my body. While there was still a long way to go, looking back sixty days, Sam and I could see significant progress and hope of more to come. This reminded me of the ancient

Chinese proverb, "A journey of a thousand miles begins with a single step," and I appeared to be making a very small step almost every week.

That week, I took Tuesday off from therapy because I needed the rest, and what a good day it was. I sat out on the deck in my wheelchair while Sam had some time to herself and went to the athletic club. That afternoon I wrote the following in my journal:

It is a wonderful, restful place here on the deck today, and I am at peace with myself for a change. Sure, I would give anything to be riding my bike or running down by the river, but I can still enjoy being outside on the deck, even in a wheelchair. Right now, today, it's good to be alive.

While I tended to push myself as hard as I could, it was on that Tuesday, sitting on the deck, when I realized I needed to focus on more than just working on physical rehabilitation. I needed time to rest, relax, and appreciate each day. Making the most of each day did not always have to be about working out. There were other things that needed my attention. Sam and I finished the day by having dinner with Kelley and Judy Johnson. They were old friends, and we had season tickets together for the Arkansas Repertory Theatre. Once again, this reminded me of my many friends who had been so supportive.

Sixty-one days after the injury, with Lou's help, I tried walking in a harness suspended from a track in the ceiling, with a mobile U-shaped support frame called an ARJO Walker around me. I kept pushing Lou to let me do more and more, so he offered me the chance to see if I could walk a little, and I was anxious to try. It turned out to be one of my most depressing moments at Baptist Rehab. I couldn't feel or control my feet at all. It looked like I might never be able to walk again. After therapy was over, Sam and I both were almost in tears, and when we returned home, I noted the following in my journal:

I have a very long way to go!

As bad as the ARJO experience was, a week later, I tried walking in parallel bars with a stiff brace on my right leg and a lower leg brace on the stronger left leg, and I found I was able to put limited pressure on my left leg, but the right leg held up only because it was in a fixed leg brace. At least I was vertical for a short period of time, so there was some hope. Anne Miskin also thought my bladder and core area were starting to develop some muscle tone, which gave me hope for some sort of recovery in those areas. Carla Branch added that she thought the muscles in both legs were showing some small improvements.

Twelve

Reflections on the Last
Sixty-Four Years

Wednesday, October 17, 2007, was my sixty-fourth birthday. Birthdays are one of those annual milestones when many people, including me, reflect on where we have been and where we are going. It was interesting to reflect back on all the things I had done—missions accomplished and mistakes made—and to think how fortunate I had been in so many ways.

As I stated at the beginning of this book, I met the love of my life, Sam, about six months after retirement and had a lot to be thankful for. My paralysis in early August of 2007 was a traumatic experience, but bad things do happen to good people for no apparent reason. It was the result of a questionable decision in not getting a second opinion and trusting a doctor I didn't know. However, I knew I couldn't afford the luxury of looking back and wondering, "why me?"

Greg drove up from Plano, Texas, to celebrate my sixty-fourth birthday, and we had a great time as usual. While I was feeling frustrated over the lack of more meaningful progress, having Greg with us was a big boost. He and I ran some errands together and went shopping for workout clothes while Sam had a much-needed day off. A few days later, Sam orchestrated a birthday dinner at the house and invited twenty people, including therapists and friends who had been so supportive and helpful in my recovery process. We had a terrific time, and once again, this reminded me of how many people were contributing to my recovery.

On my birthday, aided by some helpful counseling, I wrote down the following thoughts about loss and recovery in my journal:

What I am going through is much like losing a loved one. A very big part of my life is gone, and I haven't properly grieved for the loss. In the past, I defined myself by my physical activities, and that is no longer a part of my life. I need to understand that I have to separate the grief over my loss from the process of getting better. It is OK to take time to grieve. It is a necessary part of loss.

Dealing with the unknown is the most difficult of all. I don't know whether I will walk or bike or run or what! Not knowing can drive anyone crazy. Trying to anticipate all possible outcomes just creates more frustration and leads to more doubt. I have plenty of reasons to grieve and doubt. That is OK. But I will not let that interfere with the process of recovery.

Examining my situation at that time, I noticed that in addition to the loss of bowel and bladder control and the use of my legs, there were other changes that weren't physically apparent. Besides the frequent bouts with frustration and depression, I found I had no appetite. Frankly, I couldn't have cared less whether I ate or not. Nothing seemed to taste good, and I wasn't thirsty. Of course, with my bladder issues, I cut back on fluid intake, but even cutting back, I was never thirsty, which I knew was not normal. As an athlete, I used to drink plenty of water to stay hydrated, but even months after the injury, I didn't feel any need for fluids. Anne Miskin thought the lack of appetite was related to depression but found my lack of thirst surprising. All of this was certainly keeping my weight down. I thought that without any aerobic activities, I would be gaining weight, but lack of appetite curtailed any weight gain.

Overall, Sam and I did see some progress in October and had more hope than we did thirty days before. The eventual outcome was unknown, but there were several things I had learned: I knew, for instance, that I would not get better if I didn't believe I could. I also knew that I needed to focus on the daily process of moving forward and living in the moment. Lastly, I realized that I needed to avoid thinking about the eventual outcome, which no one could predict. If I worked hard, focused on recovery, and kept a positive attitude, I believed the future would take care of itself. While all that sounds good, it is much easier said than done.

Toward the end of the month, I had a visit from two childhood friends, Bill Miller and Jim Growdon, who was a doctor in Nashville, Tennessee. The three of us went all through school together, and it was good to see both of them. Jim thought my progress in only a couple of months was remarkable, and he believed I would walk again. Bill and Jim spent two hours with us, and we relived a lot of good times as kids growing up in Little Rock. We were so fortunate to grow up in a wonderful neighborhood with good schools and nice people. It was a different time in the late forties and fifties, when there was little crime, economic conditions were relatively good, and people treated each other with courtesy and respect. In those days, if children acted up in school, teachers called their parents and the children knew there were penalties to be paid when they got home. Kids could play outside without supervision, and before television became affordable, everyone I knew was always active riding their bikes or walking places to visit friends. It truly was a different time and place.

At the end of October, Anne and Carla believed I looked much better and appeared to be gaining ground on my recovery. The changes were frequently so minor that I couldn't see them, but they were pleased with the developments. That same week, Lou Tretter and his able assistant Jamie Stephens got me up on my feet again in the ARJO walker using the sling suspended from the ceiling. Jamie moved the walker while Lou bent over and controlled my right knee and foot, and they told me to take very small steps. I put every ounce of energy I had into trying to move my feet, and with intense concentration, I was able to generate limited forward movement. The three of us must have looked like something out of an old silent movie as we stumbled forward, but it seemed to work, and by pausing three times to rest, I was able to cover 120 feet. It wasn't pretty, and I believe it took as much out of Lou and Jamie as it did out of me. However, for the first time in almost ninety days, I was somewhat vertical and moving a little bit with my legs. When we were finished, Lou counted off the tiles on the floor to measure how far we went, just so I would have a tangible way to gauge my progress.

For my last workout of the month, Lou had me walk in the sling and the ARJO walker again, and this time we covered 240 feet. We could tell that my legs were ever so slowly coming around and getting better. Two days later, Lou got me up in parallel bars again, which was a struggle. I found that I could put enough pressure on the left leg to help support my body, but the right knee was hard to control, and the right leg offered no meaningful support. Throughout the recovery process, my right leg was always much slower to develop. No one knew why this was the case, but it occurred to me that since the nerve Dr. X was trying to treat was in my right leg, he may have damaged it more than the left. There was no evidence to support my theory based on the MRIs taken after the injury, but I thought maybe that's what happened. Regardless of the injury ninety days ago, all I could do was focus on the future. I ended the month by writing down in my journal four things I needed to remember going forward:

Unknown outcome

Need to focus on daily progress

Be in the moment instead of focusing and worrying about the outcome

Meditate and visualize the positive

At the end of October we learned a good lesson about shopping for the various supplies I needed, especially catheter tubes for my bathroom procedure. Before most people leave a hospital, they will receive prescriptions for pharmaceuticals as well as supplies they will need when returning home. It's natural to stop by a hospital pharmacy to pick up these items. There are two problems with doing that. First, many of the things one might need will not be on hand in the pharmacy, and they will have to order them from general supply. This can take a few hours or, if late in the day, you may have to pick up what you need the next day. Second, in my experience, a hospital pharmacy was usually a more expensive place to buy supplies. Also, your medical insurance may or may not cover the full (or even partial) cost for many of the things you will need. The worst example of this for us was buying catheter tubes. The first time we purchased the tubes I needed, they ran in the six- to eight-dollar range. On another of our trips, the cost for the tubes had gone up to around ten dollars a tube. The worst was the last time we went to the pharmacy; they expected us to pay $125 for only five catheter tubes. Sam was sure they had made a mistake and asked to speak to the manager, and he told her that was the correct price. As a result, we left without the tubes and searched online for a better source. The tubes I use, which are a very common size, ranged in price at several online sources from $0.99 up to $1.50 each, depending on the quantity ordered. I also have found male urinary shields, leg bags, diapers, nitrile gloves, and other supplies online at very reasonable prices, sometimes as low as half the cost we found at more than one pharmacy. However, there is one thing about ordering supplies online that you should be aware of: many sites will ask for your Medicare information first in order to send you a regular monthly supply of whatever you need and charge Medicare the maximum allowed for these supplies. We paid out of our pocket for the many of supplies I needed and saved our health insurance for the expensive prescriptions and other needs.

Thirteen

A November to Remember

On November 1, I was looking forward to a visit with Dr. U, the head of urology at the University of Arkansas Medical Center. I only saw him once because he was retiring, but I remember him vividly because of his kind manner. Like other doctors, he had never heard of anyone suffering permanent paralysis from an epidural injection and expressed his sympathy for my situation.

Sam and I were desperately hoping for some positive news about my bladder, but there was none. After a thorough examination, Dr. U couldn't find any feeling in my saddle area, and without sensation anywhere around the bladder, there was not much hope for my bladder to function again. It seemed I would have to catheterize myself and use a urinary shield for a very long time, probably the rest of my life. This was a big quality of life issue. The most frustrating part was that I couldn't tell when I needed to use the bathroom, and therefore, I frequently wet my urinary shield, sometimes soaking my pants. However, Dr. U did provide some much-needed advice about the catheterizing process. I had learned how to use catheter tubes in the hospital to empty my bladder, and the nurses were very insistent on proper procedures if I intended to reuse the tubes. This included boiling the catheter tubes for ten minutes to sanitize them. With some patients, they recommend using a catheter only once, which can be quite expensive over time. As expected, boiling the tubes at home was an unpleasant experience and took time and effort on Sam's part when she was already covered up doing everything else for me. Dr. U asked us how we managed the bowel and bladder process at home and whether we had children or pets around, which we didn't. He told us that our bodies had adapted to our own bugs, so the chance of infection was very small. With only the two of us in the house, he thought we should be OK to just rinse the tubes out and let them dry. What a relief that was. But he cautioned me that if I used a tube outside of the house in a well-used public bathroom, I probably should throw that tube away. He also commented that there is a greater chance of getting an infection in a hospital environment because of all the sick people being treated there. Therefore, nurses are much more concerned about infections and caution patients to be extra careful. Dr. U also reminded me that the penis is designed to excrete fluid, not have a foreign object pushed up the full length of the urethra and into the bladder. He concluded with the advice, "Just be careful and use some common sense."

The first week of November was especially busy, and after seeing the urologist, we had a good visit with Dr. Rehab. He continued to be pleased with my progress and said I had "come along faster" than he had hoped, but he cautioned us that there was still a long way to go. Best of all, he thought I might be able to take a few steps with leg braces and a walker after the first of the year. We were excited about the possibility and knew it had the potential to vastly improve my mobility. My first thought was that if I could walk a few steps in braces with a walker in another sixty days, then who knows what I might be able to do in a year or so? However, Dr. Rehab warned me about getting too optimistic, since my progress was likely to plateau at some point. From my athletic training, I fully understood that as the human body makes several steps forward, it needs a period to recover before moving to the next level. In nature, almost everything grows and develops and then must take time to recover. Dr. Rehab and I also discussed my ability to press down with a couple of toes on my right foot. I thought this was a major development, but he again cautioned me that "we can get really excited" when I am able to raise the toes and raise my feet. Dorsiflexion, which is raising the foot at the ankle joint, is one of the critical functions to be able to walk without braces.

There was good progress showing up in other areas, which gave me hope. My quads were beginning to gain a little strength, especially in my left leg. I was now walking in the ARJO once a week at Baptist Rehab, with Lou helping move my right leg, which I couldn't control. Lou decided to put a mirror in front of me so I could see what was going on below my waist, which was a big help. In the ARJO, I found I could balance a little bit with the majority of my weight on the left leg. Of course, inability to feel anything through my feet slowed me down. The human body is designed to balance through sensation in the feet along with visual orientation and signals from the inner ear canal. Without feeling in my feet, plus not being able to control my right knee, standing upright was practically impossible. My left thigh muscle was slowly recovering, but there was no way it could hold my weight without my arms supporting me. I was getting farther along in therapy, and hopefully I would be even better next month. Dr. Rehab, my therapists, and my friends could all see positive developments. Everyone seemed to notice different changes, but they were all connected to improvements below my waist. I usually noticed the things I couldn't do instead of those things I could. Consequently, it was difficult for me to see much improvement. However, comments from the professionals working with me, as well as from my friends, validated the value of the work I was doing to recover, and it gave Sam and me hope for the future.

While my body didn't work right, I treasured the opportunity to use my mind. Doing marketing work for my client, Metropolitan National Bank, made me feel I still had value. We had a good conference call that week about future plans for the bank, and I was able to contribute advice on some marketing issues. Plus it was nice to have extra income to help pay for all my therapy. But much more than the money, what I really needed at that time was a way to use my mental capabilities to make a contribution to the bank. In my mind, this proved I had something meaningful to offer.

Debbie came back for a visit in November, and it was great to have her in the house with us. In addition to her visit, I continued to have phone calls from friends, including two triathlon buddies. Bill Crow updated me on some of the recent races and talked about how much everyone was pulling for me. I heard from Frank Lawrence and Cory Johnson about a couple of their recent triathlons. As always, Mickey Freeman called regularly, came by the house to make sure I was behaving myself, and checked to see whether Sam needed any help. I don't know what we would have done without him. Henry Noor stopped by to help Sam bring plants in off the deck before the weather turned cold, and we had a nice visit. It was great to hear from and see so many people who were supportive and confident that I could get back on my feet somehow, someway.

While it didn't appear I would ever be able to ride any of the four bicycles hanging in our garage, my friend Bruce Thalheimer, who is a partner in Chainwheel, the largest bike shop in town, called with an offer to help. He told me he had a folding recumbent three-wheel trike that I might be able to ride. A couple of days later, Sam and I checked it out at the store, and while it was incredibly difficult to get me out of the wheelchair and into the trike, there was a chance it might work. In a recumbent cycle, the rider is laid back in a reclining position, pedaling with legs and feet out in front of the trike. By putting on my bike shoes with cleats in the bottom, I could clip into the pedals to hold my feet in place. I thought I might have enough strength, primarily in my left leg, to pedal in a very low gear at a slow pace on a flat bike trail. With two small wheels in front and a single rear wheel behind my head, it would be fairly stable. Sam and I discussed the pros and cons and decided that if we could figure out how to get me in and out of the trike, it would be an excellent way for me to get outside and exercise. This would be an incredible boost to my morale if I could ride again, even if it was just a mile or two.

We ended up going back to the bike shop and picking up the trike with the hopes of testing it out that weekend. With the backseats folded down in our Toyota Highlander, we had a lot of space, but it was still a major effort to get both the wheelchair and the trike inside the space we had. Bruce and the guys at the bike shop were very helpful, and we finally figured out the puzzle of how to load both the chair and trike in the space available. By rotating the trike's rear wheel around and under the mesh seat, we just barely had room to close the rear door. Of course, we knew this was just the first step. For me to ride, Sam would have to help me into the car and then figure out how to load the trike and wheelchair by herself.

Busy, Wild, Wonderful Weekend

The weekend before Thanksgiving 2007 was crazy. Most of my family came to town that weekend with a busy agenda, including visiting me; attending a party put on by Debbie's best friends to celebrate Somerset and Steven's wedding on Labor Day in Sedona, Arizona; and most important, seeing the Arkansas Razorbacks play Mississippi State at War Memorial Stadium in Little Rock. The Razorbacks play most of their home games in Fayetteville where the university is located. However, over the years, they regularly played two or three home games per season in Little Rock. Since the university cut back to only playing one conference game per year in Little Rock, the whole town goes crazy on that weekend. Our family had season tickets in both Fayetteville and Little Rock for over fifty years, and we loved cheering for our beloved Hogs. Greg flew in to stay with us for the weekend and to celebrate his birthday early. Debbie and David flew in from Buffalo, and Somerset and Steven drove over from Tulsa. I wasn't able to go to the game in my wheelchair, but most of the family went, including Sam. While they were at the game, Mickey came by the house and took me to Creegan's Pub for lunch. After the game, everyone stopped by the house to visit, and we stayed up until the wee hours catching up with each other and celebrating the Hogs' 45–31 victory. It was a delightful time and, frankly, I hated seeing everyone leave.

Back on the Road Again

Well, it wasn't exactly a road—more like a paved bike trail—but I was back on a human-powered vehicle again. On Sunday, after all the family left, Sam wheeled me out to the car and started the laborious process of first getting me in the car and next putting the wheelchair in our Highlander, followed by the trike. Then we were off to Two Rivers Park, which had some nice, flat bike trails. After parking the car Sam had to repeat the whole process again including getting everything out of the car, helping me get in the wheelchair, and then wheeling me over next to the trike. Getting me from the wheelchair into the trike was a challenge, but we somehow managed to do it. The whole process of loading me, the trike, and the wheelchair into the car, driving to the park, and then unloading and getting me in the trike took as much time as the actual ride. But Sam was up to the task, knowing how much it would mean to me.

My first ride went better than expected. I rode for almost forty minutes with several breaks, and it was such great fun. I could only pedal at a very slow pace, and upon reaching even the slightest incline, I had to use my hands to physically push the two front wheels to assist my left leg, which was pushing on the pedal. Without using my hands, I would have come to a stop. Sam walked along some of the trails and watched me ride. It is hard to describe the wondrous feeling of moving under my own power again. Wow! I almost felt human again, and I thought to myself, "Who knows what I might be able to accomplish?" I figured that all it takes is time and lots and lots of hard work. I knew I had the time, and I hoped I would have the patience. Riding the trike at a snail's pace was a peak experience for me. It was also a personal triumph to be able to do this after the horrible injury and all the predictions of permanent paralysis from the waist down.

Before the end of November, I rode two more times, including a fun ride with a very patient Henry Noor. Before my injury, Henry and I enjoyed riding together, usually twice a week in the mornings. I knew riding with me in the trike would be tough for him because I was so slow. In fact, I was going at such a slow pace that he had a hard time balancing on his bike and, as a result, had to speed up a little and then stop to wait for me. It wasn't much of a workout for him, but he wanted to help, and it was great to have him along. We rode on the Saturday after Thanksgiving when it was cool and damp, but I didn't care about the weather because I was able to pedal outside in a natural environment on trails that I knew like the back of my hand. Before my paralysis, I used to run on these trails and used this park as a starting point for some longer bike rides on the back roads in the area. The park was a beautiful place with over six miles of paved trails and another couple of miles of gravel trails. It is situated on a peninsula where the Maumelle and Arkansas Rivers come together. There are several large stands of pine trees where deer like to feed and can be seen through the trees in many spots along the trail by one of the rivers. From the far end of the park where the two rivers meet, there is a beautiful view looking down the Arkansas River with the skyline of downtown Little Rock in the distance. Every time I went to Two Rivers Park, there were always people out walking, biking, and enjoying the scenery. Since it was mostly flat, it was the perfect place for me to start riding again. Henry and I covered five to six miles in an hour, a distance we previously would have easily covered in twenty minutes or less. However, speed was not our objective, and I was thrilled to be out riding and enjoying the scenery for an entire hour.

Henry and me at park

November ended on a high note. Not only was I able to get out and ride three times, but I could also tell that my legs were getting a little stronger. As a runner and cyclist, I had always had strong legs, and in spite of my age, I was pleased with my endurance on longer rides. Now my legs didn't look like they belonged to me. They had atrophied, and the skin was loose and wrinkled, with very little tissue underneath. I had some limited feeling in my upper legs, but below the knee, it appeared there wasn't any change. As a result of the paralysis, the lower part of my spinal column, especially the conus, was quite stiff. Anne Miskin worked on it every week to get some flexibility there, but it was a very slow process. Consequently, with the atrophy of my leg and butt muscles, I felt like I was balancing on my tailbone whenever I sat down. As a result, I had to use a U-shaped cushion everywhere I went, including on the trike and in the car.

Counting Our Blessings, Thanksgiving 2007

For the first seven months of 2007, Sam and I were living the life we had only dreamed of. Then, on August 9, it all changed. In spite of the devastating injury from what was considered a routine procedure, we still had a lot to be thankful for. I remember reading an editorial in the Arkansas Democrat/Gazette while I was at Baptist Rehab about dealing with major setbacks in life. It said something to the effect that it is easy to live life when things are going well, but the real test is when we make a wrong turn, have something tragic happen, or are dealt a bad hand. There are things we can't control. How we play that bad hand is the real test of our character.

Yes, I was terribly frustrated at my inability to perform simple tasks. I hated when I couldn't do more at rehab, but then Sam would patiently remind me how far I had come in only a few months, and she was right. We could see progress on a regular basis. I was doing more than Dr. Rehab had hoped for, and I continued to impress Lou Tretter in rehab. Anne Miskin and Carla Branch at the athletic club could see positive changes every week or two. At the end of November, I had stopped by

107

to see one of my family doctors, Dr. M, who was very impressed with my ability to pedal a trike. My childhood friend Jim Growdon called to check on me again and was quite impressed with my progress. There was good news, and we did have plenty to be thankful for. We were fortunate to find some excellent resources to help with my recovery, and the support from family and friends continued to play a big part in my recovery. Sam had shown incredible patience and grace under the most difficult of circumstances. The loss of my legs was bad enough, but the loss of the bowel and bladder functions created issues that most people cannot imagine. Sam had to live with cleaning up after my accidents time and time again. A lot of spouses wouldn't have survived this. As I said many times, recovery from a spinal column injury is not something you can do on your own. "It takes a village" to help someone fight through this process, and the leader of my village was and is my wife, Sam. No matter how tough this process was for me, I knew the whole ordeal was more difficult for the caregiver than for the patient.

Fourteen

Big Steps at Rehab

In December at Baptist Rehab, Lou got me up in the parallel bars with a fixed brace on my right leg that came up to my hip and a plastic AFO, ankle-foot orthotic, on the left leg. The AFO held my left foot and ankle in place, which helped my balance. Amazingly, my left knee and ankle joints were in fair shape, and my left thigh continued to improve and helped support my weight.

The temporary right leg brace, which I used at Baptist Rehab, was a piece of rebar that was slightly bent at the knee, with several straps to hold it in place on the leg. Baptist Rehab kept this on hand to see whether a patient might be able to make the move to a custom brace. Amazingly, I was able to stand with the bar supporting my weight on the right side. In addition to the bar, I had an AFO on the right leg since my ankle was not functioning at all. When I put any weight on the right foot, the ankle would roll to the outside, and the entire foot would turn inward. We didn't know it at the time, but problems with the right foot and ankle would continue to be a problem for years to come. Lou also put a wide belt around my waist to keep me from falling, which we referred to as the "sissy belt." It would become a key safety tool as we continued to try new things.

Lou, Sam, and I were very pleased that I was able to walk some, even with my arms and all the braces supporting my weight. Just getting up on my feet again was an amazing feeling. Tears came to my eyes, and it was a very emotional moment. Suddenly, for the first time, I believed I might be able to walk again with braces and supports of some kind. While I told my therapists and friends I was going to walk again, in the back of my mind, I had grave doubts. I desperately wanted to believe I could walk, so I kept telling myself I could. However, the reality was that after over ninety days of working as hard as I could, I really didn't know whether it was possible or not. All the experts we saw didn't think it was likely and, at times, I thought they might be right. At the end of November, I had pedaled a trike, and now I was able to stand up and take a few steps in the parallel bars with lots of support on both legs. I wondered, was it finally possible to believe in miracles? I didn't know, but I had hope along with many doubts.

At the next therapy session, Lou and I spent the entire hour, with several rest breaks, on the parallel bars. Lou was a delight to work with and was very encouraging. From the beginning, he knew I wanted to work hard, so we started scheduling my three weekly sessions an hour before his lunch hour. After we finished the therapy sessions, I could then work on my own for an extra thirty minutes while he had lunch. He always gave me suggestions about exercises I could do on the mat, where I didn't need support or supervision.

I could feel continuing improvement in my legs, especially my left leg, and with Lou's help, I was able to get up in a walker and take a few steps. He even let me try using forearm crutches, but we could tell it was going to take a lot of time and practice before I could manage those. More than once, I found that without Lou's tight grip on the sissy belt around my waist, I would have fallen.

Lou continued to help me try to walk in a walker with braces and AFOs. It was getting a little better, but my sit-to-stand transition was still very, very difficult. Consequently, we would work on having me get up from a sitting position at the beginning and end of each rehab session. For most people, getting up from a sitting position to a standing position is just an automatic movement. Most people don't think about how they do it; they just stand up. For someone like me, it was the most difficult thing I had to learn. My legs just didn't have the strength to raise my 170 pounds off the wheelchair and into a standing position. And, like a lot of other spinal column injury patients at Baptist Rehab, once I got myself in an upright position, I needed to have something solid to hold onto, or else I would go back down again. It's amazing the things we all take for granted but only appreciate after we lose them. Urinating or having a bowel movement, driving a car, standing up or sitting down without falling, and walking with something in my hand were all things I was no longer able to do. And some of them I feared I might never be able to do again.

Mastering the sit-to-stand procedure was something I had to learn. I found that putting my right hand underneath my butt, putting my head down, leaning forward, and then pushing upward helped—assuming the chair I was in wouldn't tilt or roll out from underneath me. I learned the basic technique pretty quickly, but putting it into practice was a different story. Of course being able to grab hold of something stable with my left hand was a big help. Anything I could use as leverage to pull myself up with my arms made it significantly easier. I also found that if I twisted my body to the left and leaned forward over my stronger left leg, I could sort of throw myself forward to get up. Walkers are very stable when their users are standing, but they are designed to be light and easy to move, which means they are not stable enough to use for leverage when trying to stand up. Until my legs gained more strength, I knew that sit-to-stand would be one of my biggest challenges for some time to come. It's one of those things everyone does multiple times a day without a problem, but for me it became something I had to carefully think through every time I needed to stand up.

Going into December, I could tell I was gaining ground and getting better. I found that I had more leg control and was finally able to lift my right foot off the floor and into the bed. For the first time since I was paralyzed, I was now able to transfer from the wheelchair to the bed by myself, but Sam still had to pick up my legs and lift them into the bed. I couldn't bend over and do it myself without losing my balance and falling out of the bed. Initially, my legs were just dangling appendages, and I couldn't do much with them, so Sam had to help put me in bed. Also, without the use of my legs, it was nearly impossible for me to roll over in the bed. At Baptist Rehab, I learned to roll over by using my arms to throw myself back and forth until I eventually rolled over. However, if Sam was in the bed with me, I would have beaten her to a pulp rolling back and forth and flailing around with my arms. So she helped me into bed, and I slept on my back for the first three months at home. I was able to raise my left leg fairly early on, and before the end of the year, I could also raise my right leg so Sam didn't have to lift my legs to get me into our bed. What a relief. We had a very good visit with Dr. Rehab that week in December, and he continued to be very pleased with the recovery progress and thought the trike would be helpful to my recovery. In addition, I brought up the idea of custom leg braces, and he thought it might be possible after the first of the year.

Saturday, December 9, Mickey and I took our wives to Creegan's Irish Pub for a fun lunch. They were disappointed they didn't get to join us the day of the Razorback game, so this was a makeup lunch for them. Later that afternoon, I rode the trike again at Two Rivers Park and tried out an odometer from the bike shop so I could measure speed and distance, as if it that really mattered. However, I wanted to know how far I went so I could work on increasing the distance. Yes, I know it was compulsive behavior, but I wanted some way to measure how I was doing. That Saturday, I rode six miles in one hour and four minutes, which three months before I didn't know whether I would ever be able to do again. Sam walked a good four miles in the same amount of time that I rode six miles. Sunday, Sam and I slept in, as we both needed the rest. I had worked out seven of the last eight days, including a trike ride, and Sam had to take me everywhere we went. We had a very relaxed day and received lots of phone calls from friends. Max Mehlburger, whom I had raced with to Bermuda, called to see how I was doing, and we talked about great times sailing together. Max had introduced me to offshore sailing in Chesapeake Bay and the Atlantic Ocean, and while we had a lot of fun, it was also a terrific educational experience for me. After sailing with Max, I started doing some bareboat chartering, without hired captain or crew, in the Caribbean, which was a unique experience in gorgeous surroundings.

Bill Crow, my triathlon buddy, called to check on me and gave me the latest news on my triathlon friends and various races around the state. Henry Noor called to check in and talk about our next ride together. Henry had figured out a route where he could get in some miles on the roads and then meet me at the park for an easy ride. The most interesting call that month was from Mike Long, whom I knew from the sailing club but hadn't seen or heard anything about in several years. It turns out he had suffered a spinal column injury eight years prior in a hang gliding accident and wanted to offer help and advice. We had a nice visit, and I was surprised to hear how active he was from a motorized wheelchair. As I recall, he was a quadriplegic but had gained limited use of his arms. He wanted to encourage me to venture out and to consider traveling and enjoying life. Traveling, except by car, was something I didn't think I could do at that time. Mike talked about trips he'd made to Europe and other travels while confined to his wheelchair. He also coached me about making sure, when I bought tickets to go on a trip, to tell travel agents and airline agents about my condition and what I could and couldn't do. He also suggested following up with the airline a week or two before the trip to make sure they knew about my limitations. It turned out to be great advice. I was impressed with Mike's adventuresome outlook and appreciated the input. Once again, Sam and I were so fortunate to have the support and encouragement of so many thoughtful people. It meant more to us than they knew. That was something we could never repay, but it is a gift I will remember when I hear of someone else who has a problem and needs comforting and support. I will always remember the outpouring of love and concern we received, and I will continue to honor that gift by "paying it forward" when someone I know needs help.

I Will Walk Again!

Monday, December 10, 2007 at Baptist Rehab was the first time I was able to stand with makeshift braces and very slowly walk across the gym in a walker. As always, Lou was holding onto my sissy belt for support. Controlling my right leg on my own was a significant problem, and it caused me to stumble making a couple of turns, but thanks to Lou, I didn't fall. After we finished, he counted the tiles on the floor of the gym and congratulated me on walking 160 feet. In spite of being tired from the effort, I felt exhilarated. Lou was impressed, and a couple of other therapists I knew watched me and offered their congratulations. Sam and I were thrilled. I now believed I would be able to walk again. Regaining mobility, even in a limited way, would be such a wonderful thing. This accomplishment, covering 160 feet in a walker, felt like a major victory. It reminded me of the first time I won a sailboat race and the first time I won an age-group trophy at a triathlon. This was a watershed moment in my therapy that I would never forget.

Two days later, Lou helped me walk again in the walker, only this time he had me go through an obstacle course around small cones on the gym floor. To finish our session, he had me stand in a walker with a mat behind me in case I fell, and he and I pitched a two-pound ball back and forth to work on my balance while I kept one hand on the walker. Frankly, I was surprised at my ability to balance on my feet, and Lou was quite pleased at how well I did. Neither of us knew what to expect, but we knew it was important to try to keep expanding my boundaries. Of course, I was holding on to the walker with a death grip in one hand and catching the ball in the other. It wasn't pretty, but it was a very good start. This was another day of visible progress, and Lou gave me the best news I could ask for. He told me it was time to call Snell Orthotics and order a custom brace and AFOs for me. Over the couple of weeks since he first started getting me on my feet, I had asked him more than once when I would be ready for braces. He told me he would discuss it with Dr. Rehab, who would have to agree and write a prescription for the braces. When I asked Dr. Rehab about braces, he told me he valued Lou's opinion and would wait until Lou thought I was ready. Dr. Rehab had seen me walking on his visits to the gym, and when Lou told him I was ready, Dr. Rehab agreed. I was like a kid at Christmas. I couldn't wait to get my custom braces.

Good news continued throughout the week. Susie Smith from Metropolitan Bank picked up lunch for us from Jimmy's Serious Sandwiches, which we loved, and we had a very good visit. Our attorneys, Phillip and Bruce McMath, also came by the house to discuss progress with our legal issues. They were gathering information and had started the search for an expert witness. Sam and I appreciated them coming to the house, which made things so much easier for us. The more we worked with them, the more confident we were in our decision to have them as our advocates. This was an active week of therapy and visits with friends, and on Saturday, December 15, we decided to take a day off. This gave me a chance to update my journal and reflect on what we had accomplished.

While the holidays can be difficult times for some people, I was pleasantly surprised at how good my attitude was. Even though I continued to struggle with frustration over my inability to accomplish normal tasks, this was the best my attitude had been since Thanksgiving. I knew this had to be more relief for Sam than it was for me. While reflecting on my progress I wrote the following in my journal:

My whole life is built around my physical improvement. I couldn't care less about eating. Other activities hold little interest. This recovery process rules my life, and I will pay almost any price to get better. The downside of this is that I am totally self-absorbed in my recovery and little else. Fortunately, Sam is able to put up with me, which means a lot! Getting on my feet this week was a major breakthrough. It has boosted my spirits and improved my hopes tremendously. I can now look at the future with a more positive attitude, and I really need that.

The week leading up to Christmas proved to be even busier than the previous week, but it was still great fun. I kept up my therapy schedule, walked some more, and was learning to balance in the walker. Lou had talked with Snell about my brace, and I went to see them so they could measure my legs and get to work. I also took them a pair of shoes to attach to the metal braces. With Sam's help, I got in a four-and-a-half-mile trike ride that week on a cool day. Mark and Diane Ross included us in their annual Christmas dinner at their house, and we had a terrific time. It was delightful to see many of the people I had worked with at Bank of the Ozarks who were very supportive. We also had dinner with my former assistant, Lisa Brink, and a day later went with Kelley and Judy Johnson to the Arkansas Repertory Theatre for a performance of *Hello, Dolly!* Sam and I thought it was the best live production we had seen in Little Rock. We topped off that week with Greg coming to town for Christmas weekend.

As usual, Greg's first job was to take on some projects for us. He trimmed bushes around the house, changed out our audio system to match up with our new TV, ran lots of errands, and helped Sam with a multitude of things. I don't know what we would have done without him. He and I have always had a good relationship, but what he did for Sam and me during this incredibly difficult time was above and beyond the call of duty. He was especially supportive of Sam, and would point out to me instances in which I was demanding and not as sensitive to her needs as I should have been. And he was always right on target.

Christmas 2007

In spite of being in a wheelchair, this was one of my best Christmases ever. Sam did a beautiful job of decorating the house without much help from me. I think I actually dropped more ornaments than I hung on the tree. Having Greg with us for a whole week made our holiday. On Christmas Eve, Greg gave Sam some time off by taking me to Two Rivers Park for a ride. Afterward, we went out for dinner and to Second Presbyterian Church for the Christmas Eve service. Then we opened presents at home, and as is our tradition with Greg, we watched the movie *National Lampoon's Christmas Vacation* with Chevy Chase. It was still hilarious, no matter how many times we had all seen it. We laughed a lot, ate more than we should have, and finally realized it was two o'clock in the morning and time to go to bed.

Christmas Day we slept in. Sam made eggs benedict for breakfast and we watched parts of *A Christmas Story*, which runs continually on TV every December 25. We told family stories, both good and bad, and laughed sometimes till it hurt. Lots of family and friends called, and we had a very nice phone visit with my sister Debbie and her husband David in snowy Buffalo.

Unfortunately, Greg had to leave for Dallas the day after Christmas, and we were sorry to see him go. His visit was definitely our greatest gift. Then, with the holiday behind us, it was time to start back to therapy. However, there was one more Christmas present in store for me that week: my new braces. I don't know how Snell did this project over the Christmas holidays, when most businesses were closed for several days. I was surprised when they called me after Christmas to come and pick up my "new legs." What a treat! The president of Snell, Rick Fleetwood, was a dear friend of my mom, and he did everything he could to help us. Between him and Gary Owens, his chief brace man, they built my braces in record time over the holidays.

On Friday, December 28, 140 days after my decision to wake up every morning and focus on "The Healing Begins Today," I wore my new braces to therapy at Baptist Rehab. Lou and I spent most of the session with me in a walker, and it went surprisingly well; I asked Lou, "When can I get my own walker to take home?" Mickey Freeman came by after I got back from therapy, and we had a wonderful two-hour visit. We talked about my recovery and discussed some spiritual issues. Before he left, he encouraged me to write a book about my recovery. Mickey always thought I was a great storyteller, and he said I should keep writing in my journal and write a book about my recovery. While it was an interesting idea, I remember responding to him at the time with a shrug and saying,

"We'll see." Frankly, I was too busy with therapy to think about writing a book.

It seemed like an almost perfect Christmas, but there was some bad news about mom. A couple of days before Christmas, the doctor at the nursing home called and told me mom's condition was starting to rapidly decline. She was losing weight, and even Cassondra Sneed, our caregiver who mom liked so much, couldn't get her to eat. On Christmas Day, Greg, Sam, and I went to visit her, and Greg was surprised at her decline since he had last seen her only a month before. Mom had been unable to communicate much for a couple of months, and we knew this was the beginning of the end. The nursing home doctor told us that mom was probably in her last six months and it was time to contact hospice. We agreed, and I arranged to meet with them the following week. While this wore heavily on Debbie and me, it was not unexpected. Deb and I discussed mom's condition on our Christmas phone call, and I told my sister I would let her know as soon as there was any change. Frankly, I knew losing our mother was inevitable and in some ways would be a blessing. Her mind was gone, she had zero motor skills, and her life was now mostly sleeping. It was obvious to me that the doctor's six-month estimate was extremely optimistic.

Fifteen

Lessons Learned in Part I

The end of 2007 and the beginning of 2008 was a time for us to reflect on gains, losses, and lessons learned in this most difficult process. Sam and I had been through hell over the last five months and arrived at year's end with new perspectives on life and love and a new appreciation for the wonderful support of friends and family. I thought it would be helpful to look back and summarize some of the lessons learned in this difficult process. Writing about it helped me, and I hope this book about my experience might prove helpful to others who have suffered devastating injuries. The following is a summary of the key lessons we learned in the early stages of this battle to recover and find a way to live with my dramatically altered physical condition.

Recovery, Especially in the Early Stages, Is More Mental than Physical
After a devastating injury of any kind, it's easy to be confused and not know what to do or where to turn for help. Talk about confusing: in my case, Dr. X was convinced this paralysis would, as he frequently said, "wear off." This was in spite of the fact that the two experts he called in to read the MRIs taken before and after the epidural injection told Sam and I that I had suffered a stroke to the conus of my spinal column. They also said that the injury was permanent and that I would never walk again. Over time, we didn't find a doctor who could give us a positive prognosis, because they had never seen this kind of injury from an

epidural injection. There were some, especially Dr. Hope, who gave us encouragement and support, but they were few and far between. Was I frustrated, angry, and mad? Of course I was. However, after lying in a hospital bed for a several days, I knew that hate, anger, and fear were luxuries I could not afford. Do I hate Dr. X? No. I actually feel sorry for the man. He shouldn't be doing this procedure and, I suspect, in the back of his mind, he knows that, but I could not afford to waste time thinking about him. I knew I had to devote all my energy to figuring out how to work on some sort of recovery. Living in the past is wasted effort. Yes, it's important to learn from past experiences, but I knew I had to focus all my available energy on my recovery. Projecting too far into the future is equally dangerous. If I believed all the doctors, then there would be no future for me. All I could do was live in the now and try to find a way to somehow move forward.

All of this meant that I had to find a way to manage my frustrations and depression. I would like to be such a positive thinker that I could just will them away, but with something as devastating as my paralysis, I had to find some way to manage my negative emotions. Part of the solution, which Dr. Rehab recommended for most of his paraplegic patients, was antidepressant medication, and that helped some. At least it kept me from being suicidal. However, I still had many days—at least once a week after the injury—where I was so depressed I could not function. I couldn't get out of bed, even though I knew I needed to be in therapy. I would sleep on and off until midafternoon or later. I eventually said to myself it was OK to cry and go to bed upset and frightened, provided I could get up the next day and start over again. That only worked some of the time, but at least it was a start.

You Can't Do This by Yourself

There are probably some patients out there who have survived paralysis and accomplished an amazing recovery on their own, but I can't imagine how they did it. Only seventeen months after Sam and I were married, I was injured, and there appeared to be no hope for recovery. I offered her the chance to walk away and get on with her life and told her we could find a place to put me. She looked at me with tears in her eyes and said she loved me and wasn't going anywhere. Sam is a very strong woman who is totally devoted to me. I can say without question, I would not have made it without her. The price she paid in this process cannot be measured. Here are just two of my favorite comments from her. When I would say something negative or stupid, she would reply, "That's not helpful." And other times she would point out, "at least you haven't lost your sense of humor," which always brought a smile to my face. During troubling times, a sense of humor can often be the best medicine.

Friends and family were also crucial. Encouragement from people you love and respect is so important to any type of recovery. There were so many people who called, sent e-mails, stopped by to visit us, and offered all sorts of help, from meals and treats to just letting me know they cared. They all expressed confidence in my ability to get back on my feet. I even had what I referred to as my "Holy Trinity" for recovery, which was led by Sam, along with Greg and Mickey Freeman. Of course, Sam was burdened with the constant day-to-day activities of taking me to therapy, feeding me, consoling me, and sometimes having to clean up after me, which had to be the worst job anyone could imagine. Most important, she regularly reminded me that she loved me and that I was going to be OK. Greg made regular visits from Dallas, stayed in touch by phone, and was able to correct me when I needed it and stand up for Sam when he thought I was insensitive to her needs. Mickey was Sam's best local resource to call when she couldn't get me out of bed and off to therapy. Plus Mickey not only came by the rehab center every day in those first few weeks, but also came to see me every week at home and was always available when we needed him.

There were so many friends who made significant contributions that it is hard to thank them all. I will never forget their support and their confidence in my ability to recover. It does "take a village" to help most of us recover from major problems in our lives. I will always be eternally thankful for the support and encouragement we received during the most trying time of my life. To all our caring friends I wish to say, "I couldn't have done this without you."

You Must Take Control of Your Own Recovery

Doctors and therapists can help guide you in the right direction, but you are the one who needs to be in charge of your recovery, not them. I found it was quite helpful to tell all the professionals I worked with that I wanted to work very hard and do whatever it took to fight my way back. I wanted every doctor and every therapist to think about all possible therapy options. Sam and I also asked lots of questions and looked for anything that might help. Frankly, it is not enough to just do the minimum the therapist or doctor expects of you. In order to recover, one must work hard and put out maximum effort, while knowing there are no guarantees of a successful outcome. Recovery doesn't come easily. But if you believe and work hard, it's amazing what the human body can accomplish. In therapy at Baptist Rehab, and also with my trainers at the athletic club, I frequently saw people doing just the minimum that was asked of them, thinking that would make them stronger, slimmer, or fitter. It takes so much more than that. Over the next year, I would add acupuncture, urological therapy, psychological therapy, and anything else I thought might work. Some things worked well and others didn't, but being willing to try new things is important. I vividly remember asking Dr. Rehab what he thought about acupuncture. He commented that several of his patients had tried it, and it worked for some and not for others. Dr. Rehab added that it seemed to work for those who thought it would and not so much for those who were skeptical and didn't stick with it. Like most things in life, it takes commitment to make progress with recovering from an injury. Also, we found that most doctors tend to focus on their own specialty, where they have expertise. While this makes sense, it is easy to have lots of experts treating only one part of the body and nobody looking at the whole patient. That's why it is so helpful to have a good family doctor who knows your history and can bring everything together. While Dr. Rehab is an expert on spinal column injuries and was very good at addressing most of my issues, we found it was also helpful to have our family doctors, Drs. H and M, involved.

Physical Condition of the Body at the Time of the Injury Is Very Important

Fortunately, I was in excellent physical condition when my injury occurred, which was more helpful than I imagined at the time. As I mentioned earlier, Dr. Hope was one of the doctors called in to consult on the injury and tell me the results of the MRI following my paralysis. He told me that hospitals didn't see many people like me: in excellent physical condition in my sixties; living a healthy lifestyle with no history of smoking; and with heart rate, blood pressure, and other indicators much better than the average patient ten to twenty years younger. I was surprised that a history of smoking was an issue with a spinal column injury and asked about it. He commented that frequently, with long-term smokers, it could take up to 50 percent longer for their body tissue to recover from an injury. I knew smoking damaged the body, but I had no idea it could be so limiting for recovery from any type of injury. He told me there were no promises; however, someone with the determination to do the activities I did might be able to regain some function. He also added that my body knew that it was supposed to be active. My DNA knew I was supposed to be upright. My muscles should have had some memory about how to function, but they would have to "wake up." That gave Sam and me hope, which was a very precious thing.

Focus on Your Goals Every Morning

You must focus on the task at hand and be devoted to your goals. Mine was to walk again, and that was what I thought about most mornings and what I was dedicated to doing.

Recovery Takes Time—Lots of Time

After the first couple of months, I asked Dr. Rehab, "What will it take for me to be able to walk again?" I'm sure he had been asked this many,

many times in his career, and his answer was thoughtful and most helpful. He talked about the very slow growth rate of a damaged nervous system and told me how important it was to get feeling back in my legs and develop the leg muscles when they began to respond. He told us multiple times that it would be a very long, slow process and that there were no guarantees. And then he said something profound: "One of the key ingredients for recovery is the tincture of time." Whenever I tend to get impatient with my progress, I am reminded of his comment about the "tincture of time." I read somewhere in a triathlon magazine, that it was important to "let the race come to you." The point was that, in a long race, you couldn't force things to happen. I had to let my body adjust and not force it to do something it wasn't ready for. Now I think of the recovery process like a long race, and I will work hard but I cannot force something to happen. I will have to let the race come to me.

Shop Online for All Your Supplies

Shopping on the Internet has changed the way a lot of us shop for many things, especially items that may be hard to find locally. We found it was the best way to buy most of the medical supplies I needed. Of course, there is a wait time to get items delivered, but you can find exactly what you need and at much better prices than you will usually find at a local pharmacy. As I mentioned earlier it was the extremely high price of catheter tubes from a hospital pharmacy that pushed us to shop online in the beginning. But after finding a good resource online we also found a wide selection of most everything else I needed, and at very reasonable prices.

Part II

Sixteen

2008, A New Year and a New Beginning

While my mother's declining physical condition was much on my mind, it was time to get back to work on my therapy. Overall the Christmas break was a good time to rest and we had fun with Greg, but this was the start of a new year and I was ready to focus on therapy again. Rick Fleetwood and Gary Owens at Snell knocked themselves out over the holidays, and my new braces were a very meaningful Christmas present. The brace for the right leg, which went up to the top of my thigh, was designed to lock automatically when I straightened my leg, since my right knee would not support my weight. As a result, I had to walk with my right leg in a fixed position, which took some practice. To enable me to bend the knee to sit down, the brace had a quick-release bail behind my knee. While the brace was very bulky and took some effort to get strapped onto my leg, it was a wonderful thing. I could finally stand in a walker on my own and actually walk. This was an enormous step forward and a great way to start the new year.

For my first workout of 2008 at Baptist Rehab, Lou and I practiced walking with my custom braces. I used a walker with my arms supporting most of my weight, while Lou held onto the sissy belt around my waist in case I stumbled. It wasn't pretty, but I was finally vertical and walking! After five months in a wheelchair, this was a thrill. More than one doctor had indicated that I would probably spend the rest of my life in a wheelchair, but now I believed almost anything was possible. My body had not quit, and I was dedicated to doing whatever it took to continue the progress. January 2, 2008, was a real watershed moment that I will never forget: I spent most of an hour with Lou's help using a walker, and it went better than we both expected. Lou got so excited about my walking that he said, "The Dragon is loose." I don't know where that came from but it still makes me smile when I think about it. I could finally stand and was able to walk with Lou's assistance. There was still a very, very long way to go without any idea of what the results might be. However, being vertical and using a walker gave me hope, and the best part was still to come. At the end of the rehab workout, Lou surprised me with my own walker to take home, along with a sissy belt for Sam to hold onto when I walked. I felt much like I did as a kid when I got my first bicycle.

After we got home from therapy, I thought it was time for a celebration, so I called Mickey Freeman and told him I had a surprise and asked him to stop by the house on his way home from work. When he arrived, I walked forward awkwardly and slowly to greet him and shake his hand, which was a pretty good trick at the time. Balancing on the new braces and taking my right hand off the walker to shake his hand wasn't easy, but it was well worth it. Mickey didn't know what the surprise was, but he thought we might need a libation to celebrate. So on the way to the house, he picked up a Celebrator Doppelbock German beer to toast the event. Neither of us had ever tasted this beer, but as Mickey said, "With a name like Celebrator, we can't go wrong." Sam joined us with a glass of wine, and we took pictures to record the occasion. A fine time was had by all, and I do believe Mickey and I may have had more than just one beer. I was still spending most of my time in a wheelchair, and Lou insisted that any time I was in the walker, I needed to wear the sissy belt and have someone with me. I told Lou that was fine with me, since I was finally able to get on my feet.

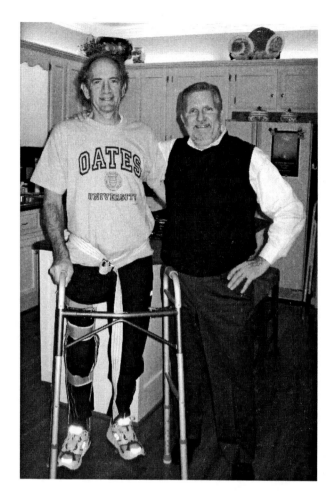

Mickey and me, first day home with walker

Being able to get up in a walker was also a breakthrough moment for Sam. She and I figured out how to use the walker to help me get into the small area in the bathroom where our commode was. I could just barely squeeze in using the walker, and now for the first time in five months, I could actually do my manual bathroom routine on the commode. This was an enormous step forward in managing my bodily functions, as Sam no longer had to dump everything in the commode several times a day.

We had a nice, warm day during the first week of the January, so Sam took me out to Two Rivers Park, where I got in a good ride on my trike, covering about nine miles. On the trike, I could tell my legs were slowly, very slowly, gaining strength. Of course, I was doing nearly all the pedaling with my left leg on the flat trails, but the right leg seemed to be getting a little bit better.

Throughout January, my use of the walker continued to improve; however, going from living in a wheelchair for five months to standing up created other problems. Using the walker put a lot of pressure on my hands and arms, and as a result, I developed some soreness in my left shoulder and had some issues with numbness in my hands and fingers. In addition to these issues, it was very difficult for me to go from a sitting position to standing up. I didn't have the strength in my legs to lift my body. So Lou and I started spending more time working on my sit-to-stand with the walker. Obviously, it was much easier to stand up when I had something stable to grab onto and pull myself up with my arms. Consequently, for a recovering paraplegic, it is very difficult and risky when there is no fixed object nearby to help. Getting up from a chair and into the walker was an enormous challenge, and I knew it would take a lot of work to master. I found that one of the more difficult problems was getting up out of a chair while sitting at a table. I could use the table for some support, but if I put too much pressure on a table, it could move or turn over. Getting out of our sofa at home was one of my toughest battles. The sofa was old, and I found I had to get up on the arm of it first before I was able to try to stand. My sit-to-stand became something that would take a lot of practice and require careful planning before I attempted to get up and into my walker. As a result, I spent a lot of time learning techniques to push and pull myself up in various situations.

Frustrations

While I continued to make slow progress with my physical issues, I still struggled with my mental condition. Sleeping was a problem some of the time, and I frequently found it hard to focus. Often, in spite of trying to maintain a positive outlook, I still felt helpless. I had to ask for help with ordinary things that I thought I should have been able to do for myself. There were times when I would remember how strong and fit I was before all this happened, and then I would remember how I ended up as a paraplegic with a damaged bowel and bladder that continued to cause problems. In early January, I wet my pants just sitting on the couch watching TV. Then, later that night, I wet the bed not once but twice. If I could just get control of my bodily functions, it would be an enormous improvement in my quality of life, but I didn't know when or if that would ever happen.

In spite of making so much progress and taking medication for depression, there were days when I couldn't get out of bed and missed some therapy sessions. Also, wrapping up the end of the year and looking at how much money we were spending on my recovery was scary. Modifications to the house, along with all my medical bills, drugs, and therapy costs, were substantial.

Sam and I were both struggling, and she had Dr. H give her a prescription for Lexapro, an antidepressant that I was also taking. I wrote the following in my journal in the middle of January 2008:

Neither of us has the same optimism that we had before the injury. Both of us are having trouble sleeping. I am not as confident in the walker and almost fell in the bathroom. It really scared me. Don't know what to do. This is hard on our relationship. I can feel it. After five hard months, this is not surprising, but it is very difficult. I take the blame for it. Maybe time will heal me and us. But right now, I don't know.

A week later, I wrote this in my journal:

It is very hard to maintain focus all the time when progress comes at a snail's pace. We all want to see results for our hard work. There is no quick gratification. It is one small step after another, repeated every day of every week and every month for some unknown amount of time. While I may not reach full recovery, I think I can beat this injury. It may be my greatest accomplishment ever.

131

Anne Miskin continued to work on me to loosen my frozen tailbone at the base of my spinal cord, in the hope that it would help the nerves communicate with my legs. She also helped me with spiritual advice to keep me from becoming so frustrated, and she wanted me to spend more time out of the wheelchair and using my walker. I had been hesitant to walk very much because I was afraid of falling. I hated to admit it, but the wheelchair was easier to use, as well as faster and more comfortable for me. As a result, I used it more that I should have. Sam was doing her best to get me out of the wheelchair and on my feet more often, but I resisted. Frankly, I was beginning to use it as a crutch.

This entire process was very tiring on both Sam and me. On the weekends, we slept in until nine or ten o'clock in the morning and usually relaxed around the house until afternoon. As I wrote in my journal:

This is the most demanding thing I have ever done in my life. And in spite of my progress, at times I still feel so helpless and useless. Life is fragile, very fragile. In spite of doing all the right things for my health and fitness, disaster can still strike. You can't see around all the dangerous corners in life.

I continued to get support from many friends, and they all could see improvements, which I couldn't. Many of my coworkers from Bank of the Ozarks visited me at the hospital and continued to stay in touch after I went home. Since retiring, I had been doing some consulting for Metropolitan National Bank, and the president, Lunsford Bridges, along with the chief operating officer, Susie Smith, stopped by and brought lunch one day. I knew how busy they both were, and yet they ended up spending a couple of hours with us, and it meant a great deal. Once again, outside comments and support added buoyancy to my attitude.

Finally, after five months, the bedsore on my bottom had skinned over enough that the doctor at the wound clinic allowed me to get into a pool. I used the pool at Baptist Rehab, where they had a chair to sit in that rotates and lowers into the water. I had an extremely difficult time keeping my legs underneath me, and since I couldn't control my feet, I scraped them up and found I would have to wear water shoes in the future. But at least I was in the water, and it felt good. Then on Wednesday, January 23, 2008, Lou had me try out some forearm crutches. Going from a stable walker with four points of contact to forearm crutches was an enormous leap, especially when I had only been using my own walker for less than a month. Nevertheless, Lou knew how hard the "Dragon", as he now called me, wanted to work. Frankly, I wasn't very stable, but Lou kept his hand on my sissy belt, and we started a new learning process. I only had one bad stumble that first time, so my spirits were good, and the following day, while working with Anne Miskin, we discovered more feeling in my legs. Afterward, I used my walker to walk from her office at the athletic club over to the indoor track and walk one complete lap around the track. That night, Sam and I went out to a movie with Mickey and Patti Freeman to celebrate.

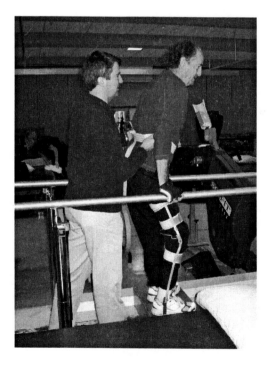

Lou working with me on parallel bars

The next morning, we woke up to sleet and freezing rain, which meant I couldn't go anywhere. It was one thing for me to walk on a dry, flat surface, but a completely different issue when it rained. While rain was bad enough, if it was cold enough for moisture to freeze on the pavement, it was much too risky for me to venture outside. As Dr. Rehab regularly reminded me, one bad fall would set my recovery back several weeks, maybe even months. It was just another issue that I had to learn to adjust to and plan around. I have never been a patient person, but this entire process was certainly teaching me to be more patient, or else! So we slept in and took it easy. Several friends called to visit, and Frank Lawrence called and said he was leaving work early and would bring lunch. Frank and I had worked together at Bank of the Ozarks, and he asked me to coach him on racing his first triathlon. It was fun to have a chance to visit over lunch. All in all, it turned out to be a nice snow day.

The Pleasures of Being Upright

It's amazing how just being upright changes one's perspective on practically everything. After spending several months in a wheelchair, I learned that the world is designed for people who walk upright. Doors, walkways, counters, chairs, tables, etc.—all of these are designed for people who can stand up on their own, and that's as it should be, since the vast majority of people are vertical most of the time. Over the last thirty years, enormous advances have been made for handicapped people, and that was quite helpful for me. However, it is difficult to appreciate the disadvantages of the view from a wheelchair until you depend on one to move around. One of the first things I noticed when I started walking in a walker was how much more I could see. In a wheelchair, I was always trying to look around people, chairs, tables, and other obstructions. Standing up, I could see much farther and see more of what was going on around me. It was a startling revelation. I had forgotten what it felt like to be vertical. Standing up, even with a walker, also made me much more mobile. I could actually go up a couple of steps again, especially if there was a railing to hold onto. Even though a walker takes up a lot of space, I found that if I was patient and took my time, I could maneuver it around most objects. Talking to people face-to-face, rather than having people stoop over to talk to me in a wheelchair, made me feel almost human again. And best of all, more people could see me when I was vertical and not hidden behind objects or other vertical people. When I started getting around with my walker, more people recognized me at the athletic club and stopped to visit. I never imagined what a visual difference it would make, just getting on my feet again. It was also interesting how tall I felt and how small everything around me looked. Even our house looked smaller once I started using my new walker.

While in public places people would sometimes stare at me in a wheelchair, there was a noticeable difference at the athletic club and at Baptist Rehab in how people saw me. Of course, in the gym at Baptist Rehab, almost everyone there is either a therapist or a patient like myself, recovering from a disease or injury. In the rehab gym, seeing all those people with their significant problems, it would be easy to feel sorry for them. But it was just the opposite. I found it to be a place full of positive energy where people were working hard and trying to get better. It also helped that the therapists saw the same patients on a regular basis in the gym and would readily notice the smallest improvements. I frequently had therapists who worked with other patients compliment me on some improvement they noticed in how I stood or walked or moved my legs. That was very reassuring, coming from experts who worked with broken bodies every day.

The feeling at the athletic club was also very positive. Frequently a club member who hadn't seen me in a week or two would come up and compliment me on my hard work and how much better I was doing. It was hard for me to see much progress over a month's time but they could. Plus I think it helped that the club was a place where people came to work out and improve their physical condition and as a result they were aware of the effort it takes to build strength and gain fitness. In spite of the compliments I received, I continued to be frustrated by my lack of mobility and my inability to do ordinary things. I made these notes in my journal about my frustrations:

With all my training, diet, racing, etc., I felt physically invincible, and yet this injury struck me down. It is hard for me to comprehend not standing on my own, walking, riding a bike, and going to the bathroom.

By the end of January, I was able to walk twice around the track at the athletic club using my walker. The track is only one-thirteenth of a mile, and for me, walking one lap took as long as it used to take me to run a 5K race, but at least I was walking. Carla and Anne watched me walk and noticed I was hunched over, so Carla made some adjustments to the walker, which put me in a more upright position, and it felt better. That same day, I saw my triathlon buddy Kurt Truax, who was glad to see me on my feet and congratulated me on my excellent progress. Those supportive comments from a fellow athlete always helped and left me with a warm feeling.

It was surprising to me the number of people at the athletic club, many of whom I did not know, who would make a point to tell me how much progress I was making. Also, many would comment about what an inspiration I was. That was very gratifying, since I don't recall anyone referring to me in the past as being inspirational. I was very grateful for the support, and it was nice that others could see progress when I felt there was so little physical improvement. I told Anne Miskin about the comments that I was an inspiration, and she thought it might be because I was living out most people's worst fears. Apparently, if I could fight my way back from being a paraplegic, it might give other people hope. As further proof of my progress, at the end of the month, with lots of help from Lou Tretter, I was able to walk 410 feet in my forearm crutches at rehab. I was slowly getting the hang of it, even though I was not very steady. After working with Lou, I went to the athletic club and walked three laps around the track with my walker. On Wednesday, January 30, 2008, after working with Lou and walking at the athletic club, I had been on my feet more than any time in the last six months. While my body was physically worn out, mentally I was proud and pumped up.

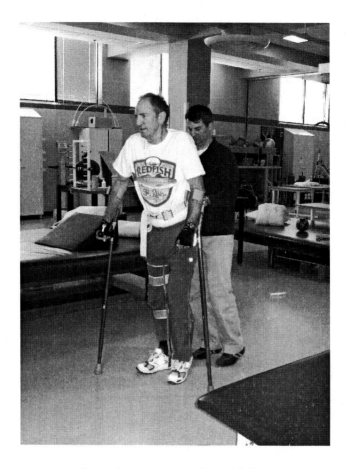

Learning to use crutches with Lou

Meaningful Progress

In early February, I continued walking farther at rehab in the forearm crutches and was starting to develop a rhythm. It was too early to even think about going out on my own with the crutches, but I was getting there. As I wrote in my journal on February 7, 2008:

I will be able to do this, just as I learned to use a walker.

137

I reminded myself that if I was ever going to walk on my own again, I had to keep this thought in my mind.

On the weekends, if the weather was good, I was frequently riding my trike. Saturday, February 2, I rode a total of nine miles in Two Rivers Park. It took some time, with a couple of rest stops, but I made it. Henry Noor was with me, and we rode the three-mile loop out to the point where the Arkansas River and the Maumelle River came together. I always enjoyed the view from there, looking down the river at the downtown skyline. At the start and finish of the three-mile loop is an incline up to the main path, and I had to use my hands to push the front wheels in order to get up the slope, but I made it on my own. Best of all, it was a beautiful day, and I thoroughly enjoyed myself.

My emotional ups and downs and continued, which reminded me of the importance of trying to maintain a positive mental attitude. In addition, I was beginning to develop a few physical problems. My left shoulder was a little sore at times, and occasionally I lost some feeling in my fingers. This was probably due to all the time I was spending in a walker after almost six months of living in a wheelchair. Now I was carrying most of my weight on my shoulders, arms, and hands since only my left leg offered any meaningful support. The right leg was virtually worthless without the full leg brace, which I kept locked in a fixed position when standing or walking.

My legs were my biggest concern, but I was most frustrated about the lack of any improvement in my bowel and bladder. Wetting my pants was always embarrassing, even when I was wearing a diaper. And having to manually evacuate my bowel three times a day was just disgusting. My digestive system was compromised from the paralysis, and I never knew what to expect.

The weekend of February 9 and 10 was the six-month anniversary of the injury. Sam and I planned to relax and have a fun weekend. It wasn't a celebration, but rather just an opportunity to look back at where I was and see how far I had come with Sam's amazingly patient support. I wrote the following in my journal Friday night:

I am so blessed to have a wife who is devoting all her energy and love to making me whole again. I don't remember feeling this kind of warm, unconditional love in a long time.

That Friday, Sam and I drove out to Two Rivers Park, where Sam walked while Henry and I rode ten miles together. The rest of the weekend, we slept late, watched TV, and relaxed. Sunday evening, we met Pete and Sandy Heister at an Asian restaurant, and they were so proud when they saw me walk into the restaurant with my walker. It was an emotional moment for all of us, and looking back several years later, I still sometimes get teary-eyed thinking about that evening. It was a special night with good food and dear friends. My friends continued to see more progress than I did, and their excitement over what seemed to me to be minor improvements continued to be very reassuring and made me want to do even better.

By the middle of February, I could tell I was making real, tangible progress. With Lou at my side, I walked five hundred feet in the forearm crutches with only one rest break. We also pushed hard to see if I could make some progress with getting up from a sitting position using just the forearm crutches. It was a difficult struggle, and my shoulders tended to be sore after some workouts, but I knew I had to learn how to sit-to-stand in the crutches. At this point in the recovery process, I decided it was time to work with the walker on the track at the athletic club after every workout. A couple of days later, I even tried walking on the track, holding on to the railing with one hand and the walker with the other. This put more of my weight on my legs and made me stand more erect, which took some of the pressure off my shoulders. The first day I did this, I wrote in my journal:

It's beginning to feel like real walking!

Back at rehab, Lou started having me attempt to walk in parallel bars without my braces. My legs weren't able to support my weight just yet, but with my arms supporting most of my weight, I believed I might be able to stand up and walk at some point. A week later, Lou took me outside to practice walking with the crutches on uneven surfaces. I had my brace locked on my right leg and only an ankle/foot orthotic on the left, and I was able to do pretty well. I knew I couldn't risk doing this without Lou, but I was vertical and moving under my own power on uneven outdoor surfaces that were more challenging.

Only six months after most of the experts thought I would never regain much if any use of my legs, I was gaining some strength in my thighs and making excellent progress. My balance was improving and, at rehab, I could walk 350 feet in the forearm crutches without a break. I was getting good enough at maneuvering in the crutches that Lou decided it was time to test my stability. He placed a small, weighted ball on the floor and had me move it in different directions using the crutches. Dr. Rehab showed up at the rehab gym while I was working with the ball and was impressed. It was an interesting experience for me, since I had to balance on one crutch and then use the other to move the ball. The doctor, Lou, Sam, and I were all pleasantly surprised with how well it went.

Seventeen

Losing Mom

While I was having a very good month, Mom was not. My sister Debbie and I were very fortunate to grow up with loving and caring parents who both lived very active lives. Our Mother, Willie Oates, was one of the best-known people in Arkansas for her volunteer activities and fund raising. We know that because when Bill Clinton was in his first term as governor, the largest newspaper in the state did a survey showing photographs of well-known people from around the state to their readers, and more people recognized mom than the governor. She served on the boards of multiple volunteer organizations, was elected to the state legislature in 1957, and was involved in politics most of her life. In her eighties, she was proud of the fact she knew one president, two first ladies and seven governors by their first names, and they all knew Willie. However, she was probably most well known for her activities as a University of Arkansas Alumni Cheerleader at, as mom always said, "The University." When the Arkansas Alumni Association came up with the idea of inviting former cheerleaders to play a part in homecoming activities each year, mom immediately stepped in to help organize the event and was very involved in all the activities. She still had her original cheerleader jacket from the early 1940s and wore it proudly the whole weekend. The night before the football game, she introduced the alumni cheerleaders at the pep rally, and the next day she rode in the homecoming parade and ran out on the field with the regular cheerleaders ahead of the team.

Willie Oates was one of a kind, and I can still remember when, in her late eighties, she went to homecoming for the last time in the first weekend of November 2005. Debbie was the smartest one in our family, and that weekend, the Arkansas Alumni Association was honoring her with a community service award for her work in cancer research. This was an award mom had received several years before, and they became the first mother and daughter ever to be so honored by the university. Even though it was difficult for mom to walk or stand without help, she went to "The University" in Fayetteville one last time. Sam and I looked after her, and everywhere she went, people wanted to have their pictures taken with her and asked for her autograph on everything from cocktail napkins to football programs. It was a wonderful weekend for our whole family, and we still talk about it at family gatherings.

Debbie and I were fortunate to have Cassondra Sneed to help us with mom even before we had to move her to a nursing home. Cassondra is a registered nurse and a delightful, caring lady whom Debbie found through a friend. From the beginning, mom enjoyed her company and looked forward to her visits. I don't know how we would have managed without Cassondra's help. Knowing that she and some of her staff were with mom on a regular basis was very comforting to us. While the nursing home had a capable staff, we still wanted Cassondra to continue to be with mom. Cassondra was someone whom she knew and trusted, which was very helpful while moving her to a strange, new place.

In the middle of February, when Sam and I went to visit mom, Cassondra told us she didn't think mom had much time left. While the end did not appear to be imminent, it was obvious she was in the final stage of her life. I had lengthy phone conversations with both Greg and Deb about mom's decline and told them I would stay in touch and let them know when they should come to Little Rock. I also had a conversation with the doctor on staff at the nursing home, and he recommended we bring in hospice, which we did.

A week later, Cassondra called me and said that it was time for me to call the family and notify them that mom would soon be gone. Greg, Debbie, and her Daughter Somerset, all made plans to come to Little Rock at the end of February. Mom passed away early in the morning of March 4, 2008. The hospice nurse on duty called Debbie at our house early that morning, as mom was having difficulty breathing. Deb was there at mom's bedside, holding her hand when she drew her last breath. She was ninety years old.

The next day, Willie Oates's picture was on the front page of the second section of the Arkansas Democrat-Gazette along with a nice story about her many contributions to the state of Arkansas. The following day, the editorial page of the newspaper featured a caricature of mom along with a heartfelt editorial. The outpouring of sympathy and support from throughout the state was remarkable.

The family visitation was at Second Presbyterian Church on Thursday evening, March 6, and we had a big crowd. The funeral home put together a nice slide show of pictures of mom, which ran on a big screen during the visitation. It was a wonderful celebration of her life, and she would have enjoyed it. Events like this always bring families together, and it was wonderful to see extended family members I had not seen in a long time. It was also an opportunity for lots of friends to see me and get a full appreciation of my condition. The outpouring of support from so many people was very comforting.

We buried mom next to dad with a private ceremony on Friday, March 7. Due to surprisingly snowy weather, we delayed the memorial service until Saturday at the church. Debbie and I talked about her headstone and decided to make an addition to the traditional name and dates on her stone. Dad had always said jokingly that mom was so busy that, when she died, he was going to put on her headstone, "This is the only stone she left unturned." Debbie and I thought Mom would have loved it, so we had the inscription added to her stone.

In spite of moving the memorial service back a day because of the snow, there was still a considerable crowd who ventured out in the bad weather to attend. We invited Skip Rutherford, director of the Clinton Library, to speak on behalf of Bill and Hillary Clinton and talk about mom's contributions to state government. We also asked Craig O'Neal, a radio and television personality who had hosted many fundraisers with mom, to speak. Debbie and I jointly composed the eulogy, which I agreed to deliver. I was able to walk into the church with my walker for the memorial service and visitation. However, I used my wheelchair most of the time inside the church, because I couldn't comfortably stand for very long.

I think mom would have appreciated how we opened the eulogy with the following:

"This week, Debbie and I lost our mother. Each of you lost a dear friend. The organizations that many of you belong to lost one of your most active members and probably your best fundraiser. The state of Arkansas lost one of its most enthusiastic ambassadors, and 'The University', as Mom called it, lost its greatest cheerleader."

I could see several heads nodding, especially with the last line, which was bittersweet. I then spoke about many of the things mom contributed to all who knew her, and closed with the following:

"Willie Oates lived a rich, full, giving life that touched many people and brightened their lives. She can rest easy now, knowing she made a significant impact on the lives of her family, on the people of her adopted state and beyond, and at her beloved University."

Delivering the eulogy was one of the toughest things I had ever done in my life, but mom deserved and would have wanted a grand send-off. Afterward, I thought back to what seemed like a lifetime ago when Sam and I were married in this same church. Yet it was only two years ago. A lot had happened since then, and all of it while we were just beginning to settle into our life together. Sam was literally a lifesaver for me. She, my son Greg, Mickey Freeman, along with sister Debbie, provided the support, encouragement, and help to keep me going when I would wander off into the "Dark Night of the Soul".

On Sunday, after laying mom to rest, the family members headed home, and Sam and I decided to take some time off. There was a lot to absorb from everything that happened, and in addition to being mentally and physically exhausted, I came down with a head cold. But there was still one more meaningful event on the calendar; the second anniversary of our wedding, which was just three days after Mom's memorial service.

Our anniversary reminded me of how blessed I was to have a wife who was devoting all of her energy to making me whole again. We had made lots of plans to travel and enjoy ourselves after we were married, but now those plans were for naught, as my ability to travel looked bleak. However, we did celebrate our anniversary with dinner at the finest restaurant in town, Ashley's in the Capitol Hotel. I was in my wheelchair, and the restaurant staff did a great job of taking care of us for dinner. The service and food were superb, and it was nice for us to have a fun night out, and I surprised Sam with a beautiful, long, black cashmere coat that Rita Harvey found for me. Rita had previously owned one of the best women's clothing stores in Little Rock and was a close friend of the family. She really came through on finding this gift, and it was a complete surprise for Sam, who was thrilled with it.

Eighteen

Coping with Multiple
Issues

The end of February and beginning of March 2008 was a very difficult time. There was a lot to absorb, and I found myself struggling again. As I wrote in my journal a few days after our anniversary:

I seem to have lost all hope and find it hard to face the future. I can feel the life force draining out of me.

I was having difficulty sleeping and had no appetite for anything. It had been a grueling few weeks, and I didn't know if I could find my way out of the darkness and back into the light. And then, we had a special visitor.

Karen Akin is the Associate Pastor at Second Presbyterian Church who performed the marriage services for Debbie, my niece Somerset, and Sam and me. Karen also presided over mom's funeral. Two weeks after mom's death, she stopped by our house to visit and was most helpful. She spent two hours with me, and we talked about all the major changes that had occurred over the last three years, and it was quite a list. I had retired from the banking business, and then, a few months later, found the love of my life, Hermine "Sam" Wellner. Sam met Debbie for the first time in the process of us moving mom from her townhouse to a cottage after she fell and hit her head. It wasn't long after that mom fell in the cottage and broke her hip, which the doctors told us was probably the beginning of the end. This happened at the time of Sam's birthday, which we celebrated in between visits to the hospital to check on mom. Not a great way for a new couple to celebrate a birthday, but Sam was a trooper and didn't complain. Next, we moved mom into a nursing home, but the first one didn't work well for her, so we moved her to another nursing facility. In the meantime, Sam and I were planning our wedding and moving ahead with selling her house in Hot Springs in order to move her to my house in Little Rock. And we were also in the process of looking for a new house for the two of us. It was a hectic time, but we eventually found a terrific house, got married, and then moved into our new place well before my injury.

I agreed with Karen that these were all dramatic events in a relatively short period of time and that it was a lot for me to swallow. No matter how strong I thought I was, Karen was right; it would take time for me to grieve the losses and adapt to the changes in order be able to move forward with my recovery. In the past, I had always been able to manage my frustrations by going for a run or a bike ride and would come home refreshed and relaxed. Now that was no longer possible. Without those normal release mechanisms, it was hard for me to cope. Karen understood and gave me several thoughts and ideas to consider in dealing with my mental issues.

Karen told me that each night before she goes to sleep, she looks back and considers what she called "the remains of the day." This was her opportunity to think back and focus on the positive elements of her day. Here is some of what she shared with me to consider, which I wrote in my journal:

> *When did I give love and when did I receive love?*
> *When did I feel God's Presence?*
> *When did I feel most alive?*

When did I feel most free?
When did I feel most creative?
When did I feel most myself?
When did I feel most whole?
Finally, look at the day with gratitude and ask for help.

Once again I was fortunate to have the right person show up at a time when I needed help, and Karen provided not only support but also gave me some valuable tools to work with in my recovery process.

Nineteen

Back to Work

After our visit with Karen, the next three days went very well. Getting back into a workout routine always made me feel good, and I was convinced that the hard work would pay off in the long run. I had an excellent workout with my trainer, Carla, at the athletic club and followed that up with a walk around the track holding my walker in one hand and the railing in the other. Friday I did a nine-mile trike ride, which boosted my spirits. Exercising outside was always a big plus for me, so I got in another ride on Saturday for six miles and was beginning to believe I might be able to walk and ride again. I still had a very long road ahead of me, but I had hope.

At this time, we also decided to add another element to my weekly rehab routine: acupuncture with Martin Eisle, a doctor of oriental medicine. The owner of the Little Rock Athletic Club, Pat Riley Jr., was very supportive of my recovery efforts, and after he saw the progress I was making, he suggested I consider acupuncture. Pat had worked with Martin on some physical issues and thought acupuncture would help me. Throughout the recovery process, Sam and I were willing do whatever might help and were willing to think outside the box of what most traditional doctors would recommend. Interestingly enough, when I brought up the subject with Dr. Rehab, he was very supportive. He told me several of the spinal column patients he treated over the years had tried acupuncture, and it had worked for some. He also said those who had the most success seemed to be those who were willing to try nontraditional methods and worked hard on their recovery. So this became a regular part of my rehabilitation. Martin had never worked with a paraplegic before and didn't make any promises. However, he thought he might be able to help, but I would need to commit to regular visits over the next few weeks before we would know if it was working. Once again, we felt fortunate to find the right resources at the right time, and Martin was able to help increase sensation in my lower legs and feet.

Easter Sunday, March 23, 2008, we attended church at Second Presbyterian, and I was able to walk in with my walker. That was a big milestone for me. After the service, I saw lots of friends who offered encouragement, and I had time to visit with Karen Akin. Then Sam and I went out for a nice lunch with our good friends Joe and Fran Holmes and Kelley and Judy Johnson. It was a very good day, and the best part was being able to walk in and out of our house with my walker instead of using the wheelchair. I was still using the walker outside the house and the wheelchair in the house; however, I was testing myself using the forearm crutches at rehab and making good progress. Lou was now working with me to walk in parallel bars with only AFOs on my legs instead of the braces.

"Be Still and Know that I Am God"

I first heard this affirmation in a Sunday school group called Spiritual Pilgrims at Second Presbyterian. It had become a popular meditation phrase in the 1960s and '70s, especially within the New Age movement, but the first time I heard it was in 2003 with the Spiritual Pilgrims group. Being back in our church for Easter reminded me of this affirmation. The leader of the Spiritual Pilgrims always started the session with a few minutes of meditation and the phrase, "Be still and know that I am God." She would say the full phrase and then say it four more times, dropping a word or two each time. So it went like this: "Be still and know that I am God," "Be still and know that I am," "Be still and know," "Be still," and finally just "Be." The group leader was a talented therapist and one of the most spiritual people I had ever met. When she said these simple words, she always did so slowly and carefully, which made sure the group paid attention to each word. It was an excellent way to start our group sessions in which we discussed one of the assigned books on various spiritual subjects. The regular group of fifteen to twenty-five people was predominantly female, and I was impressed with the knowledge and insightful comments from various members. Prior to my paralysis, I attended regularly for a year or two, until our leader thought it was time for a change and stepped down. The group didn't have the same dynamics afterward, so I quit going. After attending the Easter service in 2008, I started using that affirmation at night when I went to bed; however, I customized the final word for my situation. Instead of ending with "I am God," I chose, "I am healing." It's not that I didn't believe in a higher power, even though since my paralysis I'd had some doubts about my core beliefs. My purpose was to use this affirmation to reinforce in my mind that I was healing. I would say all five phrases to myself, thinking of the first word as I inhaled slowly and the second word as I exhaled, all the way through each phrase. It was surprising how much this helped me to relax both my mind and my body. Debbie and I have always talked about how our family tended to be more "human doings" than "human beings," and ending on the word "be" was quite meaningful to me. I would suggest to anyone struggling with major changes in their lives to consider using this positive affirmation and customizing it for their own needs.

Perceptions of the Handicapped
It's natural for many people to look at those of us who are physically handicapped in very different ways. That's not necessarily a bad thing; it's just that we all notice someone who is quite different from ourselves. For me, it took some time to get used to people staring at me in public places when I was in a wheelchair or using my walker. Children are particularly prone to stare and then ask one of their parents, "What's wrong with

that man?" This, of course, always embarrasses the parents. Also there are some people who may associate an obvious physical problem with a mental deficiency. It's rare but on a couple of occasions I have had someone I didn't know speak very deliberately and slowly to me to make sure I could understand what they are saying. At times like that I just assume they are the ones who are mentally challenged.

Most people were very sympathetic and eager to open doors and offer to help in some way, but some would walk into a store and let the door close behind them right in front me. I think the changes over the last couple of decades with more wheelchair ramps, special parking spaces, accessible bathrooms, and other modifications have made everyone more aware of issues handicapped people face on a daily basis. However, my biggest frustration is people who are not handicapped parking in handicapped parking places and using handicapped accessible bathrooms. It's amazing to me how many times there are multiple open stalls in a public bathroom and I will have to wait for the one handicapped stall while someone who is fully functional is using it. And on more than one occasion I have waited while people who have finished their business in the stall are now standing up where I can see their head and are combing their hair or checking out how they look in the mirror. I sometimes wonder if they know what that big blue handicap symbol on the bathroom stall means. Maybe they just don't give a damn. Handicap bathroom stalls tend to be larger, have nice handrails, frequently are cleaner, and sometimes have their own sink and mirror. So I assume that is why some completely functional people use them, but it is very aggravating for those of us who have to use a catheter tube to empty our bladder, or gloves to digitally evacuate our bowel, to have to wait while someone who is not handicapped ties up the only stall we can comfortably use.

"Inclusion" is a common term used by people with disabilities to promote the idea that those of us who are handicapped should be accommodated, without restrictions, to move around freely in public places. At first I was uncomfortable feeling like I was so different from everyone else around me. It was especially difficult when people who knew me but hadn't seen me since my paralysis would ask why I was in a wheelchair. Going through the process of explaining how I was paralyzed was like reliving my worst nightmare again and again. Over time, I was able to get beyond being angry and frustrated, but early on in the process, it was hard on me.

It was amazing how much misinformation there was about what had happened to me. Many people thought I was injured in a bike accident. Others heard I was hurt in a car wreck. When I told people the truth, they were surprised and would ask questions about the doctor and the procedure, which most people assumed was routine. In fact, a few people said they'd had epidural injections and didn't have any idea of the potential risks involved. One of our family doctors was scheduled to have this same procedure a month or two after I was injured, and he decided not to go through with it because of what happened to me.

One of the most common problems with using catheters every couple of hours to relieve one's bladder is the risk of infection. And sure enough, in spite of making good progress on everything else, I came down with a damn urinary tract infection (UTI) in early April. The symptoms were very similar to coming down with the flu, and I would end up in the bed for at least a day or two. This meant no therapy for several days, and it left me feeling tired and weak. Fortunately, our family doctor, Dr. H, was able to effectively treat these infections with antibiotics and help me recover as rapidly as possible.

Over the next few weeks, I expanded my trike riding by going to the river trail the city had built along the Arkansas River in Rebsamen Park, which was about seven miles west of downtown. Over several years, the twin cities of Little Rock and North Little Rock, along with the County, had greatly expanded recreational opportunities on both sides of the Arkansas River. The county judge, Buddy Villines, worked for many years raising funds and working with the Corps of Engineers to be able to build a pedestrian/bicycle bridge over the top of the lock and dam, which was next to Rebsamen Park. This bridge connected the bike trails on both sides of the river, with plans to also connect the other end in the downtown areas to form a complete loop. It took eight years from conception to build the Big Dam Bridge. The design was complex and the costs were substantial. There were times when it appeared the bridge would never be built, but the County Judge was determined, as he said, "to build that damn bridge." Before the opening of the bridge, the judge gave the planning group a tour of the bridge, and someone said, "Wow, this is big." The Judge replied, "Yes, it's a big dam bridge," and that became the name.

The opening of the Big Dam Bridge was a classic case of the now-famous movie phrase, "if you build it they will come." Parking areas had to be expanded to handle the crowds, and there were always people walking and riding in the area both day and night. It is now a major landmark for the area and is the longest bridge in the country specifically built as a pedestrian/bicycle bridge. The annual Big Dam Bridge 100 has become the biggest bike tour in Arkansas with two thousand or more cyclists expected each year.

For me the trail was a fun place to ride and see lots of old friends running, walking, or riding in the area. They would stop to visit and express their surprise at my ability to pedal a trike. The athletic community in Little Rock was pretty closely knit, and everyone had heard about my injury, so when people saw me on the trike, they were quick to offer encouragement. That meant a lot to me in my recovery and reminded me of how many people were pulling for me. Of course, at this point, I wasn't nearly strong enough to go up the modest five percent grade on the bridge, but I could enjoy riding on the paved trail. I had run in this area for many years and always enjoyed the views of the river and the park. It was on the river trail that I passed the one hundred-mile mark on my trike, which was another milestone for me.

I continued my work on learning to use forearm crutches at Baptist Rehab and was beginning to become more comfortable with them. During April, Lou and I continued working on my sit-to-stand from the wheelchair to the crutches, which was terribly difficult, but I was ever so slowly getting better at it. Anne Miskin talked about significant improvements with the way my feet looked. Without good blood circulation, my feet were very swollen, and Anne said that on the day she first started working with me, they looked like sausages. It was not a pretty picture. Plus my feet were very pale, and I worried about whether they would ever recover. Fortunately, eight months after the injury, they were starting to return to normal with less swelling and a more natural skin color. Anne saw a noticeable difference in early April and was also pleased with the increased flexibility in my tailbone. With a frozen tailbone, it was almost unbearable for me to sit down on a hard surface for more than just a few minutes, which meant I had to carry a U-shaped cushion with me if I was going anywhere without the wheelchair. On one of Debbie's trips to visit, she showed me a self-inflating cushion, which she used on the plane, and I immediately ordered a couple of them. They were a wonderful addition to the many devices I used to improve my quality of life as a recovering paraplegic.

Traditionally, our family got together every year in late March or early April for a weekend at Oaklawn Jockey Club in Hot Springs, Arkansas, for the end of the thoroughbred horse racing season. My family had a box at the racetrack for many years, and it was always a big social occasion when we went. Mother and dad loved the races, and every year, they spent the last ten days of the racing season in Hot Springs with my aunt and uncle from Missouri, along with two other couples, who were all close friends. It was more of a social event than a gambling trip, but the men were really into thoroughly studying the racing form and discussing potential contenders for each race. After dad's death, and with mom's declining condition, Debbie and I kept the box seats and continued the tradition as a long weekend and included our children and a couple of close friends. However, in my condition, with my continuing bowel and bladder issues, I knew there was no way I could go. Sam loved the horses, and I knew she could use a break, so I insisted she go and have fun with the family. She was concerned about leaving me but finally agreed to go under protest and had a great time. Part of getting her to agree to leave me for a few days involved inviting several friends to visit. The Mougeots, the Freemans, and the Noors all volunteered to stop by and even bring dinner on different nights. It was a good test for me to be on my own for a couple of days and figure out how to manage around the house. I enjoyed visiting with my friends while Sam took a much-needed break to focus on something other than taking care of me twenty-four hours a day. Henry Noor also came by one day and did several projects around the house including replacing a sprinkler head in the yard, putting metal edging at the edge of the sidewalk to control mud washing onto the sidewalk, repairing our flag holder on the porch, and unstopping one of our gutters. This was an enormous help. As I noted in my journal:

Great friends are really looking after me!

During the first week of April, I could tell that my walking was getting better as my balance improved. Also, my sit-to-stand was improving, but my damn bowel process was still a struggle, as my intestinal system wasn't functioning properly and my feces were still soft and loose. This made emptying my bowel two to three times a day a nasty and disgusting chore. Over time, managing my bowel and bladder would continue to be one of my most frustrating issues.

Plenty of Ups and Downs

On Wednesday, April 9, I had one of my best workouts with Lou at Baptist Rehab, going up some steps in the forearm crutches and doing a few moderate squats. We then walked outside with the crutches and went up the long wheelchair ramp and back down again with a couple of rest breaks. Two days later, after my regular workout with Lou, he gave me my very own pair of crutches to take home. That was another landmark day.

It was so nice to be able to use the forearm crutches inside the athletic club to walk on the track and to maneuver in and out of the weight machines when I worked with Carla. I also started using the crutches to go more places. They were so much less cumbersome than dragging the walker everywhere. As usual, both Lou and Dr. Rehab reminded me several times to be extremely careful on the crutches and not to take any chances. One stumble or fall could result in a fractured wrist or elbow or a damaged shoulder. So I continued to use the walker to get in and out of most public places, and especially to help me with my sit-to-stand procedure, which still needed lots of practice.

In spite of all my excitement over my improving mobility, by the end of the week, I came down with an intestinal bug that caused me to vomit more than once, and I spent the next four days in bed. Yuck! I could do something about working on the muscles in my lower body, but there didn't seem to be much I could do about my internal problems. Throughout several weeks in April 2008, I had good moments, but at other times I would become depressed and frustrated because of my internal issues. The damage to my legs was obvious, but the paralysis also affected my intestinal system and my body's overall ability to function properly. And there was no indication it was going to get much better.

The week I came home with my crutches was exciting until I got sick. I also had a very good conversation with Baptist Rehabilitation about the cost of continuing my therapy. My insurance was about to run out for outpatient therapy, so they offered to give me a discount on the therapy costs if I would pay them promptly, which was great news. Because it could take months for them to get payment from insurance companies, they offered patients a discount for paying within a couple of weeks. That took a lot of pressure off of us because therapy was expensive, plus insurance didn't pay anything for acupuncture, craniosacral work, or working with a personal trainer. Once again, Sam and I firmly believed that if we only did what insurance paid for, if was obvious my recovery would have ground to a halt. I also received positive news from the McMaths: it appeared they were making meaningful progress on our lawsuit, which was good to hear.

The bad news was that my bouts of depression, lack of appetite, problems sleeping, and strange dreams continued. At times I was

157

overwhelmed by my physical situation and inability to do much about it. As a result, on Saturday, April 12, 2008, I wrote the following in my journal:

How could this happen to me? Why? I have lived a good life and generally done the right things, and now it means nothing! Sometimes it feels like I am living in my own private hell. Worst of all, I was rude and hateful to Sam today. I picked at her. I see her faults and not her wonderful beauty and kindness. I wonder why she puts up with me. What's wrong with her that she stays with me? I don't know what to do. I hate myself for the way I treated Sam. I hate the way I am. When will this ever end?

Over the next couple of days, I slowly started feeling better. Once again, putting my problems on paper seemed to help. It took some of the anger out of my mind and helped me to fight my way out of my depression.

There was no question I was ever so slowly getting better, and I started testing myself around the house on my crutches. On Sunday, we rested and read the newspaper at our leisure. We also took Henry and Marcella Noor out to dinner as a thank you for all they had done for us. That was a positive end to the day and helped me sleep better that night. My body and my mind needed the rest, which I knew would help me get a good start with my therapy and workouts on Monday.

Lou Tretter continued to work on helping me get out of the wheelchair and into the forearm crutches and gave me some excellent tips on my technique. The following day, Sam and I went to the athletic club, and I walked three laps around the track in my crutches. And for the first time, I was able to walk out of the house, down the wheelchair ramp to the sidewalk, and over to our car in my crutches. At the rehab center, with Lou at my side, I walked up and down the wheelchair ramp again outside of the building. Lou and I agreed that this was my best job of walking since the injury.

Once again, Henry Noor was always glad to meet Sam and me at Two Rivers Park for a ride on the paved trails. On April 16, Henry and I did a ten-and-a-half-mile ride together, covering all the trails in the park. It was my longest ride since the injury, and while it was slow and I had to take a few breaks, I was so proud of being able to cover that much distance.

Near the end of April, Lou took me out for a real test in my forearm crutches. We walked from the rehab gym to the courtyard at Baptist Rehab and then up all four of the wheelchair ramps. I had done this before by taking a break at each landing, but this time, by focusing hard and giving it everything I had, I was able to do it without taking a break on the way up. When we got to the top, I took a short breather on a bench, and then I walked back down again. Going down a slope requires less strength but significantly more focus on balance than going up. By the end of the month, I was starting to regularly use my crutches to walk from the house to the car, into the athletic club, and even into some restaurants. Moving from the walker to the crutches was a major step forward. I was so proud. When I first arrived at Baptist Rehabilitation, I thought I would be able to walk in a couple of months. This was completely unrealistic, especially since most of the doctors we had seen didn't think I would be able to have any real use of my legs. After a couple of months, reality set in and I believed it would take me months, maybe even years, before I could stand and walk, even with braces and some form of support like forearm crutches. Nevertheless, I was now able to get around with crutches, and hopefully my recovery would continue. Of course, I could only be on my feet for a short period of time and spent all my time at home in a wheelchair, but at least my walking at rehab gave me hope.

Managing my mental state would continue to be an ongoing problem, especially with my bowel and bladder issues. Bowel issues were particularly frustrating. Often it would take me twenty to thirty minutes to digitally evacuate my bowel, and I sometimes would go through eight or more rubber gloves before I was done. This issue, along with my incredibly slow recovery, caused me to ask again and again, why me? On Friday, April 25, 2008, I wrote the following in my journal:

I was living the life I had only dreamed of, and now I am a prisoner of my injury. Why me? Yes, I have many doubts and fears.

Will I be able to run again?

Will I be able to bike again?

Will I be able to urinate and have a bowel movement?

Will I be able to have sex?

Will my feet recover?

What will be the residual damage?

How will I cope with all this?

In spite of my many frustrations and anxiety over the ultimate outcome, there were still more good moments than bad. A couple of days later, Bruce and Phillip McMath came to the house to update us on our lawsuit. As usual, they took all the time needed to clearly inform us of what they had learned and to answer all our questions. As a result of what they found through their research, they were prepared to move ahead with our lawsuit. The first step would be mailing an official notification to Dr. X and the orthopedic clinic he worked with at the time of my injury. In the back of my mind, I still had some reservations about the lawsuit, but the McMaths had uncovered enough information to indicate that my injury was the result of a faulty procedure. When an epidural is done correctly, there should be no problems. They had talked to several doctors who were surprised at my paralysis from this procedure, and all of the doctors they consulted indicated that they had not heard of this happening before. There was no doubt in Bruce and Phillip's minds that my paralysis was the result of improper execution of the epidural injection.

Twenty

Looking Ahead

After nine months of hard work, things were beginning to look up. By the beginning of May, I was trying to walk as much as possible in my forearm crutches. I still had to rely on the walker at times, especially in restaurants, due to the difficulty of going from a sitting position to standing up in the crutches. The walker gave me much more confidence and stability with my sit-to-stand. However, I was adapting to the crutches. Thursday, May 1, 2008, was one of my best days of recovery. Martin Eisle, my acupuncturist, spent two hours with me using his needles in various places on my hands, and we found good stimulation in my right foot and limited feeling in the left foot. Walking out of acupuncture that day, I could just barely feel heel strike and sensation in the arch of my right foot. I learned from Martin that acupuncture focuses on the meridians of energy that run from the right side of the upper body to the left side of the lower body and vice versa. While oriental medicine may seem like smoke and mirrors to many people, in Asia they have been doing this for thousands of years with good success, and it was working for me. Next, we went to the athletic club, where Anne worked hard on my lower back and coccyx. We were pleased, for the first time, to find some limited stimulation in the glutes on the right part of my butt. I then finished up with Carla, working on a few machines and testing my ability to walk on a very slow treadmill at only one-half of a mile per hour without using my full leg brace. Of course, I was supporting much of my weight and balancing myself by holding onto rails on either side of the treadmill, but it almost felt like walking again. It was a busy, demanding day, and I came home physically exhausted but excited about the signs of progress that gave us great hope for the future.

By the middle of May, I was becoming confident enough with my crutches that I decided to walk from the car into Baptist Rehab. On Wednesday, May 14, 2008, Sam dropped me off at the door to the rehab center where I took the elevator down to the gym and then walked from the elevator over to the gym. It was slow and took a lot of concentration, but I made it. Several of the other therapists at Baptist Rehab were pleased to see me walk in and congratulated me, but Lou was working with another patient and didn't see me come in. I was sitting on the workout bench when he came over to start our therapy session. After a few minutes, he noticed the wheelchair wasn't in its usual place beside the bench and asked me where it was. I told him it was in the car and I had walked in on my crutches. The pleased look on his face filled my heart with joy. He was so proud of what we had accomplished together. I told him I never would have been able to do it without his patience and dedication to my recovery. As a result of my progress, he decided it was time to focus more on my sit-to-stand in the forearm crutches. He also thought I was ready to try going up a single step at a time and stepping over curbs. He reminded me that these were all things I would need to do in a real-world environment. Lou also warned me to be extremely careful due to the limited strength in my legs and lack of control in my knees and feet. Just like Dr. Rehab, Lou always cautioned me about taking my time and avoiding the potential for a fall. On my next session with Lou, I was able to accomplish three very good sit-to-stands from the wheelchair to my crutches. Also, I practiced walking up steps using a handrail with my right hand and a crutch on the left. As a result of all this progress, I started using the crutches to go from the car to acupuncture, to the athletic club, and in and out of the house. I was careful to do this only in dry weather and where I was on a relatively flat surface. Sam was very helpful and supportive, and we both saw this as a major step forward in my rehabilitation.

Anne continued to find improved muscle tone in my left thigh and was getting limited stimulation in my right thigh. While I still struggled with depression and had times when I spent most of a day in bed, there was no question about the fact that I was making progress. My therapists could see it every couple of weeks, even when I couldn't. I also had a couple of opportunities to ride my trike and tried swimming on my back a little at the Baptist Rehab pool.

At times, I was still overwhelmed by my situation compared to where I was at the same time last year. May was the traditional start of my triathlon season, and here I was a struggling paraplegic who was unable to do any of the things I had done all my life. At times like that, when I was so depressed I couldn't get out of bed, I knew this process was at least as hard on Sam as it was on me. I wrote the following in my journal on Saturday, May 17, 2008:

I feel I am contributing nothing, absolutely nothing, to our partnership. She does all the work: cooking, shopping, yard work, driving me to therapy, and everything else. All I do is focus and work on my body, which is very self-centered. Sam would be better off with a dog for companionship and it would be a lot less trouble.

In spite of my frustrations, Sam got me out of the house on Sunday. We went down to the bike trail by the Arkansas River for a long trike ride of almost fourteen miles, while Sam walked seven miles. This was my first time to start on the far west side of the trail, which meant I would have to go over the small bridge crossing Jimerson Creek, and I didn't know whether I could make it. Surprisingly, I was fine using the trike's lowest gear on the bridge.

However, the next day I was struggling again. I was beginning to realize I might never walk again or ride a bike or do many of the things most people take for granted. I had been such an active person all my life. Now, after years of hard work that was rewarding both physically and mentally, I was spending most of my time in a wheelchair. When I finally had the time, money, and a wonderful partner to enjoy life with, I was a broken, crippled man without the ability to take care of myself. I loved doing yard work with Sam, especially in the spring when we would add new plants and flowers to the multiple beds around the house. Now I couldn't even do simple tasks like cooking on the grill, changing a light bulb in an overhead fixture, driving the car, and fixing small things in the house.

The next day after therapy, Sam had Mickey come by the house, and as usual, he was able to talk me through some issues and improve my outlook. Many times, this work on my "emotional muscles" was more important than the work I was doing physically. As a result, I was able to push on that week, testing my ability to walk, with Carla's help, using the walker without the full leg brace, just ankle-foot orthotics on both legs. I couldn't do much, but it went better than I expected. I also tried this with Lou at Baptist Rehab, but as he reminded me, my right leg was too weak to carry my full weight, and I should be careful and always have someone next to me in case I have a problem. However, I was starting to believe there was a better than even chance I would walk again, probably with braces and crutches, or who knows, maybe even canes.

May was a month of significant progress. I felt good enough to send out an e-mail to my family and friends about my progress. Putting words on paper (or, in this case, in an e-mail) always helped me. When I wrote about my progress, it seemed more real. It reminded me of how far I had come in my recovery. And as Lou and Dr. Rehab reminded me, only nine months into a spinal column injury is a very short time frame for recovery. The doctor would also remind me to be prepared for a plateau in my recovery, but Lou, Carla, and Anne continued to comment on my small bits of progress each week. Carla was even able to increase the weight on the machines I was working on at the athletic club. Plus, now that I was using a walker and crutches, we were able to get me into more machines to work on my lower body. I could now, lying on my back, leg press eighty-five pounds, which was amazing. Of course my left leg was doing the majority of the work, but still, an eighty-five-pound leg press for me was an enormous accomplishment in less than a year since being paralyzed. And the continuing encouragement from many people at the athletic club provided me with much-needed moral support. My triathlon buddy, Kurt Truax, always made a point to visit with me at the athletic club and compliment me on how much I had improved. It was very encouraging to have people tell me how much better I looked, especially after I started using forearm crutches instead of the walker. Throughout this process, it was hard for Sam and me to see much change from day to day. You don't see your body change on a daily basis when you are losing weight, working out, or overcoming an illness or injury. However, people who only see you every couple of weeks can frequently see noticeable changes.

The first week of June 2008, there was good news from several sources. During acupuncture, I found good feeling in part of my big toe and three other places on my right foot. Martin was extremely patient with me and devoted a lot of time and effort to my recovery, and it seemed to be paying off. That same week while I was at Martin's office, I ran into an old friend and fraternity brother, Ron Robinson. Ron and I had been through school together, starting in grade school and all the way through college. He was always a much better student than I was, and I admired his intellectual ability. At the University of Arkansas, he edited the student newspaper and was always in the know on everything going on around campus. The day was June 5, 2008, and Ron asked me if I knew what was important about June 5. All I knew was that it was the day before D-Day, when the Allies landed at Normandy. Ron was amazing about remembering dates. He shook his head and reminded me it was the forty-third anniversary of our graduation from the university. It was nice to visit about old times and remember some of the crazy things we did in school. For both of us, it was a terrific four years.

Ron's visit reminded me of how my dad was concerned about me just making it through high school; he warned me that if I didn't make my grades at the university, I was coming back home, which was what he expected. I loved the college atmosphere and worked hard at making, as my mother said, gentleman's C's. Mom was always suspicious of those who made all A's in college because she thought they were obviously not making the most of the entire college experience. Mom was involved in multiple organizations on campus and took a leisurely five years plus some summer school to graduate. While I did fully participate in the college experience, I was able to make the Dean's List my senior year. When my dad opened the letter from the university and read about my accomplishment, he thought it had been sent to the wrong family. My father was a perfectionist, and I never lived up to his expectations, but that was OK because mom thought I was special and never let me forget it. It was a strange yin and yang experience with them, but it seemed to work, and I had no regrets. Growing up, I was very fortunate to learn many positive things from my parents and grandparents, and that's one of the reasons I was able to work so hard on my recovery.

A few days later, I couldn't quit thinking about Mom. One day, while lying down to rest after a hard workout, I had this strange vision of mom with the family at Greg's house for our annual Labor Day gathering (which Greg had dubbed "Club Greg") two years prior to my injury. Greg's Labor Day weekend event was always a lot of fun, and the family knew 2004 would most likely be Mom's last time to attend. I found myself thinking back to that time, and I could see myself in almost the same situation as hers, unable to get around without help. I visualized myself sitting there just like Mom, surrounded by friends and family, knowing she was not long for this world. It made me wonder whether I was long for this world. I knew my injury was not terminal, but at this point, I was unable to do very basic things for myself. Also, my bowel and bladder situation was very much like mom's in the nursing home, which was miserable. Visualizing myself in her place was a frightening experience I would never forget.

A couple of months after the funeral, Debbie and I had a chance to talk about mom and how she had lived a rich, full life. The occasion was the initial disposition of mom's possessions, and she did collect a lot of stuff, especially clothes and stunning designer hats. Mom had five file cabinets chock full of information and records from her time in politics, and the local library, which has an Arkansas history section, was thrilled to get those records. Also, while the library was picking up the file cabinets, they noticed that mom had a large collection of cookbooks from various clubs all over Arkansas. Willie Oates was very popular as a speaker at women's clubs throughout the state, and almost every club she visited raised money by selling cookbooks each year with recipes from its members. Consequently, they gave copies of their books to the speakers at their meetings, and mom had a wall-sized collection of these that the library was happy to have. Next, we sold or gave away most of her furniture and other miscellaneous items, and then moved the more personal things to two large storage units to sort out later.

In mid-June, Debbie and her husband, David, came back to Little Rock for us to go through mom's things and decide what we wanted and how to distribute all of her possessions. Debbie had lots of good ideas about how to manage this process. She was the one who came up with the idea to call the Butler Center for Arkansas Studies at the local library. She also contacted the Old State House Museum and offered them the gowns and hats mom wore to both of Bill Clinton's inaugurations, along with some other clothing that had historical significance. Deb and her daughter, Somerset, did a lot of work sorting through the clothing, which turned out to be great fun. Debbie was the main driver, with Somerset's help, on trying to put matching hats with gowns, and in some cases, they even found pictures and newspaper articles to go with some of the outfits we gave to the museum. In addition, we invited three of our cousins—two who lived in Eureka Springs, Arkansas, and one in Dallas, Texas—to see whether there was anything of mom's they might want. Debbie, David, Somerset, Sam, and I, along with our three cousins, had a good time going through mom's belongings, and it brought back many fond memories. Mom and dad also collected a substantial amount of Razorback paraphernalia, including Mom's original cheerleader jacket from the 1940s, which we gave to the University Alumni Association. We had so much memorabilia that we warned them they would need to bring a van to haul everything back to Fayetteville.

I still have fond memories of that day, with me in a wheelchair and everyone going through all mom's stuff and coming up with interesting things she had collected over the years. All the women had fun trying on some of mom's hats and picking through her large collection of costume jewelry. We gave away many of the designer hats to several organizations in which mom was very active, and encouraged them to auction off the hats at fundraisers. Willie Oates was a key fundraiser for many charitable organizations, and we knew she would have wanted us to do this. There were still a lot of things left, including clothing, chairs, tables, quilts, and framed paintings, that we gave to the Arkansas Repertory Theatre, which is Arkansas's largest nonprofit professional theatre company. Sam and I had season tickets, and when I was able to go to the Rep again, it was fun recognizing some of mom's stuff as props on stage. Much like the alumni association, the Rep needed a van plus a car to carry everything.

The weekend after we wrapped up taking care of all that stuff, Mickey Freeman called and offered to take me to a Travelers baseball game. Before I was paralyzed, Mickey and I had a boys' night out at the ballpark every three to four weeks during the summer. Neither of us was a big baseball fan, but the games were entertaining, and the new Dickey Stephens Park was a beautiful facility with surprisingly good food and cold beer. One of the vendors was a local barbecue place, Pig 'N Chick, which served an excellent barbecue sandwich for less than five dollars. It was on an open-face bun with so much pulled pork we had to eat half of it with a fork before we could eat the rest of it as a sandwich. What a bargain. Mic knew it would be a challenge to take me to the game, but he said he was up to it. He met me at the house and loaded my wheelchair into our SUV, and we were off. The wheelchair section at the ballpark was on the main promenade where all the food and drink vendors were, and it was right behind the reserved seats. Much to my surprise, the head usher for the stadium was my former next-door neighbor when I was a child. Prior to his retirement, Robert "Bubba" Rowe had worked for a food distributor who supplied food to the ballpark. He always enjoyed going to the ballgames, and after he retired, the team's general manager asked him to be the head usher at the stadium. As the manager told him, he was always going to the park anyway, so why not get paid for it? Bubba and I had a great visit that night. He gave me his cell phone number to call him in advance and said he would make sure we had good wheelchair seats. We ended up with great seats on the main promenade right behind home plate. This meant it was easy for Mic to get food and beer, and I could easily wheel myself to the bathroom, which was also on the same level. Every time Mic and I went to the ballpark, we always ran into somebody we knew. Before the ballgame started, we ran into Chuck and Kathy Blair, whom I had known from the sailing club for many years. They had a box right next to the field and offered it to us, which was very nice. I appreciated the offer, but frankly it was easier for me to get to the bathroom in the wheelchair seats.

That weekend was also Father's Day, and Greg came for a long weekend with us. He flew in from Dallas on Thursday evening just in time to go with Mickey and me to the Travelers ballgame. The three of us had a terrific time with plenty of beer and barbecue and watched the Travelers win the game in the tenth inning.

Mickey and I had some great times together talking about politics, marketing ideas, past successes, and interesting people we had worked with, and we enjoyed the game whether the home team won or not. We laughed a lot, and Sam said I always came home with a smile after a night at the ballpark.

On Saturday, Greg, Sam, and I drove down to the bike trail by the river, and I rode my trike on the trail while Sam and Greg walked over the Big Dam Bridge. At this point, I wasn't even close to pedaling up the long 5 percent grade to the bridge, but that was a goal I would eventually achieve. I did pedal thirteen miles on the Little Rock side of the trail and paid for it the next day with considerable soreness in my left leg, which did most of the work.

Twenty-One

Redefinition

In spite of my continuing struggles, in the back of my mind, I kept thinking about Anne Miskin telling me this was an opportunity for me to redefine myself. In my mind, I had frequently defined myself by my work and my athletic accomplishments. Redefining myself in my sixties was frankly not something I wanted to do. As most of my friends would tell anyone, I was pretty proud of myself just the way I was and didn't see any need for change. However, whether I liked it or not, my life had dramatically changed, and I needed to adapt. While I was devoting a lot of time to my recovery, I still had plenty of time to think, reason, and focus on the future. As Wayne Dyer, my favorite pop psychologist used to say, looking back only works if you have a way to rewind your life. I understood that and, in the past, had frequently given that same advice to others. Now it was time for me to take Dyer's advice to heart.

My future was definitely uncertain, but I was ever so slowly getting better, and if I continued my improvement, I believed I could regularly walk again with crutches or possibly canes. At this point in time, I even thought I might be able to ride a bike again, possibly by the end of the year, which was completely unrealistic. Starting out, I knew that Sam and I needed to find a way to do some things together other than therapy. We needed some normal time just for us. She loved to travel, and I wanted for us to travel and experience new places. As Sam was fond of saying, "You need to travel while you can still carry your own bags." I knew I wouldn't be carrying any bags, but we could focus on working toward some fun vacations, maybe even outside the country. I had already received some encouraging advice from other paraplegics about flying outside the United States and getting around in foreign countries. We also talked about going to events we used to enjoy, including the horse races in Hot Springs, Razorback football games, and the Repertory Theatre. Traveling with my limited ability to walk, along with the issues I had managing my bowel and bladder, was a scary thought at first, but we thought making a short trip in the car might be the first option we could explore. At least this was something to shoot for. At this point in the recovery process, I still couldn't drive a car, but I knew there were ways to modify a car so a paraplegic could drive.

After much deliberation, I took Anne Miskin's advice and started giving some serious thought to how I might redefine myself; and here are the affirmations from my journal for the redefinition of Randy Oates:

I will relax and enjoy life more.

I will worry less about finances.

I will be more supportive and attentive to Sam.

I will be fully present in each moment.

I will focus on the now and not waste time in the past or worry about the future, which I cannot control.

I will be aware of my positive energy and not let fear pull me into the darkness.

I will change my life in a positive way.

My thoughts control how I feel, and I can control my thoughts.

I will learn and practice patience.

I will always remember that biking, running, swimming, sailing, and triathlons were special gifts.

In spite of making some strong, helpful affirmations, I still found myself struggling during the latter part of June. I had an acupuncture session with Martin in which I couldn't seem to focus my mind on the task at hand. As Martin reminded me, he couldn't do this by himself; I had to let the energy flow through my body. Part of my problem was that this was the time of year when I was usually traveling to compete in two triathlons a month and seeing old friends at these events. Sam and I had such fun on our road trips. All those things I enjoyed so much seemed gone forever. Now I felt like only half a man. At this point, Sam and I decided to take a break and had a long three-day weekend, which helped a great deal. I still did a few exercises at home with some stretch bands that Lou Tretter had given me, but it was nice to just stay home, sleep in, and not worry about therapy for a few days.

At the end of June 2008, Martin suggested we try five days in a row of acupuncture to see if some intense work would help jumpstart things, and it helped. At the end of the five days, Martin believed I was getting some very slight increase in movement in my toes, which was excellent news. While working with Lou that week, he expressed some concern about my right leg, as it appeared that the heel cord had shortened and the right calf had no muscle tone or feeling at all. This was causing the right foot to turn inward, and when I stood up in my braces, the right ankle tried to roll over to the outside because of lack of ankle support. Even with the braces, I could not control the right ankle and foot. As it turned out, this would continue to be a problem for years to come.

Sam and I agreed to take off most of the week leading up to the Fourth of July weekend. We did some workouts on Monday and Tuesday and then took five days off for a vacation at home. We also wrapped up all the paperwork the McMath brothers asked for as part of our lawsuit. They needed copies of all the medical records we had collected from doctors, insurance companies, and hospitals, which were quite substantial.

During our five-day mini-vacation, we still had plenty to keep us busy, but we could sleep in every morning, which was wonderful. We went to dinner that week at the Buffalo Grill for burgers, skin-on fries, and for me, Fat Tire Amber Ale on tap. It was a real treat. I was able to slowly walk into the Buffalo Grill with my forearm crutches, which was a big accomplishment. We were about halfway through our meal when a nice older couple that had just finished their meal went out of their way to come over to our table to compliment me on how much progress I had made. I didn't have a clue who they were, but they had seen me at the athletic club over the last couple of months and wanted me to know how impressed they were with my progress. That meant a lot to both Sam and me as a validation of my progress. What a nice gesture that was for them to go out of their way to give me a very sincere pat on the back. I still remember it vividly because it made me feel like a million bucks! And the good news continued.

Susie Smith and Barry Jackson called me from Metropolitan National Bank, and we had a good discussion about marketing issues and how I could help them. While I was physically disabled, my mind was still working well, and being asked to contribute on a marketing project was wonderful. It made me feel valuable and reminded me I still had something to offer. It also forced me to focus on something other than rehab. I spent several days working on a plan for the bank and developed some good ideas I believed would be beneficial for them.

Toward the end of the week, the Noors had us over to their house for bratwurst and beer, which was fun. Then the Freemans and Mougeots came over the evening of Friday, July 4, and brought dinner. And on Sunday, my Louisiana biking friends, Pierre, Craig, and Liz, stopped by the house on their way back from a fishing trip in northern Arkansas. Seeing Pierre again reminded me of something he said in a phone conversation we had a couple of months after the injury: "Randy, my friend, this will be your toughest race, but I know you can do it." There were many people who had more faith in me than I had in myself.

Consequently, it inspired me to work even harder and prove I was worthy of their love and support.

The month of July 2008 turned out to be one of the best months in the early part of my recovery process. Karen Akin stopped by again to visit and gave me excellent guidance about managing my mental state. She focused on the following four key issues.

1. First, she said I needed to let go of the old Randy from before August 9, 2007. Instead I should keep the good parts and start to build on a new normal. Karen echoed Anne Miskin's comments about this being an opportunity to recreate my life, and I had to, because there was no going back. Karen pointed out that the sooner I let go of the old, the sooner I could build on the new.

2. Second, she made a very clear point that Sam and I needed to have some fun. Our life was built around rehab, and we needed to build in some fun activities, starting that day.

3. Next, Karen told me to remember that I was making progress, even when I couldn't see it. This was going to be a very long process, with gradual changes, and I must learn to accept that as a fact of my new life.

4. Last, she reminded me that I needed to have gratitude for my accomplishments, no matter how small they might be. I had to put my mistakes behind me and let the past go. Only then could I have positive hope for the future, and hope would be my biggest ally.

Besides being a minister and a very spiritual person, she is also a bright, warm, compassionate person who seemed to be able to read my thoughts and offer meaningful guidance. She is one of those rare individuals who is very wise and is able to intuitively understand how to help others overcome great difficulties. Karen was certainly a blessing for both Sam and me. After her visit, I had some very good rehab sessions and was feeling better about myself. Following Karen's advice wasn't easy and accepting a new normal took some time for me. However, I did work on starting the process of accepting what I already knew, which was the fact that I faced a long, difficult struggle, and I needed to prepare myself for my new normal life.

Twenty-Two

Summertime Progress

Whiel I still had days when I was overwhelmed with my situation and frustrated at my incredibly slow progress, on the whole, there was more good news than bad. I enjoyed getting out in the warm summer sunshine. I was walking more at the athletic club after my rehab sessions, and I was working on my balance by walking on the track with one hand on a crutch and the other on the railing. It was good practice and a way to improve my balance, which was slowly coming back. Since I couldn't feel my feet, I was balancing mostly through my knees. I also found that if I closed my eyes or let my focus wander from the task at hand, I would lose my balance. Everything I did with my various therapists and trainers took incredible mental focus. In many ways, I was like a small child learning how to walk. Of course, children rarely hurt themselves when they fall, but for me in my mid-sixties, the risk was significantly greater.

The best news during the summer of 2008 was improvement in managing my bladder. I was having fewer accidents and leakage problems. Since I didn't yet have feeling in my bladder, I had to wear urinary pads in my underwear to keep me from embarrassing myself in public. While that helped prevent major accidents, the pads created other problems with irritation in the groin that would occasionally break out in a rash.

At the end of July, our friends Kelley and Judy Johnson invited us over to their lake house in Hot Springs for a couple of days. I had serious doubts about how I would manage my bathroom issues, but this was an excellent opportunity to expand our horizons and see how I could manage away from home. Plus, Sam and I looked at this as a mini-vacation, since their lake house was only an hour from Little Rock. Their house was lovely and right on the lake, with a party barge tied up to their dock. The ladies went out for some shopping while Kelley and I relaxed at the house. Sam came back with some colorful Mexican pottery, which was perfect for our deck. Then we all went out on their boat for a trip to Fisherman's Wharf for dinner. Getting me on and off the boat was a challenge, and I ended up falling on the dock next to the restaurant. This was mostly due to my own stubbornness in thinking I could manage without much help. Some things never change. I was fortunate that I didn't hurt myself, and I learned a good lesson. Overall, it turned out to be a fun time with good friends.

At the athletic club, Carla and Anne were coaching me on my walking, and we seemed to be making good progress. One of the problems with using a walker is that the patient tends to lean forward, and over time, this becomes a habit. For those who have problems walking, the worst fear is losing their balance and falling over backward. A fall like that could cause serious damage like a broken hip or a concussion. Therefore, it feels safer to bend forward and lean on the walker or forearm crutches. However, this stooped position makes it very difficult for the patient to learn to walk in an erect, balanced position. Anne and Carla continued to coach me on getting my hips over my feet and keeping my back straight. That turned out to be a difficult task, but I knew it was something I would have to learn if I was ever going to be able to walk with canes. I held onto the belief that if I could master the forearm crutches and give up the walker, then I should be able to trade the crutches for canes at some point. I knew the damage to my spinal cord was significant and that I probably would never be able to stand and walk without some sort of help. But if I could get to the point of using canes on a regular basis, then Sam and I could travel, go out to eat, and do many other things that would be considerably more difficult with the crutches.

In addition to my progress at the athletic club, Martin was finding more feeling in my legs and feet. We also noticed more movement in my toes, which was a very good indicator there was some slight nerve connection all the way down to my feet. With all the help I had from Lou, Anne, Carla, and Martin, whom I worked with multiple times on a weekly basis, there was no question that I was getting better.

Some Doubts and Questions

In August of 2008 I started having lots of ups and downs again. Looking back, I'm sure the depression and frustrated feelings were because I could vividly remember where I was at that time the previous year. The one-year anniversary of my paralysis was coming up on August 9, and in my mind, I started reliving the whole wretched experience. It's easy to say just to forget about the past because you can't go back and change what happened. But I continued to second-guess myself and hated the fact that I failed to take my time and heed Sam's advice. I still vividly remember, as we were in the car on I-430 on the way to get an MRI of my lower back, how she questioned how fast this was moving and wondered whether we should slow down and think it over. Why the bloody hell didn't I listen to her? Why didn't I ask more questions? Why didn't I get a second opinion? How could I take such an enormous risk? Why didn't Dr. X say anything at all about the risks involved? All I was thinking about was resolving this problem with a "routine procedure" and focusing on my upcoming triathlon schedule. Instead, I ended up as a paraplegic with complete loss of everything below my navel and no real hope of recovery. They say that time heals all wounds, but I'm afraid this is a mental scar I will carry for the rest of my life.

The first week of August 2008, we had a meeting with Dr. Rehab. I continue to say "we" because, as I have said many times, this was a joint effort for Sam and me. Also, while I was asking Dr. Rehab lots of questions, Sam did a much better job of remembering what he actually said than I did. I, of course, was looking for something positive and ignored his comments when they weren't things I wanted to hear. Much like my mother, I didn't want to hear the hard truth. As usual, when meeting with Dr. Rehab, there was good news and bad news. He did a thorough examination, including a pinprick test on my legs, and found that many of the muscles in my legs were firing. Below the knee it was hard to detect, but there was a connection, which was wonderful news. However, the bad news was that my bowel and bladder had no response and it was doubtful they would ever recover. He did schedule another visit to an urologist to do a more extensive test, but he didn't give us much hope.

That same week, I lost my balance walking with my crutches and fell leaving the athletic club. My right knee just gave out and I hit the pavement. Fortunately, the damage was superficial, with just a skinned knee and a sore right hand, and I didn't break anything. This turned out to be a good reminder that if I fell, I should try to tuck and roll, taking most of the impact with my butt and hips, and not use my hand to break the fall. Reaching out with my hand was a natural response, but it is a good way to crack a wrist, which would put me back in a wheelchair and limit my rehab work.

That day, my legs were probably tired from my workout, and my mind wasn't focused on what I was doing. It was critical that my mind should be focused on my legs and balance and not wandering off. When I first started walking in a walker, if I was talking to Lou Tretter and not paying close attention to the task at hand, I would stumble and have to use my arms to keep me from falling. If I lost my balance while walking in forearm crutches, it was very difficult to keep from going down. This fall on the sidewalk was a powerful reminder of how disabled I was and what a long, tough road laid in front of me.

Falling down was a frustrating event. Physically, I only suffered some scrapes and bruises, but this felt like a major defeat in my rehabilitation process. I thought to myself, "Damn it, if I couldn't even walk outside on flat pavement, how will I ever be able to regain good mobility?" Unfortunately, my mental state was frequently quite fragile, and simple things would easily set me off. It was easy for me to remember the bad moments and forget about how much progress I had made in only a year. Nighttime was when I was most fearful and would doubt my ability to recover. I frequently reflected back on what the doctors said after reviewing the MRIs of my spinal column taken before and after the epidural, and on their expectations of little or no recovery. It made me think that maybe they were right. Occasionally, I would even dream about walking or riding a bike, and then I would suddenly realize in the dream I was a paraplegic.

However, the next morning, I woke up, got into my wheelchair, and went into the kitchen for breakfast where I saw my "The Healing Begins Today" poster on the refrigerator door. It was a constant reminder that I had to put these past setbacks behind me because the only thing I could control was what I did that day. Fortunately, I ended up having a very good day with Lou at Baptist Rehabilitation. Lou knew I wanted to work hard, and he had something new for me called a tall kneel. Near the latter part of our session, he had me transfer to a mat where I balanced on my knees with my body in an upright position. He and I were both surprised with how well I did, rolling over on the mat to a prone position and then getting up on my hands and knees. Next, I used my arms to push my weight back over my knees and got into an upright position. Of course Lou was close by in case I needed help, but I wanted to see if I could do it on my own, and I did. Now that I was upright, Lou stood eight feet in front of me, and we practiced pitching a two-pound rubber ball back and forth. Pitching and catching the ball using my hands was relatively easy. The difficult part was maintaining balance on my knees, which proved to be a challenge. But I was able to remain upright most of the time, and only had to put my hand down once or twice to stabilize myself. I felt great at the end of this session, and I didn't know it at the time but this would be the beginning of a very special week for me.

Celebrating Twelve Months of Rehab

Saturday was the one-year anniversary of my injury, and Greg flew in from Dallas on Thursday to spend the weekend with us, which was a treat. On Friday, we went to Creegan's Pub for lunch with hearty dark ales and some fish and chips. Much to my complete surprise, there were thirty close friends in the back room of Creegan's to celebrate my first full year of recovery. Back in June, when Sam and I ran into Ron Robinson at Martin Eisle's acupuncture office, Sam visited with Ron about my problems with depression as the first anniversary of the injury was coming up. Ron suggested having a surprise party for me and said he would call Susie Smith at Metropolitan National Bank to help set it up. Susie and Ron had been friends for years, and they came up with a plan for the party. I was stunned when I saw everyone. The group included executives I had worked with at Bank of the Ozarks and Metropolitan, buddies I knew from running, triathlons, and sailing, and other close friends who had been so supportive. I walked in on my forearm crutches, and everyone was impressed and gave me a big round of applause. This was a heartwarming gathering of special people who had meant so much to Sam and me. I couldn't thank them enough. Kurt Truax, the most accomplished and humble triathlete I had ever competed against, gave me a card, which I still have. On the front it has three colorful drawings with the words, "Strength, Hope, Courage." Inside it reads: "Wishing you strength for each new day, hope to hold onto in difficult times, and encouragement with every sign of progress that you make." In addition to the printed message Kurt wrote the following inside the card: "Randy, I am so amazed at the outstanding progress you have made and <u>continue</u> to make. We are all in awe of your indomitable spirit, courage, and determination, and you serve as a wonderful inspiration to everyone around you. Let me know when you are ready to return for that first race, so perhaps we can "Tri" it together. Sam, please realize that you are every bit as strong and admired as your mate. Both of you keep the faith. Love, Kurt"

Many anniversaries later, when I think back to my injury, I still get teary-eyed remembering the first-year anniversary of recovery party and all the love and support I received from so many people. That extended weekend turned out to be one of my best times since I was paralyzed.

Having Greg with us was always fun, and it was especially nice to have him at the party to visit with old friends and meet people I worked with at both banks. The 2008 Summer Olympics were on television at the time, and each evening, we had fun watching the competition. I also got in a good trike ride on the North Little Rock bike trail while Greg and Sam walked along with me. Overall, August 2008 was a good month in many ways. It was an opportunity to look back and see how much progress Sam and I had made. There still were times when it was hard for me to have hope, but Sam never gave up and would point out how far we had come in only one year. I had to admit, there was a lot to be thankful for.

August was also the occasion of Sam's birthday on August 15 and the fourth anniversary of our first date, the day before her birthday. To celebrate the anniversary of our first date, we went to Bone Fish Grill and had a delicious meal. The following night, Joe and Fran Holmes joined us for dinner at one of Little Rock's best restaurants, Brave New Restaurant. We had a leisurely dinner that lasted three hours, and it was great fun. Fran had been so helpful bringing dinner for Sam's birthday on three occasions when we were in the hospital. Twice it was with Mom, and once when I was in the hospital. We had such a good time with Joe and Fran that we decided to make this an annual event around Sam's birthday.

In the first few months following the injury, going out to dinner with me in a wheelchair was very difficult. Just getting me in and out of a restaurant was a big challenge, and then there were my bladder issues. I was always concerned about having an accident while we were in a public place, which had happened on a couple of occasions. One year into my recovery, we were starting to eat out more often. I still lacked sensation in those areas, but I found if I would catheterize myself right before we went out to dinner, I would be OK for a couple of hours, provided I didn't drink too much, especially beer. Having amber ale with a meal was always a treat, but my bodily functions no longer worked properly, so I had to be very careful about what I drank. Just to be safe, any time we left the house, I always had a fanny pack with me containing catheter tubes,

K-Y Jelly, a couple of paper towels, and a spare urinary shield. Having the proper supplies on hand reduced my anxiety about having a problem, which also calmed the bladder.

I was still having difficult times and occasionally would be in bed for twelve hours. We suspected the antidepressants I was taking made me somewhat lethargic, but without them, I wouldn't have been able to cope with my condition. Also, lying in bed was the only time I felt somewhat normal. Putting my clothes on and getting up and out of bed was a constant reminder of how much damage had been done to the lower half of my body.

As it turned out, my depression that August was also related to the onset of a bladder infection. I developed chills, fever, and a headache, and was referred to a urologist who was a great help. He immediately put me on an antibiotic to take care of the infection and suggested another drug to help with my constant urination issues. In addition, we discussed my lack of feeling and control of the bowel and bladder, and he suggested a form of therapy that might encourage some return of sensation in that area. He explained that it would involve inserting an electrode into the bowel to stimulate the muscles in the pelvic floor area. He thought it was worth a try, and we were willing to do anything that had the slightest chance of getting some return of control or sensation in that area. This turned out to be one of the more helpful doctor visits we had that summer. The urologist, like all the other medical professionals we saw, cautioned us about this being a long process; however, he believed there were some ways to help me learn to manage my bladder issues. Over the last year, Sam and I had learned not to expect easy or quick solutions, but this gave us some much-needed hope about a major quality of life issue.

In spite of my ongoing mental issues, overall August was a positive month. Greg's visit, combined with the surprise anniversary party, was a big boost to my morale. And a week after the party, Mickey and I had our boys' night out at the ballpark, which always lifted my spirits. I even attempted walking at the athletic club track without crutches or a walker, just holding on to the railing for support. It wasn't pretty, but I was beginning to feel like I might be able to move on to canes at some point. I knew there was still a lot of work ahead of us, but I was making regular progress.

At the end of August, Phillip and Bruce McMath came to visit and told us they had gathered enough information to move forward with filing the lawsuit. They contacted numerous doctors and had enough information to know that what happened to me should never occur if the procedure is done correctly. One doctor they lined up as an expert witness on this procedure thought there was a possibility I would get some recovery in my legs, but most likely not in my bowel and bladder. However, almost every doctor the McMaths contacted basically said that my injury was so rare that nobody could offer a reliable prognosis. This further confirmed what we had heard many times from numerous doctors.

Twenty-Three

Looking Forward,
Not Back

O n the anniversary of major events in people's lives, it's common
for them to look back and remember where they were and what
they were doing on that particular day. I did a good bit of that in August
2008. While I was frustrated about my condition, I also could see a
great deal of improvement and progress. All my friends and therapists
could see much more improvement than I did, and the comments from
friends about my recovery at the anniversary party were a confirmation
of my progress. After a full year of dealing with paralysis, I was actually
getting used to being physically challenged and was starting to accept
my limitations. However, I made a point to tell friends, therapists, and
anyone who complimented me about my ability to get around in a
wheelchair, that my wheelchair was merely a useful temporary tool. I was
determined not to live the rest of my life in a wheelchair. By saying this
to others, it reinforced in my mind the goal of getting out of the chair
completely and moving on to crutches, canes, and who knows what.

Labor Day weekend was a traditional Oates family gathering at Greg's
house in Plano, Texas. Several years ago, Greg came up with the idea of
having family and close friends come to Plano for the weekend. After
Debbie moved to New York and her children were in Oklahoma and
Colorado, while Sam and I were in Little Rock, Greg said that it seemed

like the only time we all got together was for weddings and funerals. So every Labor Day weekend, Greg planned a three-day pool party at his house called "Club Greg." We always had a great time with lots of food and drink, Club Greg T-shirts, plus trivia games and fun in his pool. The previous year, I was going home from the hospital on Labor Day weekend, and my niece Somerset was getting married in Sedona, Arizona. Labor Day weekend 2008, the party returned to Plano, and Sam and I decided to go. This would be my first trip away from home, and I was very anxious but was determined to make the trip. Sooner or later, I had to venture out and learn how to travel with my limitations. I knew that my bowel and bladder issues would be the toughest challenge, and what better place to test myself than with family?

Sam and I went over everything I would need and packed a bag with all my bathroom stuff, where it was easy to access in the car or over at Greg's house. This included two tubes of K-Y Jelly, eight urinary shields, twenty rubber gloves, two rolls of paper towels, two urinary jugs, a package of sanitary wipes, and forty catheter tubes. We also put a dozen disposable cups in the cup holders in the backseat of the car in case I needed to relieve myself and there wasn't a convenient or clean place nearby. It was quite an operation for just a weekend, but we wanted to make sure we had everything we needed.

Greg wanted us to stay with him, but Sam and I reserved an handicapped accessible room at a hotel. I really needed an accessible bathroom, and we knew we would be more comfortable in our own place. The good news was that everything worked extremely well. It was difficult using the bathroom at Greg's, but I was able to manage. It was also a challenge for me to get in his pool, but there were lots of people to help me. I took spare ankle/foot orthotics, along with some sandals to use in the pool since my braces were not designed for pool use. Once I was in the water, I was fine on my own. With the buoyancy of the water, I felt much more normal in the pool than I did on dry land. I could stand in chest deep water, and there were plenty of floats for me to lounge on, plus I found I could swim some. I was surprisingly relaxed most of the weekend and loved the chance to be with the whole family. For our first trip out of town, everything went smoothly, and the experience encouraged me to consider venturing out more.

Razorback football started that same weekend while we were in Dallas, and the following weekend, the game was going to be at War Memorial Stadium in Little Rock, and we had tickets. After the positive results of our trip to Dallas, I decided to go to the football game. I knew the toughest part would be getting in and out of the stadium, but our seats were in a good location. I only had to walk up a ramp and then go up twelve rows to get into our aisle seats, and there was a railing next to the steps, which was a big help. I knew it would be extremely difficult to go to the bathroom in a sold out stadium, so I thought this would be an excellent opportunity to learn to use a leg bag connected to a condom-style catheter. We invited Mickey and Patti Freeman to join us and had a terrific time. This was a nonconference game for the Razorbacks with a new head coach, and we were lucky to squeak out a 28–27 win over Louisiana University of Monroe. However, as my dad used to say, "A win is a win, is a win." For me, it was a thrill to be in the stadium watching the Hogs in person rather than on TV. Crowds at War Memorial were always loud and crazy, and in a close game like this one, the stadium was rocking, and I savored every minute of it. With Sam, Mic, and Pat at my side, getting in and out of the stadium worked well, and this was another big step on my road to recovery. I believed that if I could manage to navigate through a crowd like that, I was on my way to going more places and starting to live more of a normal life. Sure, I knew there would be some setbacks, but this encouraged me to venture beyond my normal, safe routines.

The next week continued to provide hope for the future. I had a long trike ride on the bike path at the river with a very patient Henry Noor. I also met with a urology therapist at Advanced Physical Therapy to see about regaining sensation in my bladder. The doctor who recommended the therapy put me on Flomax, and that was already a big help, as I didn't have to empty my bladder every two hours. Mitzi Gibson, who became another key therapist, made no promises but thought she might be able to help me. She did a complete exam and tested my ability to contract my pelvic floor muscles. This involved inserting an electric probe into my anus, after which I rolled over on the table to watch a graph on a monitor, which showed the level of the contractions. Of course, for me the graph barely moved. Nevertheless, for a "complete paraplegic," any contraction at all was extremely positive. Mitzi was pleased with my "anus wink" and thought there was a possibility of regaining some sensation in the bladder and maybe the ability to urinate. I was excited about the possibilities but was brought back to reality that same night when I wet my pants in bed.

That week, Anne Miskin worked on me again, and she was pleased with my progress. The conus of my spinal column was becoming much more flexible, and she was convinced my mind could help my nerves and muscles recover if I focused more of my energy on that area. I also knew I needed to focus more on being in the present moment and that, if I did, I would enjoy life more. Recovery would continue to be a challenging process, but the confidence in my ability to recover was becoming stronger. After working with Anne at the athletic club, I felt strong and walked three-fourths of the way around the track and back three times, while hanging on to the railing without my crutches. The railing didn't go all the way around the track, so I had to turn around and go back to where I started. This was a remarkable week of progress for me, but Sam and I were both worn out and needed a couple of rest days. Sam had a root canal earlier in the week, and in spite of that, she still kept driving me to therapy. I don't know how she did it. She continued to be so supportive of me, and I know that without her, I would not have had the strength to do what I did.

In spite of the remarkable progress in only one year, I continued to have bouts of depression. At night, my mind would wander back to thoughts of where I was before the injury. I was a good athlete, and yet, in only minutes, I became a "complete paraplegic" with no prognosis of recovery. I thought going to court and telling my story in a public forum was something I should do, hoping more people would understand the horrific risks associated with an epidural injection.

Most people see paraplegics as people who have lost the use of their legs, but there is so much more that affects every part of one's life. In many ways, the quality of life issues were as bad as the loss of my legs. I was slowly getting some recovery in my legs, but the inability to urinate or have a bowel movement continued to be terribly frustrating. I knew that my chances of ever riding a bike, running, hiking, dancing, or participating in many other activities was out of the question. So my focus continued to be on gaining the ability to walk with braces and hopefully canes. Getting my mobility back was paramount in my mind.

Part of my depression was also linked to feeling tired most of the time. I wanted to push myself as hard as I could on my therapy, but it was becoming apparent that my body and mind needed some rest breaks. I was slowly beginning to realize that taking a day or two off from therapy was helpful for my attitude and gave my body a chance to recover. At the end of September 2008, Sam and I took a Friday off and had a relaxed three-day weekend. I suspect this was more beneficial to Sam than it was to me, since she didn't have to load and unload me from the car and drive me around town for therapy sessions. That Sunday, I planned to do a trike ride, but instead I had stomach cramps caused by an impacted bowel. Yuck! Most likely this was a result of not drinking enough water. Before I was paralyzed, I made a point of keeping myself well hydrated, especially leading up to a race or long bike ride. But when I couldn't urinate and had no feeling in my bladder, I started drinking less water to cut back on the number of embarrassing accidents, but this negatively affected my bowel. To relieve my cramps, Sam went to the drugstore and bought stool softeners. I ended up spending most of a beautiful Sunday afternoon on the commode going through about twenty rubber gloves digitally evacuating my bowel, which turned into a bloody mess. It was times like this when I would question whether life was worth living. My condition wasn't nearly as bad as that of many other patients I had seen at the rehab gym, but for someone who had been active all my life, this seemed to be more than I could bear.

October started out in a positive manner, with my therapists, my personal trainer, and my acupuncturist seeing improvements in my legs and finding more sensation in random places on my lower body. I met with Dr. Rehab that first week, and he did a full pinprick exam and also found some improvement in my legs. He encouraged me to continue my workouts and do as much weight-bearing exercise as I could. However, once again, just when things were looking up, I wet my pants one night, and then the next day I peed on myself after getting out of the Baptist Rehab pool and again while getting into the car. The next day, I had to cut my workout short with Carla due to more cramps in my gut. As soon as I got home, I had a major bowel movement in spite of thinking I had emptied my bowel that morning. All those ups and downs were so frustrating. I was getting to the point that when it seemed like my body was improving, I started worrying about what was going to go wrong next. It was obvious to Sam and me that I needed some serious psychological counseling. I had tried a couple of doctors but didn't find a good match.

One day at the athletic club, while I was walking on the track, I had a chance to visit with Cagle Harrendorf. Cagle was a retired doctor, and I always enjoyed talking with him. He frequently stopped to visit with me at the club and was very sympathetic to my issues. We discussed my bouts with depression, and I asked him whether he knew someone who might be helpful. He didn't immediately suggest a solution, but said he knew someone who was retired and thought she might consider working with me.

Twenty-Four

A New and Valuable
Resource

Cagle called a couple of days later and suggested I call Jane Roark. Jane was a registered nurse for most of her career and managed more than one doctor's office. She also was a trained chaplain and served in that capacity at a hospital and with other organizations. While she was not a psychologist or psychiatrist, Cagle thought she had all the skills necessary to help me. Jane turned out to be just what I needed. She is a very wise woman and had an intuitive sense about what I needed. Finding her was a classic example of the adage, "when the student is ready, the teacher will appear."

On Wednesday, October 15, 2008, two days before my sixty-fifth birthday, Jane Roark came to the house and we hit it off immediately. She opened the discussion by asking me about my situation, and I immediately launched into a long explanation about where I was prior to the injury and how the injury occurred, followed by a lengthy description of my recovery efforts. Afterward, I realized that I'd talked too fast, like I was trying to cram as much information as I could into a limited space. She was very patient and listened intently. However, she told me a week later during her second visit that she felt like she was being blown backward by all that I was trying to tell her at once. Our first meeting was an excellent session of getting to know one another, even though I did most of the talking. At the end of our two-hour session, she left me with the following affirmations to practice, which I recorded in my journal:

My body's DNA knows how to run, walk, and ride a bike. My muscles will remember.

I must bring my energy inside and allow my body to recover.

I need to see beyond where I am: not in crutches, but walking, running, and cycling.

I will breathe deeply, slow down, and express myself with intention.

I will not be in a hurry.

I will get back to meditation.

I will listen to music and focus my energy on healing.

I will make time to rest and time for Sam and me to play.

Over time, I have returned to these key points in my journal, and they have continued to be reminders of what I need to focus on every day. Jane had an excellent grasp of my situation and knew what I needed to focus on from our very first meeting. She was a great help, and at our next meeting, she talked about how important it was to focus on making small steps and not worry about the long-term results; she also added that if I wanted to walk, first I had to develop both strength and balance in my legs. She would remind me on a regular basis about how important it was to slow down both verbally and physically, which continued to be difficult for me. At the end of our second session, she left me with the following statement of intention: "I need to have the serenity to accept the things I cannot change." She also brought me two index cards to put on the bathroom mirror. Written in magic marker on the first card was the word "allow," and on the second card was the sentence, "My DNA can communicate with my muscles." Years later, I still have these cards in my medicine cabinet as reminders.

Prior to my paralysis, Sam and I had talked about going to the Bitter End Resort in the British Virgin Islands for my sixty-fifth birthday. I had been there a few times on a sailboat and thought it would be a great place to relax and enjoy some snorkeling and sailing. Guests staying at the resort have use of their water toys, including small sailboats to sail around in their bay. The resort is built into the side of a hill with every room overlooking the beautiful bay and beach. On sailing trips in the BVI, the Bitter End is a favorite spot to tie up to a mooring and enjoy the bar, restaurant, and music. Of course, in my condition, any thoughts of major trips like this were out of the question.

In spite of my situation, we still managed to have a fun birthday. Greg was with us again for the weekend. He sent us Omaha Steaks in advance to cook that weekend, and he added to my collection of Razorback clothing. Our next-door neighbor, Patrick Mathieu from Dijon, France, showed up with a six-pack of 1664 French beer. This is the same beer Pierre and I had enjoyed several times during our bike trip in the Loire Valley. One of my biggest surprises was Carla delivering a twelve-pack of Samuel Adams holiday beers, which I always enjoyed. Sam bought me some clothes for traveling, which was a statement of her confidence that we were going to be able to travel again.

Sinus problems had been an issue for most of my life, and Sunday, after my birthday, I came down with a bad cold and was in bed for most of the next four days. I had chills and a mild fever for about thirty-six hours, and the whole episode left me depressed and unable to function. Sam ended up calling both Jane Roark and Mickey Freeman, asking them for help. Between all three of them, I was finally able to get back on my feet and return to therapy. In the past, it was easy for me to do something physical to release my anger. A run or bike ride always let the frustration and negativity drain away from me like the sweat falling off my body, but now that coping mechanism was no longer available. However, I did find some help in writing about things that troubled me. In the first week of November, I wrote the following in my journal:

How could this happen to me? I am unable to walk, run, bike, have sex, drive a normal car, urinate, or have a bowel movement. Wish I were dead. Unknown, will I recover? What will come back and what won't? Is life still worth living? Where do I go from here?

While this kind of ranting would seem to reinforce negative thinking, getting it out of my mind and onto a piece of paper seemed to help. For most of my life, I found that when I had a problem, if I wrote about what was bothering me, it would make it easier to manage the problem. It wasn't always a complete remedy, but there were many times when it was very helpful, and this was one of those times.

Twenty-Five

Another November
to Remember

I don't know what it was about the month of November, but in spite of my ongoing issues, November 2008 was another very good month for the Oates family. With the help of Sam, Mickey, and Jane, I was able to get up and get back to work, and the results were surprising. The first week of the month, Lou Tretter had me start working at Baptist Rehab with a cane in one hand and a crutch in the other. It was a strange combination, but this was the way to start moving toward canes and giving up the crutches. I still struggled with my sit-to-stand in the crutches, but it was getting better. Anne and Carla were both seeing improved motor control of my legs, and they were coaching me on walking in a more erect position.

While I still had a few problems with bladder leakage at night and had a few frustrating days, I continued to make progress. My mind was starting to make a connection with my pelvic floor muscles, and urological therapy was producing positive signs. Everyone working with me could see improvements, and I was getting around well enough that Sam and I agreed it was time to get rid of the wheelchair ramp on the front of the house. I called Dorothy Willoughby, who had given us the ramp, and told her that if she didn't need it, we would like to donate it to the Arkansas Spinal Column Commission. She thought that was a great idea, and when I called the Commission, they were thrilled to have the ramp. As it turned out, they desperately needed a fourteen-foot ramp for a recently injured patient who was being released from the hospital in a few days. Thursday, November 13, 2008, was a landmark day for Sam and me, as three men from the commission arrived, disassembled the ramp, and delivered it to another spinal column injury patient, who was probably as pleased to have it, as we were to give it up. After they left, I started looking back to my journal notes from the previous November, and it was amazing how much progress we had made. Sam and I could vividly remember the first time Lou got me up in a sling suspended from the ceiling and tried to see if I could walk by supporting myself on a very heavy ARJO walker. He thought it was too soon, but I was anxious to try it, and it was a disaster. A year later, on the way home from therapy, we reminded ourselves that after fifteen months of hard work, the wheelchair ramp was gone, and I was walking with forearm crutches and braces on my legs. That was real, meaningful progress. Going up and down steps was still a struggle, but I was getting there. After the ramp was gone, I thought it was time to see if I could get up the steep, grassy slope to the sidewalk by the street in front of our house. Our house was eight feet below street level, so the front yard had a steep upward slope. I knew better than to attempt going up our sloping concrete sidewalk with several steps to the mailbox. Consequently, I worked my way at an angle across the yard where, if I fell, hopefully I wouldn't hurt myself. It took me about fifteen minutes, but I made it on my own with my crutches. Wow!

That same week, Sam and I continued my hamstring exercises on the bed with some positive results. On November 15, lying face down on the bed, I was able to do seven hamstring curls with the right leg without any help. It was interesting that the hamstring muscle in the right leg was making some progress, while the hamstring muscle in the left leg was very, very weak. Sam had to lift the left foot off the bed in order for me to curl it once or twice. The left leg was developing more quickly in almost every other area, but not with the hamstring. We could see good improvement in the left thigh muscle, while the right leg still looked withered and had significantly less feeling than the left leg.

I also heard from several of my friends that week, including a long talk with my childhood friend, Dr. Jim Growdon in Nashville, Tennessee. Jim continued to be impressed with my progress over the last few months and was convinced my recovery would continue. I also heard from Mickey, Jane, and Henry, who all offered their encouragement on my progress. I ended the week with a couple of emails back and forth with Susie Smith, the CFO at Metropolitan National Bank. We talked about issues she wanted me to help them resolve, and she expressed her appreciation for my contributions. It was important for me mentally to believe I still had something to contribute. It's common for some people to assume, when they meet an individual with substantial physical problems like mine, that the person may also have mental deficiencies. While I did have my struggles with depression, it was reassuring to be able to provide marketing support to a major bank that needed my help and valued what I did for them.

As the good news continued leading up to the week of Thanksgiving, I started sleeping better and wasn't getting up as often at night to empty my bladder. Lou had me walking more with two canes, and I was getting the hang of using my "sticks." I also convinced Dr. Rehab, with Lou's help, that I was ready to try driving a car with hand controls. Baptist Rehabilitation had a car set up with hand controls on the patient/driver side, and some controls on the passenger side for the instructor to help in emergency situations. It was an interesting setup, with the gas and brake controlled by a single handle on the left side of the steering wheel. The gas throttle worked much like a motorcycle by turning the handle with my wrist. For the brake, I just relaxed the gas and at the same time pushed the handle forward, which was connected to a rod that pressed down on the brake pedal. This method allowed a paraplegic to steer the car with the right hand and use the left on the gas/brake handle, while allowing anyone else to drive the car in a normal mode using the brake and gas pedals. The instructor had me practice for a few minutes in the parking lot, and then it was time to get out and practice in traffic. I was pleasantly surprised at how well I was able to manage the car. The Baptist Hospital campus is on the west side of Little Rock just off of Interstate 630, six miles from the heart of downtown. To test how I could manage in traffic, we drove over the interstate to Markham Street, which is a four-lane, east-west corridor parallel to the interstate. I was anxious about using the hand controls for my first time at the wheel of a car, but everything went very well. We drove all the way down Markham, through the heart of downtown, and returned by way of the interstate. Without stoplights and lots of turns, the interstate was the easiest part of the drive.

After we returned to the Baptist Rehab parking lot, my instructor said he thought I did very well and would sign off with Dr. Rehab on moving ahead with converting our Toyota Highlander to hand controls. Arkansas doesn't require a doctor's approval for a handicapped car conversion, but with a prescription from a doctor, there is no state sales tax added to the conversion cost. Regardless of the tax deduction, Sam and I didn't want to rush into this until Dr. Rehab and I were comfortable with my ability to manage driving a car by myself. Speaking of taxes, in spite of having good health insurance, our income tax returns in 2007 and 2008 showed that our out-of-pocket expenses that insurance did not cover, for doctors, therapists, drugs, my bowel and bladder supplies, and everything else that was a part of my recovery, amounted to enough to buy a new car each year (not a BMW, but certainly a Honda Accord). As I tell everyone who asks about my recovery, relying only on therapy paid for by insurance is not nearly enough. Sam and I agreed early on that we would spend whatever it took to get me back on my feet, and we were fortunate to have prepared well for our retirement. Frankly, our original plan was to spend that money on traveling, but fate had changed our priorities.

Thanksgiving Week
Sam and I cancelled all our therapy for the week of Thanksgiving, and Greg flew in again to spend the whole week, which was a wonderful thing for

both of us. He helped Sam with a lot of projects around the house, and he and I enjoyed watching college football over the weekend. The Razorbacks usually played the LSU Tigers on the Friday after Thanksgiving, and this year the game was in Little Rock. In spite of cool temperatures and light rain, we decided to go to the game and had a terrific time. It helped that the Hogs rallied from being behind by sixteen points to win 31–30 in the last minute of the game. The crowd, including me, was on their feet for the last ten minutes of the game, and it was a great victory for Arkansas. Getting into and out of the stadium was a challenge with the massive crowd, but with Greg's help, I managed to navigate into our seats without a problem. I also wore a leg bag again to manage my bladder issues. This enabled me to celebrate the victory with a couple of beers in the parking lot after the game.

Father and Son celebrate the victory

The modifications on our Toyota Highlander were completed a couple of days before Thanksgiving, so we used it to go to the game. Being able to drive myself to therapy was a big boost for us. It gave me much more independence, and it was a major benefit for Sam, as she didn't have to drive me all over town with me coaching her on how to drive. Now Sam could run errands on her own and get things done around the house while I was in therapy. She still went with me most of the time to the athletic club to work out, but she didn't have to go and wait on me at acupuncture, urological therapy, and Baptist Rehab. She still went with me for all the doctor visits and occasionally went to some therapy sessions to keep up with what I should be doing at home.

Each Thanksgiving after I was paralyzed, we made a point to look back on where we were in August 2007 and how much improvement we could see since then. The progress seemed slow to me, but looking back and remembering how little hope there was for any recovery and then taking stock of my physical status on Thanksgiving Day was most reassuring. Sam and I had many reasons to be thankful. We had found excellent, well-trained professionals to help us. The lower half of my body was continuing to gain sensation and motor function, and while I was mentally prepared to plateau at some point in my recovery, my therapists continued to see regular progress. It was small progress, but as Anne Miskin said more than once, "No matter how small, any progress at all is important." In her career, Anne had worked with hundreds of clients and continued to be amazed and proud of the fact I had not plateaued in my recovery. Throughout this ordeal, we had meaningful support from friends and family, which provided both of us much-needed encouragement. And best of all, I had an incredible, patient, and loving caregiver who was the "love of my life." As I said to myself many times, as much to remind myself as to brag on Sam, "You cannot do this by yourself." Yes, we both had a lot to be thankful for in 2008.

Twenty-Six

Good Progress in 2008

Monday, December 1, 2008, after a fun and restful week, it was back to work and we had a full agenda with some sort of therapy or workout every weekday. I was so proud I could drive Sam and myself to the athletic club, take her home afterward, and then go to urological therapy on my own. The ladies at Advanced Physical Therapy, where I did my urology work, were surprised when I showed up by myself and wanted to know where Sam was. I was pleased to tell them that, with modifications to the car, I was able to drive myself and that it gave me a great feeling of independence. Just driving a car again made me feel more normal and less handicapped.

As the year was coming to a close, I couldn't help but reflect back again on how much Sam and I had been through together. It was a good exercise, which always helped my mental outlook. December 10, 2007, I took my first real steps in a walker and covered 160 feet, with Lou's help holding onto my sissy belt. Only one year later, on December 10, after therapy with Carla, I walked over eight hundred feet with two canes! I was still using my forearm crutches to get to and from the car and only using the canes on the track or in therapy, but I was getting better and better with the canes. I was also getting better contractions in my pelvic floor muscles and finding increased stimulation in my lower legs and feet. Plus, I was sleeping better and only getting up a couple of times at night while experiencing fewer accidents in bed. What a relief that was.

Christmas week 2007, I was just getting fitted for my braces and struggling to balance enough to walk in a walker. By Christmas of 2008, I was walking everywhere in forearm crutches. My sit-to-stand, which for any recovering paraplegic is an enormous challenge, was getting better even from low chairs and benches. It wasn't perfect, but it was improving.

For Christmas, my niece Somerset and her husband Steven invited the entire clan to come to their home in Tulsa, Oklahoma. This was about equal distance from family members in the Dallas area and from those of us in Little Rock, so it was a natural gathering spot for a family holiday. Somerset made reservations for us at a hotel near their house, which was a big help, as I needed an accessible bathroom and some privacy to manage my bowel and bladder issues every morning and again at night. It turned out to be one of the best Christmases with the whole family that we had experienced in many years. We had ten family members all together for a great visit. We told old and new family stories, laughed a lot, caught up on what everyone was doing, and ate too much of everything.

The family was very impressed with how far I had come in my recovery, and of course, they all wanted to help me in and out of the car and up and down steps. I thought I could do most of these things on my own and managed to step out of Somerset and Steven's house onto a damp front porch and took a tumble. Fortunately, I didn't hurt myself, and afterward, I let anyone who was handy help me up and down steps and on slippery surfaces. Leaving Tulsa, we could say in confidence, "A good time was had by all."

Back home for New Year's, I continued to reflect back to what we had accomplished that year. I started 2008 in a wheelchair but was able to bring a walker home with me in January. A year ago, my hands and arms were frequently sore from holding myself up in a walker, and now I was going everywhere in forearm crutches. The crutches were a big leap from the stable walker; however, I wasn't able to use them on a regular basis until April. Now I was practicing with canes at the athletic club and had become very comfortable with the crutches. I could walk around

201

the track at the athletic club in crutches in a little under ten minutes, which was half the time it took me to get around in my walker. My spirits were better and my energy levels were improving. At the end of 2008, Carla and I were pushing harder to build strength in my legs, while my upper body, which was still supporting most of my weight, was probably stronger than before I was paralyzed. I never in my worst nightmares imagined anything like this ever happening to me; however, by the close of 2008, I was definitely getting better, and I had hope for even more progress in the coming year.

Twenty-Seven

Lessons Learned in Part II

Take Your Caregiver with You on Visits to the Doctor
When visiting with a doctor, the patient is frequently thinking about all the questions to ask and sometimes may not be paying close enough attention to the answers. Having Sam with me on all important doctor visits was critical. She would make notes and asked good questions, and when we got home, she seemed to remember more specific points than I did. Also, since she was my primary caregiver, the doctor would frequently explain to her how important some routines and medications were and tell her that she needed to make sure I followed the doctor's instructions. We quickly learned that no two spinal column injuries are the same and what works for one patient may not work for another. Consequently, Dr. Rehab would discuss several possible alternatives, and any decisions required both Sam and me to participate in the process.

Think Outside the Box and Try Anything that Might Help
The recovery process is long, hard, and expensive, with no guarantees of positive results. However, if you are dedicated to your recovery, you should examine every possible option to help your body regain some function. I have tried acupuncture, meditation, several personal trainers, craniosacral therapy, and a few psychologists, some with more success than others. Sam and I talked to Dr. Rehab, about every possible option that might help me recover, and he was receptive to trying options

beyond traditional medical treatment. He told us that many of his patients had tried alternate therapies, and it seemed like the ones with the most success were those who believed it might help and devoted the necessary time to see if they could make any progress. He also reminded us there were no magic bullets. Whatever I did to recover would take consistent work, and my body would also need the "tincture of time," which was one of his most memorable sayings.

Be Thankful

This may sound simple, but some of us have a hard time accepting compliments. When someone would come up to me and tell me how good I looked and how much progress I had made, instead of saying "thank you" with a smile, I would frequently talk about how slow my recovery was and how I wasn't getting better quickly enough. It took practice for me to learn to just say "thank you" and let people know how much I appreciated their support. Thanking my therapists and trainers was easy to do because I trusted their professional opinion more than other peoples. Over time, I found that when someone offered to help me get out of a chair or go up some stairs, I should let them help me. I learned this lesson from someone we met on a trip who offered to help me up out of a chair. I, of course, said, "I can get up by myself." He immediately responded, "Randy, that's your problem; you are just too hardheaded. Let people help you. It will make them feel better and your thanks is all they need." I am getting better at accepting help, and I try to make a point of thanking all my supporters, therapists, and friends who have played such an important part in my recovery. As I remind myself every day, I couldn't do this by myself, and I should be thankful for the progress I have made with the help of others. There is an African proverb that says, "It takes a village to raise a child." Well, it also takes a village to help a paraplegic walk again. Trust me, I know.

Part III

Twenty-Eight

Starting Another Year
with High Hopes

In 2008, I struggled with my mental state and experienced a great deal of frustration and anxiety about my condition, which frequently interrupted my therapy. Having said that, it seemed that, with the passage of time I was better able to manage my attitude. Part of that process was learning to live with my severely comprised physical condition and admitting to myself that I would never be able to do many of the things I did before I was paralyzed. The word "paralyzed" was something I never said prior to the injury, and it continued to be difficult to use that word to describe my condition. Also, thinking of myself as handicapped was beyond my comprehension. Consequently, I made an effort to come up with some other way to refer to my situation. As I told all my therapists, trainers, and friends, the wheelchair was just a tool to use until I could stand and walk. Now I needed a better way to think of my physical condition, other than handicapped or paralyzed. So I decided to focus on my condition as being "physically challenged." I first used that term on the one-year anniversary of my injury in August 2008. Now I was determined to keep that thought in my mind. Those two words implied the ability to grow and recover, and they meant this was not a permanent condition. Hopefully I could make one more positive step in adapting to my new normal.

Looking back in my journal at the beginning of each New Year I frequently would find examples of how naïve I was about the speed of my recovery. On January 2, 2009 I wrote the following goals for the year in my journal:

I will ride a bike this summer. I will walk regularly with canes by the end of the first quarter. I will start urinating this summer.

I thought it was a good thing to set goals for each year, but this dramatically demonstrated how unrealistic some of my goals were. Walking with canes was certainly doable, but riding a regular bike and urinating were not. More than one expert told me that the use of my bowel and bladder would be the last thing to come back. I was desperate to regain some control of my bladder, and this would continue to be one of my major priorities.

After a nice rest over the holidays with friends and family, I got off to a good start in January. I was always concerned that taking too much time off from my rehab training would set me back, but once again I found that the rest paid off both physically and mentally. Back working with Carla and Lou, I found that my balance was better while walking with both my canes and my crutches. I was taking bigger steps and moving faster. I found that getting into a rhythm was important, and once I started walking, I didn't have to stop and rebalance myself as much. Also, I was able to do a few sit-to-stands in my canes. Wow, if I could do that on a regular basis, it would be a major leap forward in my mobility. Carla even said she believed my learning curve on walking was accelerating.

The first week of January, Sam and I make a trip to Target to pick up some new workout clothes to add to my wardrobe. It was one of those lovely, rare January days in Little Rock with bright sunshine and temperatures in the low seventies, and I wanted to take advantage of being outside. I used to enjoy running at Pinnacle Mountain State Park, just twenty minutes from our house. It was also a popular starting place for bike rides on beautiful country roads. On nice weekends, the park was always full of families having picnics, people climbing the mountain, and folks just enjoying the beauty of nature. After our shopping excursion, I suggested to Sam that we go out to the park. With Sam's help, I wanted to attempt walking around the half-mile paved path by a stream that ran through the park. While I used my wheelchair to get around in Target, I wanted to test myself in the park on canes. We were pleased beyond words that I was able to walk the half-mile path using my canes and only needed to take one rest break. Once again, I was so pleased with this accomplishment that I overestimated my ability to recover and wrote the following comment in my journal:

I am going to walk this year on my own.

Oh, well; it was nice to have strong convictions and significant goals, even if they were completely unrealistic.

Walking with canes at the park

That same week, while my bladder problems continued and I wet my pants in bed again. I also experienced a strong tingling feeling through my body, especially in my legs and feet, while lying in bed. I was able to move my toes a little and was able to focus my energy on repeating the experience. It was an exciting development. In addition to this, Carla helped me get on a stationary bike, and I rode it for thirty minutes. My left leg was doing most of the work, but it felt a little like old times on my bike. I felt good about all these developments and asked Sam to help me get into our Jacuzzi tub so I could soak in the hot, bubbly water. It seemed like a positive start to 2009.

Then, on January 8, Mickey came by for one of his regular visits and had some bad news; he had prostate cancer. Suddenly, his news made my problems seem very small. Mickey's dad discovered he had prostate cancer at age seventy-three, and it was successfully treated, and he was now in his nineties. Fortunately, Mickey had regular checkups and discovered it ten years earlier than his dad, but at a younger age, it could be more serious. In spite of the bad news, he had high hopes for recovery and was working on exploring several options for treatment. As he said, he was lucky they found it early, and he believed it was treatable. I was certainly struggling with my paralysis, but situations like this reminded me of how much worse things could be. My condition was frustrating and dramatically changed my life. However, it was not potentially terminal, and if I worked hard, I believed I would slowly get better and better. At this point, while most of the doctors had originally thought I would never be able to stand, I was now walking frequently with canes. Things could have been much worse.

It's interesting that most of the women in my family were born in January. This included my dad's sister, Susie; my mother; my sister, Debbie; her daughter, Somerset; and Somerset's daughter, Savannah. Mom was born on January 14, 1918, and January 14, 2009, was the first birthday without her. Debbie and I talked on the phone and shared some of our favorite stories about mom. Willie Oates was special, and this birthday was harder on me than I expected. I had my hands full with therapy and my rehabilitation, but on January 14, she was much on my mind. Losing one's parents tends to be a reminder of one's own mortality. Much of the time when depression would get the best of me, my death didn't seem like a bad alternative to living with all my limitations. But thinking about Mom and how much she got out of life reminded me of why I should appreciate every day and live my life to the fullest. Her birthday in 2009 was a sobering day for me.

At the end of January, Greg made another trip to see us for a long weekend, and he was pleasantly surprised with the improvements I had made since his last visit at Christmas. He could tell my leg strength was improved, along with my motor skills. He also was surprised to see I had removed the top part of my brace on the right leg. The brace was very cumbersome, coming up to the top of my leg. It helped support the right knee, but it was difficult to put on and take off, plus it made it very difficult to get my pants down to catheterize myself several times a day. Lou, Dr. Rehab, and I had discussed the pluses and minuses, and Dr. Rehab agreed to let me test out the new configuration for a few days. It seemed to work out well and made my life much easier. I still had to be careful since the right leg was very weak, but it was slowly getting better. The bigger concern was the condition of my right foot, which was not improving. Lou was very concerned about the way the foot was turning inward, and the Achilles tendon was definitely getting tighter, making it almost impossible for me to get my heel down on the floor with the leg at a ninety-degree angle to the foot. Dr. Rehab gave me two possible solutions to correct the problem with the Achilles tendon. The first would be a Botox injection, and the second would involve surgery, which would put me in a boot for four to six weeks and limit much of my therapy. Dr. Rehab thought we should try the least invasive approach first and see if a Botox injection would loosen the tendon enough to allow it to stretch back to normal. Sam and I discussed the alternatives, neither of which we liked, but we knew that something had to be done and decided to have the Botox injection.

The first week in February, Sam and I decided to give ourselves a treat and drove to Hot Springs for a weekend at Oaklawn Park for the horse races. Sam loved betting on the horses; the races were exciting, and we always ran into old friends whom we saw every year at the track. I was able to get to our box using my canes, and the two couples in the box next to us were very excited to see me standing up with canes. Frank, Della, Jim, and Betty couldn't get over how much I had improved from the previous year when I was in a wheelchair. Also, sitting in the box in front of us was ninety-five-year-old Betty Blake, who was a legend at Oaklawn. She and her late husband owned Bett-B-Farms, where they raised race horses, and she and Mom had been great friends. We had fun sharing stories about Mom, and Betty was so pleased to see me on my feet. Sam and I also had dinner with her dear friends Marti and Robert Dalby. Marti is a minister, and she presided over our wedding, along with Karen Akin. It was fun to see them, and they were so proud of us making progress with my rehabilitation and being able to go to the races. This was a major break from our normal routine, and we enjoyed a fun weekend with nothing on our minds but enjoying the horse races and having dinner with friends.

We had a lot going on in February. I did another half-mile walk on the paved path in Pinnacle Park and was pleased again with my ability to balance on a somewhat uneven surface. Carla helped me start walking on the track at the club with one cane while holding onto the railing. I was doing well enough at this point that Sam and I decided to move the walker to the attic, which was a personal triumph for me. And then we had dinner with the Freemans to celebrate eighteen months of recovery. Except for the problems with my right foot and Achilles tendon, things were looking up. Being able to drive with hand controls and walk some with canes and removing the top of the brace on my right leg helped my attitude and gave me much-needed hope for the future.

Carla and me at athletic club

Also things were finally starting to move ahead with our lawsuit. Bruce and Phillip McMath had done a lot of research, and it was time to start collecting information regarding the doctor and the clinic where he worked at the time of the injection and my paralysis. Lawsuits like this move very slowly and appear to be intended to wear out the plaintiff. Henry Noor, who worked in the insurance business for most of his life, told me early on in this process, those lawsuits like ours usually take three to five years from the incidence of the injury until either they were settled or they went to trial. However, in our case, there were several unique issues that might encourage the defendants to resolve the lawsuit in a timely manner. First of all, this should have been a routine procedure, and the McMaths had to do a lot of research to find any

213

situations similar to mine. Most doctors had never heard of an injury like mine from an epidural steroid injection.

Since Dr. X had left the clinic he was with at the time of my injury, there were two law firms involved in this process on his side, with one law firm representing the clinic and another representing the doctor. And then there were the insurance companies involved. These companies had a major stake in the process because they were the ones who would ultimately have to satisfy any settlement or judgment. As a result, they would prefer to drag this out as long as possible. They asked us to supply reams of documentation from my medical records over several years, plus all kinds of personal information like tax returns for multiple years, which had nothing to do with the lawsuit. Of course, the McMaths challenged much of this and were able to cut down some of the paperwork, but there was still a lot we needed to put together. Looking back on the whole process, I would not want to go through it again, but I wanted to tell my story about how potentially risky this procedure could be, and I wanted someone to be held accountable for the devastating damage done to me.

Thursday, February 19, was a very special night for me. The Little Rock Roadrunners Club, one of the largest running clubs in the state, invited me to speak at their regular monthly meeting about my injury and my fight to recover. This club, which was founded in 1977, is for runners and walkers of all ages who share an interest in fitness. The club has regular meetings, usually with guest speakers, publishes a very informative monthly newsletter, and organizes training runs, and races. Their website describes the club as: "LRRC is a great way to meet other runners and reach your goals, whether they be to qualify for the Boston Marathon or simply to be able to run a mile without stopping". At one time I was a very active member, and for several years wrote a column for the club's newsletter. Consequently, I knew many of the members and was pleased to have a chance to talk about my recovery process.

In my presentation, I did my best to convey what I had been through and talk about things that are important to any kind of recovery, from a minor injury to my paralysis. For the first time, I also talked about "Lessons Learned," which I have included in this book. My goal was to be as positive as I could and yet still be open and honest about the terrible difficulties Sam and I dealt with, which were quite substantial. I told the group that we knew there were no easy solutions and that I would never get anywhere close to full recovery. However, if I could just find a way to get back on my feet, I could gain some much-needed mobility. And on this night, I was very proud of being able to walk into the room on my crutches and do my talk standing up. I told the group that I still continued to second-guess my decisions leading up to the epidural and wished I could go back and change things. However, looking back was not helpful and wouldn't change anything. I had to focus on the future and let the past go. Worrying about the past only works if we have a rewind button in our life. Focusing on my therapy was where I needed to spend my time and energy. I hoped my talk would provide hope to others who experience tragic injuries, and I enjoyed talking about the recovery process in a positive light. At the end of my presentation, I was overwhelmed by the standing ovation I received from the group. Afterward, many of my old running buddies came up to visit with Sam and me, offered their encouragement and support for my recovery, and told me what an inspiration I was. It was a wonderful night that I will never forget.

Twenty-Nine

Facing Surgery

I continued to have lingering problems with my right foot, which concerned me, but I put off doing anything because I knew it would be a major interruption in my therapy. My Achilles tendon was shortening due to my ankle rolling outward, and I had so little strength in my right leg that I couldn't put the foot firmly on the ground. Plus, whenever I was off my feet, the right foot naturally dropped because the tendons and muscles wouldn't work to hold it up. I had tried some temporary solutions, but it was becoming apparent to Dr. Rehab and me that I would probably need surgery to correct the problem. Based on my previous experience with a flawed medical procedure, I dreaded the thought of surgery on any part of my body. Then there was the recovery time, which would involve having a cast on the right leg for six weeks and then a boot for another six weeks. This was another one of those times when it seemed like I just couldn't get a break. As a result, the last week of February 2009, I was angry and frequently flared up over little things and managed to upset Sam more than once. At that time, I didn't like living with myself and I'm sure Sam didn't either, but fortunately she was able to hang on in spite of my attitude. It was times like this when I would have been just as happy not to wake up the next day and would pray to be able to just pass away in my sleep. Sometimes I just could not find a way out of the darkness of my mind.

Unfortunately March got off to a bad start. March 4 was the one-year anniversary of Mom's death, and I missed her much more than I thought I would. While I had an uneasy relationship with my dad and never lived up to his standards, mom and I were always close. I look a lot like my dad but have more of my mom's personality. She would always support me in anything I wanted to do and was proud of my accomplishments. She was a very loving and caring person and was a force to be reckoned with in the community. She also had her father's infectious laugh and was the ultimate positive thinker. I sure could have used some of her positive thinking in March of 2009.

To add to my frustrations, one day I fell on the way to the car from the athletic club; I banged up my left thumb and hip but didn't break anything. Of course, whenever I would fall in a public place, people would always run up and want to know whether I was OK, which always made me feel like a helpless invalid. I also noticed in the mornings while shaving that I was looking older and felt like the aging process was accelerating. When I was sailing and racing triathlons, I used to feel ten years younger than my age. Now I was feeling ten years older and wondering about how much longer I had, especially in my condition. I just didn't have the enthusiasm for life that I had prior to the injury. Before that, I was always looking forward to the next challenge or adventure, but now all I had to look forward to was more therapy with very little hope of full recovery. I hated feeling this way, especially when I saw so many people with spinal column injuries who were living in a wheelchair. Here I was getting around pretty well with braces and canes, and yet it was so very far away from the Randy I knew before I was paralyzed.

After much thought and looking at various alternatives, Sam and I decided it was time to move ahead and have surgery on my right leg to extend my Achilles tendon. Unfortunately, the best day to do the surgery was March 10, which was the day before our third wedding anniversary. This meant I would be spending our anniversary in bed at home. Consequently, we made plans to celebrate a couple of days early with dinner at Ashley's in the Capitol Hotel. As usual, the food, service, and evening at Ashley's were very special and a nice break from our normal routine.

Based on my previous experience with Dr. X, I was anxious about doing another major medical procedure, but I knew it was critical to my long-term recovery. The surgery went extremely well and was my best medical experience since I was paralyzed. The doctor gave me a very complete explanation of what was going to happen, and I found all the doctors and nurses at Ortho Arkansas to be very professional. They understood my issues and were very sympathetic to my problems.

The procedure involved tearing the heel cord by inserting a sharp, X-shaped blade into the tendon, twisting it just enough to create a small tear in the tendon, and then twisting it back and withdrawing it from the tiny incision it made in the skin. The X-shaped cut on the skin was very small and healed within a week, leaving no scar. I was impressed with the procedure and wished I had gone to this group of doctors nineteen months ago instead of the clinic with Dr. X. I believed that if I had gone to this group, I would still have use of the lower half of my body. However, as I told myself again and again, looking back and trying to change the past is wasted effort. My focus needed to be on recovery and what I could accomplish in the future.

Prior to the surgery, Sam and I had talked about making another trip to Oaklawn Park Race Track in Hot Springs and invited Mickey and Patti Freeman to join us. Due to the surgery, I was laid up in bed for that weekend but insisted that Sam go ahead with the Freemans and have a fun day at the track. Sam had a particularly good day betting the horses and collected a daily double and a trifecta, which paid well. This was one of her best days of playing the horses since we had been together. Maybe not having me along to give her advice about the horses, whether she needed it or not, was a positive thing.

I tried to get back to therapy with a cast on my right foot, but it was a struggle. Standing for any length of time put too much pressure on my right knee, which started causing some problems, and I developed some minor swelling in the knee. As a result, I had to back off from most of my therapy work, which was frustrating. Not working out made me feel as though I was losing ground on my recovery. Over time, I began to find that when I took a break for a week or so, I really didn't lose any of my fitness. As most of my therapists told me, my body would benefit from rest. I was prone to pushing as hard as I could, thinking the harder I worked, the better I would be, but that was not the case. Occasional rest was a very good thing.

As usual, my psyche therapist, Jane Roark, was quite helpful. She reminded me that I "needed to be centered, relaxed, and careful about cranking up my intensity." She also suggested that I relax and remember that recovery will take time. That was not something I wanted to hear, but I knew she was right. After my counseling session with Jane, I wrote the following in my journal. This was not original but was something I had come across several years before, and I customized it to resonate with my beliefs.

Each day I will

Work some;
Play some;
Love some;
Dream some;
Rest some;
Celebrate even small victories;

And at the end of the day, I will be grateful!

At the end of March 2009, just as I was getting back to a somewhat positive attitude, I developed stomach cramps and had to leave a therapy session. As I expected when I got home, my bowel was impacted. Damn! I spent almost an hour going through multiple gloves cleaning myself out. Yuck! That left me exhausted, and I had to go to bed for an hour or so. Before I was injured, my intestinal system worked beautifully, but now

I had to be so careful because the injury completely changed the way my system functioned. I had to start over again and try to figure out how to keep my system on an even keel. Managing my bowel would continue to be one of my biggest frustrations.

Thirty

Good Times and Bad in April and May 2009

While I was still battling depression at times, April 2009 got off to a good start with our annual family gathering in Hot Springs for the horse races at Oaklawn Park. Because of issues with my right foot, I only went to the track one of the three days. Sam had another good outing and came away the big winner of the weekend. Being around the family always boosted my spirits, and Greg was very attentive to helping me. The week after that, Mickey and I had a fun time at the ballpark despite unusually cool weather. Then it was time to get the cast off my right foot and switch to a boot. The doctor gave me the OK to get back to therapy, which was very helpful, especially for my mental attitude. I also was making good progress at Advanced Physical Therapy with my pelvic floor contractions. The owner, Mitzi Gibson, noticed that my "anus wink," which they measured with a probe, was improving, and I found I was finally getting some sensation in my bladder, so I could better anticipate when I needed to go to the bathroom. It wasn't always reliable, but it was getting better. If I could gain some control of my bladder, that would me a major step forward.

Losing Joe

While things were going well for me in April, they were not going so well for two of my dearest friends. The same week that Mickey decided to go ahead with surgery for his prostate cancer, I received devastating news from Joe Whitesell in Apalachicola, Florida. Before my injury, I spent a week or two every year for over ten years with Joe, and we always had a great time together. Surprisingly, I hadn't heard from him but maybe once or twice in the nineteen months since I was paralyzed. In the past, we frequently e-mailed each other, but Joe hadn't responded to my e-mails, so I mailed him a letter and asked what was going on in Apalachicola.

The reason I hadn't heard from him was revealed in his letter, which told me he had cancer in both lungs. Joe had been a long-time smoker but gave it up many years before he retired and moved to Florida. I knew he had some chest pains over the past couple of years, and he thought it was from a fall one morning when he was out running. He had seen doctors in Apalachicola and also Tallahassee, but they were unable to identify the problem. His girlfriend and regular dance partner, Betty, who lived in Tallahassee, insisted he go to the Mayo Clinic in Jacksonville. So Joe and his son Pete, who also lived in Tallahassee, made the trip together. The clinic ran multiple tests and found he had advanced tumors in both lungs, which were pressing on his rib cage and causing the pain in his chest. They believed he had only about three to six months to live, and I didn't receive his bad news until several weeks after he got back from the clinic. I was devastated when I read his letter. While my problems were significant, they certainly were not terminal. After getting the news, I called my sister Debbie at Roswell Cancer Institute and asked her how bad this was and how much time she thought Joe had. She checked with some of the staff and got back to me right away with the bad news. She believed the clinic was trying to be optimistic, but the time was likely to be much shorter than a few months. She said if I wanted to see him again, I better go right away.

I called Joe on the phone, and we had a good visit even though he sounded very tired. I also talked with Pete and told him that I wanted to come down to see Joe and that we would stay over on St. George Island for a few days. Pete warned me about how much weight Joe had lost and said he could only tolerate visitors for short periods of time. I understood but still wanted to make the trip.

The first week of May, Sam and I checked on Mickey at the hospital after his surgery and again after he got home. He was doing well and everything looked good. We told him about Joe and informed him that we were going to be gone for about a week.

It was about a twelve-hour drive to Apalachicola, and it would be the longest trip I had made since I was paralyzed. On the trip, I had to empty my bladder about every two hours or so, and we couldn't always count on finding a clean and sanitary bathroom. To manage that issue, we took several twelve-ounce plastic cups and would pull off the road at times to let me catheterize myself into a cup and dump it on the roadside. We did find good bathrooms at some of the fast food restaurants where we would stop to eat, which was helpful. I was able to do a good part of the driving on the trip to Florida, and it turned out to be a good learning experience and gave us confidence in doing other road trips.

As soon as we got to Apalachicola, we went straight to Joe's house. I vividly remember stopping at his house and walking into his open garage, which also served as his woodworking shop. While Pete had prepared me for how much weight Joe had lost, I was still surprised when I saw him. He apologized for not having a T-shirt on because they felt heavy and uncomfortable. He was much thinner than I expected, and his skin looked like it was just hanging on his bones. It reminded me of pictures I had seen of survivors of prisoner of war camps in World War II. However, his attitude was good, and he was pleased to see me walking with my forearm crutches. We had a nice visit, but it was obvious Joe was tired and we shouldn't stay too long. Pete was working on varnishing a wooden shower curtain rod he had built, and Joe was giving him lots of guidance. We laughed some and talked about old times, but I could see Joe was not long for this world. I didn't know it then, but that would be the last time I saw him. Finally, Joe said he had to go lie down, and Sam and I took off for the short drive over to St. George Island.

On my many visits, Joe and I frequently went over to the island to walk on the beach, swim in the gulf, and eat at the Blue Parrot overlooking the beach. The drive from Joe's house to St. George Island was always beautiful. I never got tired of going over the Apalachicola River and looking at the bay, and then on to the St. George causeway to what was a bit of old Florida on the island. I called Joe every day while we were there, but he wasn't up to seeing anyone and was in bed most of the time. He apologized for not being up for a visit, but after seeing him in person, I understood completely. Sam and I had fun on St. George with a hotel room overlooking the beach. We walked on the beach every day, and I was pleased with my ability to walk with the forearm crutches in soft sand. I did stumble one day taking a shortcut through the sea oats, but I was able to get back on my feet by myself, which was a big accomplishment. However, after that experience, I made it a point to take the regular path out to the beach instead of the shortcut. Sam did more walking while I spent most of my time reading on a lounger under an umbrella. We ate seafood every day, sometimes twice a day, at the restaurants in Apalachicola and also on the island. It turned out to be a good vacation for us, even though I didn't have a chance to see Joe again. In my daily phone calls, I got the feeling he was uncomfortable with visitors. He probably didn't want people to see him in his withered condition. His body had atrophied to the point that it was difficult for him to stand, walk, or do much of anything.

On Wednesday, May 6, 2009, I called Mickey and found out that his follow-up lab report was back and that the doctor was very pleased with the results, which was great to hear. I still called Joe every day, but it was obvious he was struggling. In spite of this, Sam and I managed to have a relaxed vacation, and I gained confidence with my ability to get around with the crutches and sometimes the canes. I used the crutches on the sand and occasionally the canes on solid, level surfaces. We also brought the wheelchair along in the car but never needed it, which was very good news. The weather was perfect for the whole week, with bright, blue skies every day, nice sea breezes, and comfortable temperatures. Sam and I enjoyed the beach and the smell of the ocean and agreed we needed to do more of this.

When I talked to Pete on Thursday, he said he had called hospice and they set Joe up with an oxygen tank to help his breathing and ease his pain, so I knew the end was near. Saturday was our last full day on the beach, and I had a very nice visit with Joe over the phone. He apologized again for not being able to have me over to the house, but I understood and told him it was OK. I also thanked him for all the great times we had over the last ten-plus years. We talked about paddling on the Wakulla River, dancing with the ladies at the Spoonbill Lounge, eating and drinking beer at Boss Oyster, and of course sailing on his boat, Second Hand Rose. She was the most-sailed boat on all of Apalachicola Bay. Joe loved her, and she was always shipshape and ready to sail.

We left for Little Rock on Sunday morning, and while on the interstate between Birmingham and Montgomery, Alabama, Joe's daughter Beth called from California to tell us Joe died that morning. We pulled off at a rest stop for me to gather myself and call her back to get the details. I knew this was going to happen, but the finality of his death really hurt me. He was a dear friend and an excellent sailor, and we had some terrific times together. When Sam and I got back home, the Y-Flyer Fleet of the Grande Maumelle Sailing Club got together to celebrate Joe's life and talk about all the fun times we all had together. This gathering helped me get some closure on Joe's death. However, he is still missed by those of us who sailed with him.

The two-day drive home gave Sam and me a chance to reflect on our lives, what we were doing, and where we were going. I called Debbie to tell her about Joe, and she told me this was a good reminder that we needed to take some time off for life and not spend all our time on my therapy. This was what Sam had been saying for some time. The week-long trip gave me confidence about doing some more traveling. My ability to walk was improving, and I gained confidence in my overall mobility during the trip. Sam and I continued to discuss how much we loved being near the ocean and the beach, which would eventually lead to a major, life-changing decision in the future.

Just a couple of weeks after getting back home, I lost another old friend, Tom Steves, who died in a motorcycle accident. Tom and I had worked together at First National Bank in Little Rock, which was the beginning of my career in bank marketing. Losing another friend was a stark reminder of why I needed to focus on enjoying life as best I could, even with my limitations.

When the boot was removed from my right foot in early June, I was able to do more therapy, but it was like learning to walk all over again. I was also able to get into the pool and do some exercises in the water. This started when we spent a long weekend with Greg in Plano and I tried to do some things in the pool that Carla and I had worked on back in Little Rock. At this time, I was spending most of my time in the forearm crutches to help my right foot develop properly. Anne Miskin was pleased with the results of the surgery and spent much of her therapy trying to loosen up the ankle joint and reduce swelling in my right foot. It was a battle, but we both believed the surgery was the right thing, and there was no question that my legs were getting stronger. At the beginning of the summer of 2009, I was still having problems with hyperextension of the right knee and eventually had to go back to a knee brace.

We also had good news from the McMath brothers, who finally were able to get a court date for us in early April 2010. I knew this would be a long process, but it seemed like it took forever just to schedule this court date.

During June, my therapy work continued to pay off in small but meaningful ways. My bladder control was continuing to improve, which was a blessing, and my bowel procedure was becoming more routine. (Frankly, digital evacuation of the bowel will never be considered routine, but it was improving.) I was definitely walking better and could feel some sensation in my right foot when I put weight on it. The second week of June, Carla Branch could see an increase in my leg strength, while

Anne said that my right foot looked much better and my skin tone and movement were much improved since removing the boot. Independent of these comments, my acupuncturist, Martin, saw more movement in the right ankle and foot connection, as well as in the toes. To have three of my key therapists commenting on this kind of improvement in the same week was a significant boost to my morale and gave me increased hope for the future.

The following week, I had lunch with Lunsford Bridges and Susie Smith from Metropolitan National Bank, and we had a wonderful visit. They needed my help on a project, and I appreciated them giving me something to focus on other than my therapy. I found the intellectual challenge to be very stimulating, and it was a great boost to my morale to be needed for my marketing ability. It reminded me that in spite of my crippled physical condition, I still had something valuable to offer.

Thirty-One

Intestinal Issues

At this time, most of my energy and focus were on being able to stand up and walk comfortably with canes. In the meantime, I hoped my bowel and bladder issues would follow in time. July 2009 was a real wakeup call for me about my internal organs. Before the injury, my bowel process was as regular as a clock. Starting in July, I was having problems involving constipation that were very difficult to resolve. If I used a laxative, I could relieve the pain in my gut but would lose complete control of my bowel. In the middle of July, I was blocked up for forty-eight hours, and once I was able to get things moving, I couldn't get it to stop. I spent over an hour one day on the commode going through multiple gloves, and it was a mess. I finally had to cancel all my therapy for over a week as I tried to get this under control. My regular doctor sent me to a specialist, and everything we tried with him just seemed to make it worse. I was having accidents on a regular basis and had to start wearing adult diapers. Even after empting my bowel on the commode, I would get up and a few minutes later defecate all over myself. One time, after what I thought was a complete emptying of the bowel, I got in the shower to bathe and clean myself up and promptly defecated all over the floor. I was afraid to leave the house for several days and wondered whether this would ever calm down. Also, with all the stress on my intestinal system, I broke out with fever blisters all over my mouth. I could count seven large blisters and numerous other smaller ones. It was painful and I looked like I had been in a fight. On August 22, 2009, I wrote in my journal:

What else can happen?

Fortunately, during all this misery, I had a visit scheduled with Jane Roark at our house. Jane said the same thing the specialist did: that I had an irritable bowel, which I already knew. More important, she encouraged me to get off all the medications for the bowel and immediately start with some yogurt and probiotics to get my bowel back to a more normal state. She also said I could take a small dose of Imodium when having problems but warned me not to depend on it. As she said, I needed to get my bowel back to a more natural state. She also echoed what Dr. Rehab had said about needing to get more fluid in my system, especially in hot weather. I knew fluids were important, but I was reluctant to drink too much since it caused me to wet my pants. However, if increasing fluids would solve the bowel problems, then I could learn to deal with the bladder issues.

Jane was a wonderful resource, and as a nurse with a long history of working with a variety of patients, she had a lot of experience to offer. She coached me about my nutrition and how to get my system back to a more normal condition. She also was concerned about my lethargic condition and tendency to frequently sleep most of the day when fighting depression. While she believed taking the antidepressant Lexapro was a good initial plan for me, she encouraged me to talk to Dr. Rehab about switching to something like Wellbutrin as an alternative. Dr. Rehab agreed, and the change in medication worked quite well. Within a few days, I was waking up with more energy and was able to do more at therapy.

By most estimates, the number of people in the United States with spinal column injuries is between 250,000 and 300,000, and paraplegics make up slightly more than half of that group. This makes those of us with spinal column injuries a very small segment of the population at about 0.1 percent. As a result, I found that except for Dr. Rehab, many doctors didn't fully understand all the issues involved with a patient who has little or no use of his body from the waist down. My bowel, bladder, and digestive system didn't work like they should, and when I had problems, they were not easy to correct. Therefore, I had to be particularly careful about what I ate and drank and what medications I took. For example, before my injury, I used to love popcorn, but I had to give it up because it is very hard to digest and gave me stomach cramps. Before the injury, I always drank plenty of water to stay well hydrated for all my athletic activities, but after the injury I cut back to avoid wetting my pants, especially in public. Since I needed fluid to keep my digestive system working properly, I had to learn to achieve the delicate balance of getting just enough fluid but not too much, while also avoiding foods that were hard to digest. Honestly, at this time, I didn't have much of an appetite, and having to manually evacuate the bowel decreased my desire for food. There were many days during this time when I would have been just as happy to give up most foods and live on Clif Bars and water, with an occasional cheeseburger thrown in once a month.

While I was still working on my bowel issues, other things were looking up. Sunday, August 2, 2009, was a banner day. Henry Noor, Sam, and I met down by the Interstate 430 Bridge. Sam was going for a walk on the trail while Henry and I went for a ride along the riverfront. We rode about twelve miles down and back to the base of the Big Dam Bridge, a pedestrian/bike bridge built over the lock and dam near I-430. I told Henry I wanted to see how far up the bridge I could go. He waited to see if I could get about halfway, and when I continued, he rode up to the top and encouraged me to keep on going. Having him cheering and encouraging me kept me going, and surprisingly, I made it all the way to the top. I was in my granny gear, going barely two miles per hour, but I made it without stopping. What a thrill that was. We were both so proud of how far I had come. As we came back down the bridge, we saw Sam passing the bridge, assuming we had already ridden back to the car. Henry and I took our time and came up behind Sam, who was surprised to see us behind her. She was also thrilled to hear I had ridden all the way up the bridge. Henry had to head back home after the ride, but Sam and I went to Pizza Café to celebrate. And there was still even better news waiting for me the next day. Bruce Thalheimer called from Chainwheel Bike Shop and told me he had a great opportunity for me if I was interested. The shop had built a special trike for a customer who was having back surgery and would probably not be able to ride a regular bike again. However, over eighteen months, he made remarkable progress and was back on a two-wheel bike again. He asked Bruce if he knew someone who would really appreciate and enjoy a trike like his. Bruce told him my story, and the man, whom I never met, told Bruce he would make me a very good deal on the trike. It was a top-of-the-line recumbent Catrike, which was custom fitted with excellent components, including small wheels with high-pressure tires up front and an expensive, full-size racing wheel on the back. I told Bruce I was definitely interested and excited about the prospect of the new trike.

That same week, Anne finally got my right ankle to loosen up some, and we were confident this would improve my ability to walk. Also that week, I received a wonderful compliment from fellow sailing buddy and former fleet champion, Dudley Rodgers. The sailing club had asked me to write an article for the monthly newsletter about Joe Whitesell and what an important contribution he made to the club, both with his woodworking skills and also with his delightful attitude and wonderful sense of humor. Dudley called to thank me for writing the story and said that I really captured Joe and that reading the article brought tears to his eyes. That may be one of the nicest compliments I ever received for my writing.

As my bowel finally calmed down, it was time to get back to my workouts. At the end of August 2009, Carla and I devoted time to working in the pool. Getting in and out of the pool was still a struggle, but I enjoyed being in the water and was determined to use it for some of my therapy. I was surprised that an hour in the pool wore me out more than a normal hour of therapy, and then I realized that while in the pool I was on my feet for a full hour. Instead of doing any real swimming, Carla had me balance by holding on to the edge of the pool and doing leg exercises, including moving each leg sideways, backward, and forward, and also including some squats. The buoyancy of the water was incredibly helpful, and I found I was able to move my legs much more than I could on dry land. I also had another good visit with Cagle Harrendorf at the athletic club after my session with Carla. We talked about working on my attitude, coping with depression, and managing the issues involved with my bowel and bladder. As a retired physician, he was exceptionally helpful and empathetic.

After I got home from the club, Mickey Freeman and I had our last "boys' night out" of the season at the ballpark. While we kept up with the game, this mostly was a time to visit about marketing, banking, and some politics. As always, we enjoyed beer, barbecue, hot dogs, and salted-in-the-shell peanuts. There is something special to me about shelling peanuts and drinking beer at a baseball game. I don't even recall whether the Travelers won or not, but I do remember that I felt really good about myself that night and was looking forward to the future. As usual, Sam said I came home refreshed and with a smile on my face. September of 2009 turned out to be a very good month for me physically and mentally. Adding a few fun events to my regular workout routine helped.

Thirty-Two

Having Fun and
Making Progress

At this time, the McMath brothers were making meaningful progress with our lawsuit. Phillip informed us he had made contact with the lawyers representing the other side and hoped this would enable us to move forward sometime this year with depositions. From our standpoint, any movement at all would be a positive development.

The beginning of September was our annual family gathering in Dallas for "Club Greg" on Labor Day weekend. The five-hour drive to Greg's house in Dallas was another good test of my ability to manage my bladder, and things went surprisingly well. I didn't have any accidents, and we had a delightful time with family around Greg's pool. Many of his friends hadn't seen me since the previous year and were very complimentary about my progress, which was always a boost to my morale.

The Grande Maumelle Sailing Club had been a big part of my life for twenty years, and while I had given up racing sailboats when I started competing in triathlons, I still had lots of friends at the club. In September 2009, the club celebrated its fiftieth anniversary, and I appreciated being included in all the festivities. Prior to the celebration, there were many activities, and one of them was meeting with a group at the clubhouse to film a video about the history of the club. As a former Commodore, I was included and had a wonderful afternoon visiting with sailing buddies and telling stories about all the great times we had together.

Three weeks later, on the Friday evening prior to the actual celebration on Saturday, Max and Kaki Mehlburger had about fifty of us over to their house for a reunion of those who had been instrumental in the development and growth of the club. I was surprised to see many former members and officers of the club who had moved out of town and came back for the fiftieth anniversary celebration. It reminded me of how much I enjoyed racing sailboats with all these people and how important the club was in my life. Seeing many old friends brought back a rush of memories of wonderful times together when we were all younger and full of ourselves. It was almost like stepping back in time. I could close my eyes and feel the motion of a sailboat under me, the wind in the sails driving the boat across the water, and the pull on the tiller as we raced for the next buoy. The following evening was the actual celebration with a big crowd and even more old friends. The anniversary party included a video with pictures from the past, interviews with older members about the history of the club, and several skits poking fun at many of the key players in the club. It was a special evening for Sam and me, and I was asked to finish it off with a toast to the club. I said a few words about how blessed we were to have inspired leadership and a racing program that had developed outstanding sailors, many of whom had brought home trophies from regattas throughout the country. I finished with the following: "So here's a toast to the spirit of the Grande Maumelle Sailing Club. May she continue to give future generations what she has given to all of us: a full measure of joy, pleasure, and excitement, and most of all, a unique learning experience that you only get with wind, water, and sail." While I was no longer able to sail due to my injury, I was thankful for dear friends and all the memorable times I had racing sailboats. This included everything from small two-man dinghies to crewing with Max on his thirty-eight-foot Swan and winning the Marion-to-Bermuda yacht race. That was an amazing experience I will never forget. Being with so many sailing friends reminded me that regardless of my tragic injury, I had been blessed with a rich, full life.

In September, I finally decided it was time to move ahead on selling our collection of bikes. It had been two years since the injury, and I realized my chances of ever riding a two-wheel bike again were very remote. I had my new trike, which I enjoyed, and I would have to be satisfied with that. Sam and I had acquired a beautiful, bright yellow Cannondale tandem bike we had enjoyed on several rides, but there was no way we would use it again. We put it up for sale and advertised it through the bike club and also with my biking friends, including those in Louisiana. As luck would have it, our friend Pierre knew a couple who were looking for a quality tandem, and they ended up buying it, along with our expensive but easy-to-use tandem rack for the car. I was pleased to get a good price for the tandem, but watching them drive off with our bright yellow bike was tough. I had a sinking feeling in the pit of my stomach. For a couple of weeks, every time I went into the garage and the tandem wasn't hanging on the wall, it was a painful reminder that I would probably never ride a two-wheel bike again. I got a lot of pleasure from riding, and when I moved to Shreveport, the local bike club became my social group. We had regular club rides on Tuesday and Thursday evenings and Saturday mornings. Several of us also went to bike tours in east Texas. Pierre, Craig and Liz Rambin, and I even put together an annual two-day tour on parts of the Natchez Trace. We all had a great time together, and I was putting in about two thousand miles a year on my bike and loving it. Giving up biking along with running left a big hole in my life. Parting with my triathlon bike was especially difficult. I had the bike custom made for me by Johnny Cobb in Tyler, Texas, who had worked with some of the best cyclists in the world. I bought my first good road bike, a carbon fiber Specialized model, from Johnny when he had a shop in Shreveport, and I knew he would make me a great bike. My tri-bike had a custom paint job with my name on it and was a terrific race bike, but it was time for it to go. We also decided to sell Sam's hybrid bike. My much-loved Trek road bike and my mountain bike went to Greg.

At the end of September, my Louisiana riding buddies came to stay with us and ride the Big Dam Bridge 100 bike tour. The first time they came to see us, we all rode together, but after I was paralyzed, Sam and I still wanted them to come back and stay with us for the weekend. Having Craig and Liz along with Pierre pay us a visit was always a treat. Pierre came a day early, and we all went out to dinner to one of my favorite places with the Freemans. We told stories about riding, laughed a lot, and had a terrific time. At times like that, I still felt like the old Randy before the injury. I would forget about my paralysis and revel in the warmth and laughter of good friends. The next day, Pierre and I met Mickey, Frank Lawrence, and his young son Jack for a ride on the river trail. I couldn't have asked for a better weekend. My Louisiana friends, who hadn't seen me in several months, were very impressed with my progress, and that was good to hear. Also, Frank and especially Jack were surprised at how well I was doing on my trike. This reminded me that even though I couldn't see much progress, the hard work and dedication to therapy were paying off.

At this time, Sam was getting ready for a Mediterranean cruise on a small 60-passenger motor/sailor, *Le Ponant*, with Henry and Marcella Noor. We were supposed to do a riverboat trip in Europe with them two months after I was injured, but of course that was canceled. They went ahead and now, two years later, found another great boating trip and wanted to see if we were interested. I knew it would be too difficult for me on a small ship, but I believed Sam could use a break from our routine, and I was doing well enough to take care of myself for a week. Also, I knew how much Sam loved to travel, particularly in Italy, which was a big part of the ship's itinerary. My recovery was far enough along that I could manage getting around the house and continue driving to therapy while she was gone. I also called the Mougeots, Freemans, and Heisters and planned some activities to keep me busy on the weekend while Sam was out of the country.

During Sam's absence, I was busy with my therapy and proud of my ability to take care of myself on my own. However, I ended up missing her so much more than I thought I would. The days were fine, but I really missed her at night. I was surprised after living alone for so many years how hard it was to sleep without her next to me. On September 30, 2009, I wrote in my journal the following:

> *I especially miss her when I go to bed; it seems so lonely. I don't know how I lived all those years alone. I couldn't do this recovery without her.*

During the time she was gone, I was able to have some good times. Mickey and Patti came over to watch a Razorback football game and brought dinner. I also had dinner with the Heisters one night, and the next day the Mougeots brought food from Whole Hog BBQ for dinner, which was outstanding. Whole Hog in Little Rock is still the best brisket and pulled pork I have ever had, including barbecue at some of the famous spots in Memphis. Then, shortly before Sam returned from her grand adventure, Mickey and I went out for cheeseburgers and beer at the Buffalo Grill. With my therapy and various friends coming over, I was a pretty busy boy, but I still struggled to go to sleep at night without my bride. Sam was due home in a few days when I wrote the following:

> *Can't wait to see Sam in a couple of days. I need her more than I know. She is very precious to me. I hope she is having fun.*

During this period, several of my therapists were seeing good improvements. I sometimes thought they commented about improvements in my legs just to make me feel better, but it was obvious that almost everyone was seeing progress in different places. Anne Miskin found lots of energy in both my feet and my legs, and helped me stand up on my bare feet with me holding onto the therapy table for balance. Even though my arms were doing most of the work to hold me up, it was a very good feeling, and I was surprised at my ability to balance my body in that position. Anne believed my ankles had much more flexibility, and the skin tone on my feet was the best she had seen, and she believed I was on the verge of big improvements. The next day, I had a therapist help me practice walking with one crutch for a short distance, and I did pretty well. The day after that, I practiced on my own walking with canes at the athletic club. I used the running track, which has a railing next to it, and I was pleased with my ability to walk and keep my balance with two canes. However, I was still having problems with hyperextending my right knee, which would turn out to be a long-term issue.

Things were definitely looking up, and I had lots to brag about to Sam when she came home that week. She had a great time on her cruise and took plenty of pictures to share with me. I know she missed me, and she looked great. It was obvious the trip was a very positive experience for her. She loves to travel and explore other cultures, and I was happy she was able to go on this cruise.

With Sam back home, we had a party at our house for close friends and all my therapists on the Friday night before my sixty-sixth birthday. It was a good opportunity for the key people involved in my recovery process to get to know each other and have them all together in our home. Greg surprised me by showing up late that night after the party. Then, on Saturday, Debbie and Somerset arrived for the weekend. They all stayed with us, and it made for a terrific birthday weekend. Everyone thought Sam looked great and enjoyed hearing about her trip. I made up a slide show of two hundred of her pictures to show on my MacBook, which was fun.

Thirty-Three

Therapy, Lawyers, and Planning a Vacation

Overall, I knew I was making good progress, and apparently it showed in both my attitude and my improving mobility. Debbie sent me a very nice e-mail after she returned home, stating that she thought my emotional state was much improved and that she was very impressed with my progress. I showed off some over the birthday weekend by trying to use my canes as much as possible, and everyone was impressed. The following week, I used my canes to walk into Advanced Physical Therapy. I could park right in front of the door, so it was easy for me to maneuver around to get into the building. Also, it was on a flat surface, which made a big difference. I still used crutches to get into the athletic club from the parking lot because it was a longer walk on a sloping surface, and I found it to be quite difficult to safely manage with the canes.

That same week, I had an excellent session with Jane Roark. We discussed Debbie's observations on my improvements and, as always, we talked about the importance of looking forward and not looking back at where I was before the injury. I told Debbie that Sam and I were beginning to explore possibilities of traveling, and Jane thought that was a major step forward. As she and Debbie both reminded me, I should be "rehabbing to live and not living to rehab." My bowel and bladder issues were still a problem, and the thought of getting on and off an airplane concerned me. However, I knew lots of spinal column injury patients who were confined to a wheelchair but were still were able to get out and travel. So, for the first time since my paralysis, I began to think about how and where we might go for a vacation. I had done pretty well driving to Apalachicola and now was beginning to think about other possibilities. Jane was strongly encouraging me to think about getting away for a real vacation. As she said, driving to Dallas to visit Greg and going to see Joe for a few days in Apalachicola were not real vacations, and I knew she was right.

Therapy, especially at the athletic club, continued to go well, and I felt I was getting better each week. Carla was increasing the weight on a couple of the machines we used, and I could tell that I was gaining strength and my balance was improving. I tested myself at the club by trying to walk with one cane next to the railing on the track and fell. I liked pushing myself to see what I could do, but this was a somewhat painful reminder that I needed to be more careful. My right hand was sore for a day or two, but fortunately, I didn't break anything. The fall frustrated me and was a reminder of my inability to walk. As a result, I again felt overwhelmed with my condition and angry about my situation. Most of the time, my body was making better progress than my mind, and I knew I had to keep my mind focused on my progress if I was going to continue to get better.

Finally, in November, it looked like our lawsuit was moving forward. The McMath brothers were able to schedule a deposition with Dr. X for the middle of the month. I decided to take a week off to work with our attorneys, rest, and prepare to sit in on the deposition. Just seeing Dr. X again would be a vivid reminder of how dramatically he changed my life, and listening to his explanation about what happened would be extremely difficult. However, this was my life we were discussing, and I was anxious to move forward with this process.

Sam and I had a lot on our plate at this time, and we took Jane's advice and discussed where we would like to go for a vacation. We both loved the water and enjoyed the Gulf Coast of Florida. Sam's twin stepdaughters in

Virginia had a condo on Captiva Island, which is connected to Sanibel Island, and Sam enjoyed being with them and their husbands on the island. My aunt and uncle in Missouri went to Naples every winter for over twenty years, and Debbie and I had frequently visited them. Eighteen months before I was paralyzed, Sam and I had talked about a trip to the southwest Florida coast and decided Sanibel would be a great place for a vacation. I did some research on the area and contacted the Sanibel/Captiva Chamber of Commerce for information. They sent us their brochure, along with an abundance of information on rental property on the island, which we filed away for future use. After talking with Jane about a vacation, Sam pulled out our file and we found what appeared to be a lovely condo overlooking the beach and I called the owner to book a couple of weeks in early December before the rates went up. We didn't know it at the time, but during "the season," which starts in mid-December and goes through early April, the rates double along with the population of the island. On Thursday, November 12, 2009, we made a reservation for December 2–19 on beautiful and warm Sanibel Island. Even in the off-season, the condo was still expensive, but we deserved a break and certainly needed a real vacation. We even talked about making this a regular trip every year, assuming we liked the condo and enjoyed our time there. Little did we know at the time that this trip would lead to a major change in our lives only nine months later.

On the following Friday, things didn't go very well for me. I almost fell walking to the car in our garage and had to catch myself on the car. Then I didn't seem to have much strength in my legs while working with Carla. I even had difficulty just going from one machine to the next. It just seemed like I couldn't balance very well. Part of the problem was my mind, which was focused on the deposition coming up on Monday, and I wasn't concentrating on my workouts.

On Monday, November 16, 2009, we started making meaningful progress on our lawsuit. This was the day for Dr. X's deposition, and Bruce McMath, who does most of the litigation, was in charge of questioning the doctor. Sam and I met Bruce and Phillip for lunch to discuss what was going to take place that afternoon and then met with the doctor and his attorneys for the deposition. In this process, Sam and I were spectators while Bruce did all the questioning. Bruce and Phillip McMath had done considerable research nationwide on issues with epidural steroid injections and found some expert doctors who were willing to discuss what may have caused my paralysis. Bruce was well prepared and did an excellent job questioning the doctor about the procedure. The deposition lasted for five and a half hours, and afterward we had a brief discussion with Bruce, who wanted to know what we thought. There was no question in my mind that Bruce had done an excellent job and that the doctor was in trouble and knew it. In fact, I told Bruce that after sitting through this, I would hate to be in a courtroom with him questioning me. While Sam and I were exhausted at the end of the day, we were glad to be moving forward, and it helped us prepare for our deposition, which would be in early 2010.

Two weeks later we spent our third Thanksgiving since my paralysis by ourselves, which was a good thing. Both of us had been working hard on my recovery and we had a relaxed long weekend and started planning for our upcoming trip to Sanibel Island. Thanksgiving Day was an excellent opportunity for us to look back at how far we had come since I was paralyzed, and how thankful we were for many, many things. Here is the list of what I wrote in my journal:

We are thankful for

Our wonderful house that Dorothy Willoughby found for us with a master bedroom on the ground floor;

Our solid financial situation, which enables us to pursue anything that might help my recovery;

The support of my sister, Debbie, and especially Greg, who has gone above and beyond to do everything he can for both of us;

Many dear friends, especially Mickey Freeman, who was at the rehab hospital every day and has been so helpful throughout the last twenty-eight months;

All my therapists, who have been supportive and dedicated to my recovery and continue to devote a lot of time and energy to this effort;

My body and my history of working out and training, which have helped me fight through my paralysis. My body is coming back, but very slowly. However, my physical training for over thirty years helped prepare me for this challenge.

Thirty-Four

Vacation on the Beach

The Monday after Thanksgiving, we loaded the car and took off for our first real vacation since my injury. Although I was anxious about traveling with my bladder and bowel issues, I managed by stopping every two to three hours to catheterize myself. On interstate highways, there are usually fairly clean rest stops, especially once we got to Florida, where we could find one every hour or so. While many states like Arkansas have closed rest stops, Florida has built many convenient rest stops whose bathrooms tend to be very clean. I'm always concerned about getting a urinary tract infection, so I needed to be very careful about where I did my business.

We had a good trip during our two-day drive and arrived without any major problems. We also tested out a new Garmin, and it was extremely valuable. It was very helpful in finding convenient places to eat and giving us estimated time of arrival and other valuable information. After using it for this trip, I couldn't imagine making another trip without it. New technology, once you learn how to use it, can be very helpful. Mickey Freeman introduced me to books by Carl Hiaasen, and he has become one of our favorite authors. He is a columnist for the Miami Herald and also writes humorous novels set in and around Florida that usually contain a character with a strong environmental agenda. I bought his book, *Tourist Season* on CD, and Sam and I enjoyed listening to it on the road trip. It made the time go by quickly while on the road, and we enjoyed it so much that at times we were reluctant to stop for lunch until we got to the end of a chapter. I highly recommend Hiaasen's books as a companion on a long trip.

Once we arrived at the condo building, unloading the car was a tough chore for Sam. About all I could do was pull bags out of the car, and she had to load them on the elevator to go up to the second floor, and then wheel them down to our unit at the end of the building. The condo we rented turned out to be spectacular. When we first walked in the door and saw the view, we were thrilled. It had floor-to-ceiling windows with sliding glass doors across one entire wall of the living room and about halfway across the other wall. We were right on the beach, and since the building was located at an angle to the beach, we could see up and down the beach on both sides. This was a two-bedroom unit, which was more than we needed, but we were glad we paid a little extra and planned to reserve this condo for a trip to Sanibel Island the next year.

Sanibel is a beautiful place and is very popular in season with snowbirds from up north and a surprising number of tourists from Canada and Europe. However, during our two and a half weeks on the island, there was very little traffic, not many people on the beach, and no waiting lines at the wonderful seafood restaurants on the island.

One of the big decisions we made about this trip was to leave my wheelchair at home. Sam, along with my therapists, had encouraged me to spend as much time on my feet as possible and not depend on the wheelchair. I agreed that the wheelchair was a crutch, but it made getting around the house so much easier, and I was reluctant to give it up. I knew that sooner or later I would need to give up my dependence on the chair, and this trip seemed be a good time to test my ability to function without it. We did bring my crutches, along with my canes, and I was determined to work hard on using the canes on a regular basis. Sam and I were pleased at how well I did with the canes maneuvering around the condo, walking on the beach, and going out to eat. Walking in soft sand was a challenge but one that I was willing to take on. I believed that if I could walk on a beach in my canes, I would develop better balance and be able to use the canes as my primary means of support.

Enjoying the beach on Sanibel Island

Two days after we arrived, we received an e-mail from our attorneys about completing depositions with two nurses involved with my procedure. It was good to hear that after many months of not making much progress, things were happening. They also wanted me to help set up a meeting with Dr. Rehab to discuss my condition, as well as with another doctor who had reviewed the MRIs taken before and after the epidural injection. I could tell that the McMaths were working hard on our lawsuit, and I felt like our cause was in very good hands. Once Dr.

X had settled on a law firm to represent him, the McMaths finally had a contact that could respond to requests for depositions. A few days, later we received another e-mail confirming their visits with Dr. Rehab and another doctor, which were very helpful.

After only a couple of days in Sanibel, Sam and I had settled into a delightful, laid-back routine of enjoying the beach and discussing which restaurant we wanted to visit for dinner. We slept in and enjoyed a late breakfast looking out over the gulf. Then we would set up camp on the beach with an umbrella, some chairs, a cooler, and our Kindles. Sam would spend at least an hour or two picking up shells while I read. I made an effort most days to walk on the sand for about a quarter to half a mile. Listening to the sound of the surf, watching the pelicans diving for fish, and feeling the warmth of the sun were very therapeutic. I wrote the following in my journal on Wednesday, December 9; 2009, about how relaxed we were:

> I can't recall being as relaxed as we are here. We have no agenda other than enjoying the beach, reading some, and Sam finding shells. What a way to live. It's warm with bright, blue skies and waves lapping on the beach just steps away from my beach chair. Except for the setting sun and an occasional walker going by, the world seems to stand still. I am at peace. I was made for this. Even in my crippled state, everything has worked so well.

Later that day, there was more activity on the beach, with a family that included two small children. I spent almost an hour just watching the parents help the kids build sandcastles, which were really just small piles of sand. The kids laughed and played at the water's edge, fell down occasionally in the sand, and looked for shells in the surf. The whole scene looked like something out of a Norman Rockwell painting. On Thursday morning it was foggy, so Sam, with my encouragement, took off for some shopping at the many shops along Periwinkle Way, Sanibel's main street. After Sam left, I sat out on our balcony to read and look out over the beach. I could only see six people within half a mile of us.

A month later, that same stretch of beach would be full of snowbirds escaping from the frozen north. We enjoyed the condo so much that within five days of our arrival, we e-mailed the owner and told him we wanted to book the unit again for the next year. He agreed and told us when we checked out to confirm the dates with the real estate firm that managed his condos.

For our last week on Sanibel, we did some exploring beyond the beach. We toured the Ding Darling Wildlife Refuge, which occupies about a third of the island. It is a spectacular area with an abundance of wildlife, including two alligators that had ventured out near the road. Apparently this is fairly common, as there was a ranger on hand to make sure people gave the gators plenty of space. The ranger made the point that we were only visitors and this is home for the gators. After driving through the refuge and exploring some of the wooden paths out to an overlook, we decided to go back another day and do a kayak tour through the mangroves. The two-hour guided kayak tour turned out to be one of the highlights of our vacation. It was a beautiful trip in the mangroves, and our guide was very helpful and made it an educational experience. She pointed out many birds and explained how important the mangroves are to the protection and development of the island. We enjoyed it so much that we planned to do it again on our next visit.

At first I was concerned about getting into and out of the kayak, but I did pretty well with significant help from the two men who rented the boats. Most of the kayaks were open two person boats, and I had the two guys stand on either side and hold onto my arms while I stepped into the boat, which was resting partially on the beach. Then they helped lower me into the second seat and I gave them my canes to keep until we returned. Since the kayak was mostly open I had plenty of room for my legs, even in my braces. They then helped Sam get in, handed us our paddles and shoved us back into the water. I had to coach Sam some on paddling but she learned quickly and paddling around in the mangroves was easier than I expected. When we returned getting out of the boat was also pretty straightforward. The rental guys pulled the boat onto the beach and helped Sam out first. Then they grabbed my arms on either side and lifted me up so I could step out while holding onto one of them. It's amazing what a recovering paraplegic can do with the help of a couple of strong men.

On Sam's Mediterranean trip with the Noors, she became friends with a couple who live in Englewood, Florida, which was about a two-hour drive from Sanibel. So before we left to go home, we drove up to spend the day with Frank and Carol Lugo. They are very nice people, and we had a good visit with them, plus the trip also gave us a chance to drive through some of the surrounding area on the way.

On Friday, December 18, it was time to get our stuff organized so we could head back to Little Rock on Saturday. I was so glad we made the trip. Jane Roark was right; we needed this vacation more than I realized. The night before we left I wrote the following in my journal:

This has been a terrific holiday—very refreshing, relaxing, and healing.

Thirty-Five

State of Recovery, 2010

. . .

It was rough on both of us to go back to cold weather in Arkansas the week of Christmas and give up the beach, sun, and seafood. We loved our house and had a relaxed holiday, but I had to admit, Sanibel was still very much on our minds. I wasn't scheduled to go back to therapy until after New Year's Day, so we had some time to adjust and enjoy visiting with friends. To start off the New Year, I noted in my journal the following on my current situation and resolutions for 2010:

State of Recovery: It's been two years and five months since the injury. While I am gaining strength and balance in my upper legs, my progress below the knees is very limited, which is a concern. Not much feeling or movement below the knee. Lack of feeling in my feet really limits my ability to walk. I am working on walking with one cane, but all my balance and strength are from the knee up.

New Year's Resolutions:

Walk with one cane regularly.
Get better control of bladder and be able to urinate.
Control diet, keep weight down, and firm up core muscles.
Focus on "rehab to live," not "live to rehab."
Relax, enjoy the moment, and plan to travel more.

250

Once again, in retrospect, my expectations were well beyond my ability to accomplish these goals. Yes, it is important to give yourself something to aim at, but goals also need to be realistic. However, since I had already accomplished more than anyone thought I could, I continued to set a very high bar for myself.

On my return to therapy after a month off, I was very pleased to find that rather than losing ground on my recovery, I was actually a little stronger and my balance was better. Of course, the biggest change was that I was more relaxed and had a positive outlook. The first week back, I definitely pushed myself a little harder than I should have and ended up with some sore muscles. Most of this resulted from training with Carla on weight machines at the athletic club and then spending forty minutes on a bike in spin class. The spin class was too much and I knew it. My left thigh was sore, especially on the inside of my leg, and I developed some cramps in my right calf. I didn't do any real damage and just needed an extra rest day before the next workout. That week, I also spent about twenty minutes walking with one cane on the track next to the railing and was fairly stable. In addition, my right knee was working better, and I was not having as many problems with hyperextension of the knee.

By the middle of January, we had a firm date set for the other side to depose Sam and me on our pending lawsuit: February 4, 2010. We would be glad to get this done and then would start moving ahead on preparations for the trial. My workouts were continuing to go well, and I did the spin class again but only for thirty minutes and took it easy. Carla was changing my workout routine, and Anne was having me stand up barefooted again while supporting most of my weight with my arms holding onto the massage table. Best of all, my bladder control was getting better, which helped my sleep patterns. At Anne's suggestion, I also tried some reflexology with a therapist she knew. It seemed to produce some limited sensation in my feet, so I planned to add this to my routine every couple of weeks.

After our wonderful trip to Sanibel Island, I thought it would be fun to produce a photo book from our best photos of the trip. I had made a printed photo book after Mom's funeral for both Debbie and myself, with some special pictures of mom and the family. After doing that book, I thought I would do the same for our vacation. There are several online services that produce these hardcover books in full color with custom captions to go with the photos. They are reasonably priced, and I found it to be a great way to remember special events. Our book arrived in late January, and it brought back wonderful memories. I was so pleased with the book that I wrote the following in my journal:

Now any time we want to, we can open the book and relive the memories and feel from the pictures what we felt at the time: love, peace, relaxation, happiness, warmth, and more.

On Thursday, January 22, I made a special point to stop by Baptist Rehabilitation and visit with the various therapists I had worked with. It was my first time back there in several months, and I wanted to thank everyone who had played a role in my initial recovery. The inpatient therapists were so very important to me in those first three weeks after I was paralyzed. At that time, I had so little hope, and all indications were that I would spend my life in a wheelchair, but they gave me hope, which was scarce among the doctors I had seen. The therapists were thrilled to see me walking with canes and congratulated me on the improvements I had made since the last time they saw me. Of course, my outpatient therapist, Lou Tretter, is the one who got me to the point that I could walk with canes, and he had told the inpatient therapists about my progress. However, hearing about progress is a lot different from actually seeing a former patient who left in a wheelchair and now could walk with canes. Seeing their excitement over my progress was wonderful. It was always helpful to have friends tell me how good I looked and how much progress I had made, but having professional therapists who deal with paraplegics every day tell me how far I had come was special. It made me proud of what I had accomplished and gave me great hope for the future.

Moving Ahead on the Legal Process

Being a plaintiff in a lawsuit is not an easy task, and the McMaths had warned me that it would be a long and difficult process. I had great confidence in them, and the more time Sam and I spent with them, the more we were glad to have them on our side. They were incredibly patient with me and took whatever time necessary to discuss all the issues involved.

One of the techniques they used in some cases like mine was to produce a video with pictures of me before I was paralyzed and footage of me working out at the athletic club and doing therapy. They also wanted to do an interview with Sam and me to discuss how much my injury had changed our lives, as well as what we had been through in creating a new life in which I had lost the use of my legs, bowel, and bladder. Going through old pictures from bike tours, triathlons, and other activities wore me out more than I expected. While it was fun to relive some old memories with good friends, it was also exhausting to look at where I was and then realize what I was going through to learn to live as a recovering paraplegic. As a result, I had a meltdown at the end of the day because I was so overwhelmed by my situation. I was unable to do anything for the next two days, but I had doctor appointments coming up and had to get over my depression and get back to work. I had a good visit with Dr. Rehab, and he was again impressed with my physical progress, which was a boost to my morale. He also signed off on making some modifications to my braces to adapt to my improving ability to use my legs. I also met with my urologist about my bladder issues, and he had some thoughts about medication that might improve my condition.

The next two weeks were a very busy time working with Phillip and Bruce in preparation for our deposition on Thursday, February 4, 2010. I didn't realize it initially but found out that Sam would be deposed along with me about everything leading up to the epidural injection and the disastrous results. Fortunately, I did have some delightful interruptions to my work on preparing for the deposition. Mickey Freeman invited me to speak to a night class he taught on marketing at the University of

Arkansas in Little Rock. I loved talking to students about the marketing process. It had been my life's work, mostly in the banking business, and it was fun to share experiences and successes resulting from properly designed and well-targeted marketing projects. It was a nice break from all the anxiety of preparing for a deposition.

The week of the deposition, we met with the McMaths on Monday and again on Wednesday. Phillip did most of the pre-deposition preparation with us, and Bruce took the lead on the actual deposition. We spent a good deal of time going through 350 pages of Dr. X's deposition plus other materials related to the lawsuit. On Thursday morning at eight thirty, we met with Phillip and Bruce at their offices, and then at nine o'clock we went into their boardroom for the actual deposition. There was a court reporter on hand to record everything, along with three attorneys for the other side. There was one attorney representing the clinic where Dr. X was employed at the time, in addition to two other attorneys representing Dr. X himself. I was surprised that a new attorney whom we had not met replaced the lead attorney who was very involved in Dr. X's deposition. It seemed strange to me that a new attorney would be the one conducting most of the deposition, and Dr. X was not present.

They started the process with basic questions about age, physical condition, work experience, and other facts about Sam and me. The two attorneys representing Dr. X grilled me mostly but also quizzed Sam for about ninety minutes about events leading up to and immediately after the epidural injection. The attorney for the clinic asked a few questions, mostly to clarify a point or two. It was a fairly straightforward process with no real surprises for us, but there was one gotcha that caught the attention of the other side. Amazingly, we had received absolutely no disclosures of any kind, either verbally or in writing, about the risks that might be involved with this procedure. Neither the clinic nor the doctor asked me to sign anything. Dr. X seemed eager to move ahead with the procedure and didn't have his nurse or anyone give me any disclosures. I think they already knew we had received no disclosures of risk, but they wanted to make sure, so they presented me with the clinic's standard disclosure form for this procedure and asked if I had ever seen it before. I told them I had and pulled out the same blank form, which the clinic had mailed to us approximately ten days after I was paralyzed. When I pulled out the form and told them when we received it, the attorney for the clinic visibly winced and turned his head away. The attorneys for Dr. X tried to show no emotion, but it was obvious they knew that the lack of any disclosure was a major issue. After going over in great detail what happened and my time at Baptist Rehabilitation Institute, I asked for a break and broke down and cried. Sam helped me get over this and refocus so we could go on with the deposition. We finally finished up at five thirty, and I was worn out, physically exhausted, and mentally spent. We visited briefly with Bruce afterward, and he thought it went very well for our side. Now the next step was to get prepared for the trial.

The next week we had snow, which in Little Rock only happens occasionally. However, it was enough to keep us at home for most of the week, and while it was nice to get some rest, it was frustrating. In my condition, it was impossible for me to attempt to go out in conditions like this because one slip on the ice and I could be seriously hurt. After we'd spent three days in the house, the snow had melted on the street, but our driveway, which was on a steep slope didn't get much sun, and was still covered with ice. Sam went out and used a garden hoe to break up the ice, and I would slowly drive the car up as far as I could and then roll back, after which she would break up more ice on the tire tracks. It was exhausting for her and took close to thirty minutes to get the car up to the street. This was a big reminder of the difference between being on the beach two months before and now chipping ice to get out of the house. A week later, after the snow was gone, we made a trip to Dallas to see Cirque du Soleil with Greg and Amy, who was his partner for several years before they finally married. That was a nice treat and well worth the drive, which is about five hours each way.

March 4 was the second anniversary of mom's death, and Debbie called to talk. I think both of us were well past our grieving for mom, but she was a powerful force in our lives, and it was nice to share some family stories with Deb. Also that week, I got my haircut and came across a magazine about places to retire with a cover story about Charlotte County, Florida. After our vacation on the beach in December and then the recent snow, it was tempting to think about living in a tropical climate year-round. I didn't say anything about the article to Sam until I had some time to think about it. Like my dad, I had grown up and lived most of my life in Little Rock. I loved the city, we had a wonderful house, and I had many very good friends. However, two and a half years ago, our lives had changed dramatically. I could no longer do many of the things I loved, especially biking and running with my friends. Also, it was still very difficult for me to do a lot of normal activities, due partly to my lack of mobility, but mostly because of my bowl and bladder issues. I was starting to get a little more control and sensation in my bladder but still wet my pants from time to time. I had experimented some with a leg bag attached to a catheter, but it was not comfortable and required me to wear long pants, which was another issue. Getting slacks on and off over my braces was a struggle, and I had to resort to relaxed-fit, lightweight, warm-up pants. Eventually, I found some nylon slacks that looked better, but even those required me to take off my braces to put the pants on, and then I needed help to put the braces back on. This was another one of the many things I once took for granted that now was a major effort to accomplish. Also at this time, we learned that the Spinal Column Commission needed me to return the wheelchair, which they had lent me two years ago. I was surprised I hadn't heard from them earlier, and I knew it was time we bought our own. A lightweight, easily transportable wheelchair is not cheap, but it was what we needed so that Sam would be able to load and unload it into and out of the car. We had a sales rep from one of the medical supply houses recommended by Baptist Rehab come out and measure me for a new chair. Chairs like this offer lots of custom options, including quick-release, lightweight wheels, choice of colors, and different seat and brake configurations, which was very helpful. Costs can run from two to three thousand dollars, depending on the type of chair, and insurance won't cover much of that. But this was what I needed and was something I expected to use for a long time.

After sleeping on the idea of even considering picking up and moving to coastal Florida, I told Sam about the magazine article and suggested she pick it up from the hairdresser. I enjoyed the Gulf Coast and loved boating. There is something inviting about the smell of salt air and the sound of water lapping against the hull of a boat. Sam and I both liked fresh seafood and enjoyed the mild climate of southwestern Florida, so maybe it was something for us to think about. The magazine article mentioned Charlotte County being one of the most affordable places to live on the coast and having convenient access to the water. The article included an interview with a real estate agent, and I went online and looked up the firm. As it turned out, there was a retired bank marketing director who worked at the real estate company, and since I had a similar working background, I decided to call him. Tom Thrasher had lived in Homestead, Florida, for many years before retiring and moving to Charlotte County and working part-time in real estate. Tom and his wife, Connie, turned out to be delightful people and a prime source of information about the area. Tom even volunteered to contact the local chamber of commerce and have them send us some information. I told him we hadn't made any big decisions but appreciated his help. In the meantime, we had a lot of other things on our plate.

We finally had a firm court date coming up in a month, and the McMaths had found and interviewed a doctor in the New Orleans area who they thought would be an impressive expert witness for us. The doctor had a long history in the field of epidural spinal injections and had at one time taught doctors how to properly perform the procedure. He had reviewed the fluoroscope films from the procedure and was confident that he knew what went wrong and believed Dr. X should have aborted the procedure early on in the process. In the meantime, with the trial date less than a month away, Bruce and Phillip were baffled by the lack of attention and action by the attorneys on the other side. They didn't appear to be prepared and were not responding to our requests for information. Bruce suspected they were going to ask for a delay in the trial because they were not prepared, but they had yet to take any action. In the middle of this process, I continued my workouts and was making some progress. In addition to my regular workouts, I added an occasional spin class with Carla, and Anne was pleased to find increased feeling in my left calf muscle. They both were very supportive and continued to remind me that while my recovery was slow, we were still seeing improvements, and that was important. Anne frequently said to me that in any recovery process like this, it is very common for the body to plateau at times, but that was not the case with me.

Shortly after reading the article about Charlotte County and visiting with Tom Thrasher, I had a session with Jane Roark and brought up the idea of maybe moving after the legal process was finished. I wanted her input on making such a major change in our lives and also wanted to make sure I wasn't running away from something. Surprisingly, she was very supportive of the idea and said after what Sam and I had been through, a change of place might be a very positive thing. While I had many friends in Little Rock and worked with first-rate therapists and trainers, I was starting to do some serious online research about the Charlotte County area. But first we had major legal issues to resolve, and there was no predicting how long that might take.

With the trial only three weeks away, Bruce was finally able to make progress in setting a date for the opposition to meet him in New Orleans to depose our expert witness. After the deposition of our witness, Bruce called us before flying back to tell us that it went very well and that he could tell that the opposing attorney realized they had some serious issues to address. That night after Bruce returned to Little Rock, he got a call from one of the attorneys representing Dr. X informing him that they intended to ask the judge to postpone the trial date because they needed more time to prepare. Bruce called again the next day to tell us he thought the judge would probably grant the delay. Damn!

A couple of days after we heard about the potential trial delay, a film crew spent the day with us, filming me working out and then interviewing

Sam and me at home about what we had been through and how my injury had dramatically changed our lives. It was an emotional, exhausting day for us, especially the interview. The lady conducting the interview was very empathetic and more than once broke down in tears. All I could think at the time was that hopefully this video would be beneficial when shown in a courtroom, if we ever get there.

After all this, Sam and I booked a room at the Stagecoach Inn across from Oaklawn Park Race Track for a couple of fun days at the horse races. Mickey and Patti came over on Saturday to join us for the day, and we had a terrific time together. We didn't win any money, but we did relax and think about something other than therapy and legal issues. When we returned home, we had a lot of mail waiting for us about Punta Gorda, Florida. In a follow-up conversation with Tom Thrasher, I told him what we were interested in, including boating. Tom thought Punta Gorda, the only incorporated city in Charlotte County, would be something we should look at. As we found out, Charlotte Harbor covers two hundred square miles with lots of small islands, beaches, and what appeared to be interesting places to explore. It is protected from the gulf by a series of barrier islands, and this made for good fishing and boating in the area. Punta Gorda is right on the bay, and the small town with its canal system looked interesting.

The last week of March was busy for us. Bruce McMath came to visit us at the house and go over where we stood. All the details, including some follow-up on the deposition with our expert witness, were wrapped up, and it appeared he would be a strong advocate for us when and if we went to trial. That was the good news. Bruce then informed us that the trial date had been pushed back by a year to the next February! That was painful to hear. However, as part of the attorneys' discussions with the judge about the trial date, Bruce pushed hard for a court-ordered mediation with both parties, and he had one tentatively set with a professional mediator for June. At this time, I really wanted to tell my story in open court and warn people about the risks of this seemingly "routine procedure." Again, Bruce reminded us that it would be a long and very difficult trial, and he had high hopes for getting a settlement. Sam and I wanted to find closure, but we weren't going to walk away from the fight. Still, the thought of dragging it out for another year was very hard to take. And of course, this is what insurance companies want. The longer they can drag things out, the more it wears on the plaintiffs, and the easier it becomes to settle out of court.

In the meantime, we needed something to look forward to, so Sam and I had serious discussions about taking a hard look at Punta Gorda. The more research we did online, the better we liked the possibility. I didn't know whether I could leave Little Rock, but I told Sam I thought we should make a trip to Punta Gorda and spend a few weeks renting a house with a pool on a canal. I wanted to get a feel for living there, shopping in the stores, eating in local restaurants, and learning as much as we could about the area. And if we were going that far, why not add on two weeks on the beach in Sanibel, which was only an hour away from Punta Gorda. Since it was the off-season, we were able to find a nice house to rent in Punta Gorda at a reasonable cost, and also were able to rent the condo in Sanibel we had enjoyed so much back in December. It all came together much more easily than we anticipated, and we planned to arrive at the rental house on April 21 for three weeks.

Before leaving again for Florida, we had our annual family weekend at Oaklawn Park for the races. Debbie and David flew down from Buffalo, and Greg and Amy drove up from Dallas for the long weekend. Our dear friend Meredythe Kimbrough also drove up from Dallas and brought bunny ears for the girls to wear on Saturday since Easter was that Sunday. It was one of the best times I could recall with everyone. Sam and I didn't do well picking horses but still had a terrific time. Greg and Amy hit three trifectas on Saturday and also had two winners bet across the board with good payoffs. I was fortunate to recoup some of my early losses with a very nice exacta in the feature race. Overall, everyone enjoyed themselves with lots of fun cheering on the horses and enjoying

Oaklawn's legendary corned beef sandwiches along with a few adult beverages.

With only a couple of weeks to go before leaving on our second Florida trip in only five months, we had a lot to do. I continued my regular workout and therapy schedule and continued to make good progress. My therapists, especially Anne Miskin, were continuing to see positive signs. Anne had been working hard for months on trying to get some flexibility in my coccyx (tail bone), and it was finally beginning to move a little. We were confident this would help open up the neural pathways in the lower half of my body, and it seemed to be working.

I was still anxious about our trip and the possibility of moving, but I was also excited. The combination of excitement and anxiety was making it hard to relax and get the sleep I needed. Sam and I agreed that we were not in a position to make any big decisions until we settled our lawsuit, but I thought it might be helpful to talk with Greg and Mickey Freeman about the possibilities. At this point, we had not discussed the idea with anyone except Jane, my psyche therapist. I talked to Greg first to get his input, and to my surprise, he thought at this point there wasn't much keeping us in Little Rock and asked why we hadn't thought about this before. He talked about how much fun I had on my trips to Apalachicola and said this sounded like a great idea. I was concerned about being farther from him, but he told me he would love to fly to Florida and visit us there. Mickey and I had a boys' night out at the ballpark scheduled a couple of days later, and I had the same conversation with him. This was also the first time to test out my expensive, new, lightweight wheelchair. Getting it in and out of the SUV was easy, and I loved how fast and easy to maneuver it was. Like Greg, Mickey was also very supportive and said that after all my trips to Apalachicola, he thought I would move there. We discussed my concerns over missing good friends, and Mickey pointed out that with my outgoing personality, I could make friends anywhere, just like I did in Shreveport, plus he and Patti would love to come visit us on the coast. He added that it wasn't like I would never make some trips back to Arkansas. It was extremely comforting to me to find that two of the people I was closest to were so supportive. Greg and Mickey both commented on how much my life had changed since I was paralyzed, and they agreed that Sam and I should take care of ourselves first and do what we thought was the best thing for us.

Thirty-Six

Discovering Punta Gorda, Florida

W e took three leisurely days to drive down to Punta Gorda. The car was packed to the brim with clothes, two beach chairs and an umbrella, plus my wheelchair and all my bathroom materials. Leaving home for several weeks was like organizing a major expedition, but Sam did a great job of taking care of everything. I could pick out clothes and pack a few things, but she had to do all the loading and unloading. I was fortunate just to get myself from one place to another.

Pulling off the interstate and driving into Punta Gorda was a treat. The city has a long history, dating to the late 1800s, when it was the farthest south anyone could travel by train in the country. At that time, it was a major shipping point for cattle going to Cuba, and fish and produce going to Key West, St. Petersburg, Mobile, and New Orleans. The highway off the interstate took us right through the heart of downtown with its brick streets lined with palm trees, quaint buildings, and historic homes. City leadership had obviously done a good job of protecting its history and developing linear parks along the waterfront for recreation. We easily found our rental house, and it was better than we expected. The back opened up onto a pool with a canal just steps away.

On our second day, we met Tom Thrasher and a real estate agent he recommended to show us around Punta Gorda. It was tough to leave the lanai and pool; and while we weren't interested in buying anything we wanted to look at some houses and get a feel for the area. The agent was a nice woman but didn't seem to grasp what we might be looking for. Fortunately, the lady we rented the house from kept trying to get us to meet with a real estate agent she had used for years, buying and selling property throughout Charlotte County. She introduced us to Jeff Cardillo who turned out to be a wonderful resource for everything about the area. After walking through three or four houses, he understood what we might be interested in and lined up several properties to visit. We enjoyed shopping at the local Publix grocery store, which had a wide selection of fresh fruit and produce, bread and pastries baked fresh daily, and of course seafood, all at favorable prices. Tom told us about the Punta Gorda Club as a workout facility, and we checked it out. It was significantly smaller than the Little Rock Athletic Club, but we believed it would be fine for our needs. During our first week in town, we tried out a new restaurant almost every night. There were lots of options, all locally owned. Of course, the seafood was terrific, and Laishley's Crab House had not only excellent seafood but also a spectacular view of Charlotte Harbor from their second-story deck.

Our second week in town, we met Tom and Connie Thrasher on top of the Wyvern hotel for drinks and dinner. From the bar on the Wyvern roof, we could see the whole area with a 360-degree view. It was a beautiful spot to meet them and enjoy the view. They are delightful people and were excited to hear about our exploration of Punta Gorda.

After we had our fill of looking at property in the area, we decided to drive over and explore Gasparilla Island. Tom and Connie had talked about what an interesting place it was, and Jeff also suggested we take a day to see the island. Gasparilla is only a six-and-a-half-mile-long very narrow barrier island, which borders the gulf on one side and Charlotte Harbor on the other. Boca Grande is the town on the island, and it is very quaint. It is so small that while I was standing at the main intersection in town, a driver pulled up and wanted to know where Boca Grande was, and I said, "You are there." He wanted to know where the main part of the town was, and I told him he was in the middle of town! Services are limited on the island, and they don't have a gas station. Consequently, most of the locals use golf carts for transportation, and many of them are customized in a variety of configurations to look like sports cars, pick-up trucks, and other fun designs. It's also the most expensive property in the area. Every Christmas, the entire George Bush family comes to the island to stay at the historic Gasparilla Inn and play golf, go fishing, and enjoy the laid-back island lifestyle.

No trip to Punta Gorda would be complete without a tour of Charlotte Harbor on one of the tour boats at Fisherman's Village. At one time, the village was a long pier out into the harbor, which originally had fish houses where local fishermen could sell their catches. After Hurricane Charley destroyed a lot of the village in 2004, it was rebuilt into an open-air mall with rental units on the upper level, along with restaurants and a wide variety of shops on the lower level. Fisherman's Village is on the water and includes a newly rebuilt marina with over a hundred boat slips, along with several tour boats, and it has become a major tourist destination right in the heart of town.

Sam and I enjoyed our stay in Punta Gorda, but it was time to move over to Sanibel for two and a half weeks on the beach. We had a very positive visit and found everyone in the city—including store clerks, waiters, our land lady, real estate agents, and other locals we met—to be lovely people with a positive attitude. And, of course, Tom and Connie felt like good friends by the time we left. In fact, we enjoyed their company so much that we invited them to come over to Sanibel and stay with us to enjoy the beach and our lovely condo.

At the end of our stay in Punta Gorda, I wrote down the following observations about where I was in my life and the possibilities of moving, which would be an enormous task. While I wasn't ready to commit to anything as long as the legal process was slowly moving ahead, I was beginning to think seriously about our long-term plans.

I have done most of the activities I have wanted to do in life—sailing, triathlons, multi-day bike tours with friends, bareboat chartering in the Caribbean, hiking in Sedona, and more. Now, in the last chapters of my life, while I am crippled and hurt, I have Sam, the love of my life. She is someone to share the rest of my days with, and why not do it here, in a mild climate, in a very pretty town with nice people.

After we moved into the condo on the beach in Sanibel, I took some time to reexamine my condition. I was worried that my progress was slowing down. Above the knee, my legs were improving slowly, but below the knee, I still had major problems. Without my knee-length support hose, the lower part of my legs looked like skin and bone. I did get in the pool at our rental house and at the condo several times to practice walking with sandals on both feet and an ankle foot orthotic (AFO) on the right leg. In chest-deep water, I gained enough buoyancy to balance fairly well by keeping my hands in the water to help me move around. I tried this once without the AFO, and the right ankle would not support me. Surprisingly, the left foot and ankle worked well and could support my weight while in the water. But both feet still dropped at the ankle, and on dry land, I had to have an AFO on my left leg and a brace on my right leg for support. Walking on the beach in braces and canes, I found that my balance was improving, but I was beginning to realize I would never have use of my bowel and bladder again. It was frustrating, but I would just have to learn how to manage those issues.

Tom and Connie joined us for a couple of days on the beach, which was a lot of fun. After some beach time, we invited them to join us for a kayak tour of the mangrove islands in the Ding Darling National Wildlife Refuge. Sam and I enjoyed our previous guided kayak tour of the area, and we knew Tom and Connie would have fun exploring with us. The guys who managed the kayak and canoe concession were very helpful getting me in and out of the kayak. Getting in was pretty easy, but I never could have gotten out of the boat without a guy on each side helping pull me up. It's a beautiful place, and fortunately it was protected from development in the 1940s, largely through the work of Pulitzer Prize-winning political cartoonist J. N. "Ding" Darling. He spent winters in the area and led the campaign to protect the natural wildlife habitat on Sanibel Island and in other areas around the country. The refuge is part of the largest undeveloped mangrove ecosystem in the country and is one of Florida's finest natural treasures.

It was tough to leave Sanibel after two and a half beautiful, warm weeks, but it was time to head back to Little Rock. We carried home Sam's growing collection of shells, plenty of photos, and wonderful memories. For us, it was the right vacation at the right time.

Thirty-Seven

Progress and Setbacks

June 2010 was a very busy time. I had emailed Dr. Rehab from Sanibel
about moving to permanent, custom-made braces, and he agreed
it was time. Rick Fleetwood and Gary Owens at Snell Orthotics were
incredibly helpful in this process and went to work right away on new
braces. Also, as I came to grips with living in braces and canes for the
foreseeable future, I knew it was time to start working on downsizing
my clothing, much of which I wouldn't need anymore, including dress
slacks, suits, dress shirts, ties, and of course, all my biking gear. What I
needed was casual pants and shorts that were easy to put on over my
braces and comfortable for walking.

Sam and I settled into our regular workout routine at the athletic
club and were pleased to find that our latest vacation actually seemed to
help my progress. I had some good workouts and was practicing walking
with one cane next to the railing on the track at the club. My walking
was smoother and more balanced, and I was able to take ten to twelve
steps on the track without having to touch the railing. By the middle of
June, I was able to make it all the way around from one corner of the
track to the opposite corner without having to grab the railing. A week
later, I did another lap with one cane, but this time, I kept going after
the railing stopped near the weight machine area, and I made it all the
way around to where I started. That was meaningful progress.

At this time, Anne believed that my feet had more energy and their skin color was much improved. Carla was trying out new exercises for me, and things were looking up. Also, Carla and I started meeting down at the river once a week for a bike ride together. She was very patient and a lot of help. She also encouraged me to get back in the pool and gave me some exercises to do in the water. I tried to work out in the pool at least once a week and, on one occasion, tested my swimming ability by doing ten laps in the pool. I was very slow, and it was hard to swim properly without use of my legs, but I still completed ten laps.

In spite of positive signs of progress, I was still frustrated at times. I developed a sore on my left shin and was having terrible problems with the right anklebone rubbing on the new brace. Every time I put weight on my right leg, the right ankle and foot rolled outward, which meant the braces would have to be adjusted again. And then we had bad news from the McMaths about our upcoming mediation in July. As usual, the opposing side once again asked for a delay, and the mediation was pushed back a couple of weeks to July 20. We hoped this would be the last major delay. When everything seemed like it was going so well, I frequently would get knocked down again. I had sores on both legs, and now the next step in the lawsuit was delayed. Because of this and other issues, Dr. Rehab wanted me to get off my feet for a few days and back in the wheelchair. On June 25, I wrote in my journal the following:

Damn, this is a terrible setback. Going back to the wheelchair is devastating. I am truly frightened! What do I do now? I don't know if I am ever going to be able to live any kind of a worthwhile life.

For the next couple of days, I had a hard time mustering the energy to get out of bed. Another visit to the doctor helped, along with pain medication for my back. Also, backing off of my workouts helped some. Anne thought this was not all bad. She believed that the pain I started feeling in my back was a sign that things were waking up, especially around the base of my spine where I was paralyzed. She believed this was mostly good news.

We drove to Dallas to celebrate the Fourth of July weekend with Greg and Amy and had a very good time. It was apparent that I would never be able to ride a two-wheel bike again. So, before the trip, I had Chainwheel overhaul my mountain bike and took it with us to give to Greg as a surprise. There is a nice bike path near his house, and I knew he would enjoy riding the bike. We had fun playing in Greg's pool, but I had trouble getting out of the pool and had to ask for help. I hated being so helpless. I always believed I didn't need anyone to help me. I thought I could take care of myself on my own, but no more.

After a fun weekend with Greg and friends, I felt good and was ready to get back to therapy. My bladder was beginning to develop more sensation, and while I suspected I would not be able to urinate again, if I could get enough sensation where I could tell when the bladder is full, that would be a blessing. I thought my bladder problems were partly related to being anxious about being out in public and wetting my pants. If I could just learn to relax, I knew things would get better, but that was easier said than done. I was still having some problems walking, with a little pain in my right hip, but was on the mend.

Thirty-Eight

Face-to-Face with Dr. X, Attorneys, Insurance Executives, and a Professional Mediator

W e were fast approaching the mediation date, and it looked like it was finally going to happen. The opposition had not asked for another delay and they did have an expert witness, whom the McMaths were ready to depose. However, prior to the deposition, the witness backed out for "personal reasons," whatever that meant. Now all our attention was focused on the upcoming mediation. We had been looking forward to the mediation date for six months since the judge had agreed to delay the trial until the following February. We were hopeful to settle this but were also prepared to be disappointed, and in my mind, I wanted to go to trial and tell my story in a public forum so people would be aware how dangerous this procedure could be in the wrong hands. I seriously wanted my day in court. However, Bruce and Phillip counseled me several times on how difficult and time-consuming a trial would be, and they told us several times that it's impossible to tell what a jury might do. If we could settle this without a trial, we could get on with our lives. The night before the mediation, I was anxious and didn't sleep much.

I had to get up about every two hours to go to the bathroom to urinate and had trouble going back to sleep afterward.

Mediation, Tuesday, July 20, 2010

This was one of the longest days of my life and also one of the most difficult. Years later, I can remember it vividly as if it were just a couple of days ago. We started at nine thirty in the morning in the boardroom of the mediator's office with myself, Sam, Bruce and Phillip McMath, and the man who produced our video on one side of a long table. On the other side was Dr. X with his lawyer, plus a lawyer representing his former clinic, along with two executives from Dr. X's insurance company. One was the Arkansas representative for the insurance company, and the other was a senior executive from their office in Nashville, Tennessee, who we assumed had the ability to make a decision on settling the lawsuit. While the lawyers did most of the talking, the truth is, the key decisions were going to be made by the senior insurance executive. At the head of the table was the mediator who explained how the process worked. After some opening comments, he told us that each group would retire to a separate office and he would meet with each group and present their financial offers to the other side.

The doctor's attorney opened the initial discussion in the boardroom by saying that he wanted everyone to understand that we were not there to beat up on the doctor, which I thought was a strange comment. Everyone in the room already knew this process was not about assigning blame. This was an opportunity to settle the lawsuit monetarily without the time and expense of going to court. Bruce agreed and said we didn't intend to attack the doctor, and then explained the rationale for the video, which demonstrated how dramatically this injury had changed our lives and what I was doing to recover. Obviously, showing the video at this point demonstrated to the opposition what we planned to use in front of a jury. Bruce and Phillip believed the video was a powerful tool that vividly showed how drastically my injury had affected our lives. Nothing tells a story better than showing pictures of the injured party prior to and after the injury. The video of me walking with braces, using a wheelchair, and working out was very powerful. The video ended with Sam and me discussing how much my paralysis had changed our lives forever.

The mediation was somewhat like buying a house. One side, the seller, states a price, and the buyer makes an offer. If the buyer is serious about buying the house, he or she puts forth a strong offer and hopes the seller will either accept the offer or counter with something in between the initial price and the offer. However, in a medical malpractice suit, while the injured party may make what they think is a reasonable offer, the defendants' insurance company will usually respond with a much smaller amount. Obviously, the insurance company's goal is to pay as little as they can and draw the process out as long as they can. They would be happy to wait until the day before the trial begins and then make a reasonable offer. On the opposite side, the injured party would like to settle and get on with their lives.

Sam and I, along with the McMaths, settled into our separate office and left the opposing side in the boardroom. We discussed what we thought was a reasonable offer based on the McMaths' substantial experience in this process. In Arkansas, the dollar amount of damages in a malpractice lawsuit has limits due to lobbying by the medical profession, which pushed a bill through the state legislature limiting settlements in these cases. In response to our offer, the opposition came back with an offer of less than 10 percent of what we proposed. Their offer would not have covered our substantial out-of-pocket expenses since the injury, much less anything for pain and suffering. It was a ridiculous offer and indicated to me they were not serious about trying to come to an agreement. The McMaths calmed me down and explained that this was how the process worked and that it would take some time before they would put forth a serious offer. I was still pissed off but trusted our faithful attorneys, and we continued the process on through lunch and into the afternoon. It was beginning to appear that we would never reach an agreement, and I was ready to leave. However, the professional mediator proposed that we make one last offer, and he would tell the opposition that this was our best offer and that if they didn't respond with something more meaningful, this would probably end the mediation. They took a while to respond to our offer, and when their final, meager amount was presented to us, I exploded. I slammed my hand down on the table, stood up and passionately said in front of the mediator and the McMath brothers, "F—— this! I've had enough! I'm leaving, and I am going to tell my story in a public courtroom!" At this point, Bruce McMath jumped in and tried to calm me down. It was obvious that he understood my frustration, and he told me again that he thought we could still settle this without having to go to court. I didn't see any possibility of settling and told him so. However, the mediator had a suggestion. In cases in which it appears that both sides are unable to come to an agreement, he could come up with an offer and put it in an envelope, which he would give to both parties. If either party said no, then there was no settlement and the mediation was over, which was just fine with me. Bruce had been keeping track of every offer and counteroffer throughout the day and asked Sam and me to consider what our absolute bottom line might be. We spent some time on that discussion, which also involved the McMaths getting paid for their work and expenses. Bruce was crunching numbers and said to his brother, "Phillip, if we gave up our expenses, we could offer to settle for this amount." Before Phillip could respond, I slammed my hand down on the table again and said, "No, you are not going to give up your expenses! You are going to get what you are due." Bruce went back to crunching numbers and came up with something he thought might work. It was now after five o'clock, and all of us were worn out. The mediator went to work and came up with a number to present to both sides. The amount was lower than I wanted, but we thought we could live with it, and much to my surprise, around six o'clock, the opposition also accepted.

At this point, all we needed was for both groups to meet back in the boardroom for the lawyers to sign off on the paperwork. While the attorneys were doing the paper work, Dr. X got up and walked to a corner of the room and stared out the window with absolutely no emotion. Then he came back to the table, picked up his briefcase, and walked out without a word to anyone. After he left, the attorney representing the clinic came over to me and said, "Randy don't think twice about the settlement amount. Forget this whole process and get on with your life and continue your recovery." And then, as the insurance people left the room, the senior executive paused and said to me, "I hope you can use this to continue to make progress with your recovery." They didn't have to say anything to me, but it was obvious they felt sorry for me and hoped I could get on with my life. Bruce and Phillip finished up the paperwork, reassured us we had done the right thing, and said they would be back in touch in a few days. It was six thirty when we left the building, and after nine very long hours, we were all worn out, but it was finally over. As we went to bed that night, I turned to Sam and asked her if it was really over. She reassured me it was. I asked her again the next morning and again she reiterated that it was all over. That day I wrote in my journal:

We are relieved and feel like we have a new lease on life. Today is the first day of the rest of our lives. I feel a heavy weight has been lifted off my shoulders. Now we intend to focus on living life to the fullest. Sam and I feel like we are starting our life over again, and we are going to have a very good time!

The day after the mediation, we slept in and relaxed. We really needed the rest. Then, on Thursday, we called Greg to tell him the good news. He said we had to celebrate, so he got in his car and said he would be in Little Rock in time to meet Mickey and me for a boys' night out at the ballgame. Mickey and I had planned this outing some time before the mediation, and I had no idea it would be a celebration. As luck would have it, we ran into Bruce and Phillip at the ballgame and had a chance to introduce them to Greg. As I told Greg, they were so much more than just our attorneys. They were family friends who counseled us and led us through this exhausting process. I couldn't have imagined going through it without them.

Greg stayed through the weekend, and we had a great time. He and I ran some errands and bought some workout clothes for me, along with other stuff. After he left, we called Jeff Cardillo, our Charlotte County real estate agent, to tell him we were planning another trip to Punta Gorda. He immediately recognized our phone number and said, "Randy Oates, I have your name on the top of a yellow pad as a reminder to call you. A couple of days ago, I walked through a house that is exactly what you are looking for. It's a little more than you wanted to spend, but it's a great house. I don't think it will be on the market very long. Are you coming down here anytime in the next month or so?" Sam and I told him we still had several things to take care of in Little Rock but hoped to drive down to Punta Gorda in the next seven to ten days. Jeff offered to send us online information and pictures of the house, along with several others he thought we might like. As soon as we got off the phone with Jeff, we called the lady who had previously rented her house to us and asked if it was available. She was pleased to hear from us again and said that, during the summer, the house was empty, so we could rent it for as much time as we wanted, and she would give us the same monthly rate and prorate it for the time we needed. She was also tickled to hear we were working with Jeff, whom she had recommended.

After getting over the trauma of the mediation, we spent some time talking seriously about moving to Punta Gorda. This was an enormous decision for me. I was a second generation to be born and grow up in Little Rock and lived there most of my life. I spent a few years in Houston, Seattle, and Shreveport, but I always came back to Little Rock. It's a lovely city, and I had lots of good friends there. It was also where I eventually retired from my banking career with Bank of the Ozarks. As my accountant said when I discussed our potential move with him, "Randy, you can't leave Little Rock. You know so many people in town; you can pick up the phone and call anyone." However, the more Sam and I discussed this major change in our life, we thought that in many ways it was time for a fresh start. My paralysis dramatically changed our lives, and I was unable to do many of the things I enjoyed so much about

Little Rock. I had to put the fun I'd had sailing, running, and biking with friends behind me. I was beginning to believe it was time for a fresh start, and Punta Gorda had so much to offer us. We loved the thought of being on the Gulf Coast with mild weather and the possibility of having a boat in a canal behind the house. In addition to our accountant, we also visited with our attorneys, our investment broker, and our local real estate agent. Dorothy Willoughby had found a beautiful home for us in Little Rock, just a couple of years before my paralysis. We told her we were thinking about moving, and she reminded us that the market was depressed and she didn't know if we could get all of our money out of the house. We understood that, but we also knew that the Florida real estate market was even more depressed, so it was a good time to buy in Charlotte County. We told our key contacts that we had not made a decision yet and asked everyone we told to keep our plans confidential, but we wanted their input on a potential move.

It was a busy time, but we were getting excited about the trip back to Florida. We spent a good deal of time researching the houses Jeff sent us online, and he was right. The house he thought we would be interested in looked exactly like what we wanted. It was beautifully landscaped, had a pool with a spa, and was on a canal close to Ponce Inlet with easy access to Charlotte Harbor. Frankly, online, it almost looked too good for the price, and we wondered if there was something negative about the neighborhood. We talked to Greg a couple of times before we left for the trip, and he said that when talking to us about the house and Punta Gorda, we sounded like kids preparing for Christmas. Mickey stopped by the day before we left to wish us bon voyage. We showed him the house online, along with some of the other houses Jeff sent us. He was excited for us and said he and Patti would definitely come for a vacation if we did move. The support we received from Mickey, Greg, Bruce and Phillip McMath, was very encouraging.

Thirty-Nine

Moving in a New Direction

On Friday, July 30, 2010, only ten days after the mediation, we took off on our grand adventure. Again we decided to make it a leisurely trip, taking two and a half days to drive to Punta Gorda. It still was a tiring trip, especially going through Georgia in the rain. Turning off the interstate at the Punta Gorda exit immediately after crossing the Peace River was a relief. Again we drove through the heart of town and were as impressed as we were on our first visit with the pretty and quaint downtown area, with its brick streets lined with palm trees. From there, we continued through the historic homes section and decided to go out of our way to view the house that Jeff thought we would like. It was dark by then, but we still had a chance to look at the house from the street and tour the neighborhood, which was much better than we had expected. The house was beautiful at night, with lovely landscape lighting on the house and the palm trees in front. The street was very quiet because it was only one block long and ended at a street facing the rim canal, which had cul-de-sacs at both ends. Sam and I were excited about the possibilities.

Monday morning, Jeff Cardillo showed up at our rental house, and we talked about the five houses we had selected from his online site. Jeff had everything lined up, and we told him we wanted to first visit the house on St. Thomas Drive, which we had driven by the previous night. In the daylight, the house looked terrific, and when we walked through the front door, we were thrilled. Jeff was right. It was what we were looking for. On stepping into the house, the first thing we noticed was the large, open living, dining, and kitchen area looking toward the expanse of large glass sliders, which opened onto a beautiful lanai and pool. The pool was built with a raised landscaping area around the back and sides, which made the pool and lanai look like it was part of a small garden. The majority of the houses in this part of Florida are built with a screened "pool cage" covering the area to keep out the bugs, and it was connected to the roof as part of the house. This made it possible to leave all the sliders open in good weather so that the pool and lanai were an extension of the house. The view from the kitchen, dining, and living area overlooking the lanai and pool also had a view of the canal behind the house. This was the Florida lifestyle we'd hoped to find. We spent close to an hour looking over the house, and the owners, who were living in the house at the time, were very nice people and eager to show us around. After we finished asking questions and looking around, we then toured the other four houses on our list, none of which came close to the St. Thomas house. Jeff drove us back to our rental place, and we had a long talk about making an offer. We decided to make one more visit that day to St. Thomas to take pictures and get a few measurements of the rooms. After touring the house a second time, we tried not to show our excitement, but we thought this would be perfect for us. When we went back to our rented house, I was worn out from all the walking and standing, but we wanted to move ahead and talked with Jeff about making an offer. He said this house wouldn't be on the market long, and with the decline of the housing market, the house was favorably priced. We came up with what we thought was a strong offer, and that evening, he delivered it to the owners' agent. Jeff expected that they might counter our offer, but he felt it was good enough that they might accept it. Sure enough, the next morning, they accepted our offer. We were going to move to the Sunshine State.

Then we met with Jeff to discuss what needed to be done next on the purchase. He lined up an inspection for the following day, and we started making notes on the many things we needed to accomplish over the next week. Wednesday we met with the home inspector, which went well. Then we had a very nice meeting with the owners. They said, "We wanted you to have this house. It has been a place of healing and a time of recovery for us." They also indicated that they had found a condo in town to buy and wanted to move ahead quickly on turning the house over to us. As it turned out, they were actually ready to move much sooner than we were. They provided a great deal of information about the house, along with improvements they had made over the last five years, including all-new appliances in the kitchen and laundry room, which stayed with the house. The owners were very helpful over the next several days in providing a list of companies they used for the pool,. phone, Internet, television, home insurance, and pest control, along with documentation on the appliances that went with the house. They also provided good information about the area and the neighborhood, and encouraged us to call and come back anytime we needed to check out anything on the house. This was very helpful, as we were planning to buy some new furniture for the living area in the house, and we wanted to remodel the closets in the master bedroom to use the space more efficiently. Plus we were going to have to make some changes in the bathroom to accommodate my needs. Of course, Jeff continued to be an excellent resource for anything we needed to know about Punta Gorda. He and his wife, Ellen, had lived in Charlotte County for twenty-plus years, and they became great friends.

Thursday was another full day for the Oates family. We visited three furniture stores, which Jeff and the owners suggested and found a designer at Bacon's Furniture who turned out to be another valuable resource. She agreed to meet us at the house the next week to help us decide on furniture for the living area and arrangements in the house for our furniture that we planned to move from Little Rock. That evening, Tom and Connie Thrasher invited us to join them for "Thirsty Thursday" at the Stone Crabs baseball game. We had a great time with hot dogs and discounted beer, and the Crabs won a close game in the bottom of the ninth inning. More important, we had a chance to relax and get to know Tom and Connie, who became dear friends and were a big help when we moved into our new home. That evening reminded me of how much fun Mickey and I had in Little Rock at the Travelers games. It was another one of those things that made me feel good about making the move.

Friday we met with representatives from the insurance company that insured the house and then took the afternoon off to relax and regroup. It had been a whirlwind week, and we celebrated by going out to dinner at an Italian restaurant downtown that, like everything in Punta Gorda, was ten minutes or less from our rental house. Saturday we made a trip to the Apple store in Fort Myers to resolve some issues with my MacBook. The store is in an upscale, open-air shopping center, and I thought it would be helpful having an Apple store only fifty minutes from our new home. At the time, the closest Apple store to Little Rock was in Memphis or Fayetteville. The shopping center also had a Chico's store, which Sam shopped at in Little Rock, and she found some things she needed. After driving back to Punta Gorda, we had another delightful dinner at Laishley's Crab House while watching one of the many beautiful sunsets we would enjoy after we made the move.

The next week continued to be busy, as we tried to resolve as many things as we could before returning to Arkansas. We bought a dinette set and living room furniture for the house. We had enough time before moving to allow Sam and the store designer to order the fabric for the living room love seats and the dinette chairs. The designer's husband did remodeling work, and we had him work up a design for the closets in the master bedroom. We met with the owners of the house several more times, and they were most helpful about explaining how the pool, spa, and fountain worked. They also told us they would leave their records about appliances and pool information when they moved out of the house. They were moving ahead on buying the condo and hoped to move within thirty days or so. This process appeared to be moving forward more quickly than we were prepared for, as we needed to sell our house in Little Rock; but we had no regrets and knew we would enjoy the house and living Punta Gorda. Before we left for Arkansas at the end of that week, Jeff and Ellen Cardillo invited us to dinner at the fine restaurant in the Wyvern Hotel. That was very nice of them and was the beginning of a wonderful friendship. It appeared we were going to be on the road for Sam's birthday on August 15, so Tom and Connie invited us to go to dinner to celebrate her birthday at the Perfect Caper, which became our favorite restaurant for special occasions.

Forty

Conclusion

After returning home to Arkansas, we had a lot to accomplish. One of the first things we had to do was get our house ready to sell. On the drive back, we called Dorothy Willoughby and told her we needed to sell the house we had just moved into a few years before. Next we had to prepare to downsize from a 2,700 square foot house with plenty of attic storage to 2,075 square feet and no attic.

Shortly after we had returned to Little Rock, the owners contacted Jeff and indicated that they would be moving soon and would like to close on the house in early September. Wow, was that quick, and we hadn't even listed our house yet. It was beginning to look like we might be the owners of two homes at once in a slow real estate market.

Having so much to do in a short time was overwhelming at times, but we were moving ahead as quickly as we could. We started making daily trips to Goodwill to get rid of clothes and other things we didn't need. We gave away some furniture and hired a company to put most of our other furniture in an estate sale. We met with a moving company to start the planning process for our move to Florida, including packing up Sam's grandfather clock and her beautiful antique chandelier for the dining area. Moving both of these involved building custom boxes to transport them, which was not cheap. After getting rid of a lot of stuff out of the attic and throughout the house, we asked Greg if he would to come to Little Rock and haul a bunch of stuff back to Dallas. We had some things we knew he could use, and he said yes. I told him we would buy plane tickets for him and a buddy to fly up and drive a U-Haul truck back to Texas. He and his friend Dutch flew up on a Friday, and Greg wouldn't let us pay him for the tickets. The two of them spent part of Friday and most of Saturday loading the big truck with house and patio furniture, plants, tools, some clothes, and other stuff. Greg also took great pleasure in helping me, with Dutch looking on, reduce the amount of clothing in my closet by throwing away many items, which in his opinion, were either ugly or terribly out of style. I had one sweater I really liked, which he thought looked just like one of the crazy, wild sweaters that comedian Bill Cosby wore. Greg insisted I get rid of it and still kids me about it in his best Cosby voice. By Saturday afternoon, they had the truck packed as full as it could stand, and he and Dutch were happy to have all the stuff except the, according to Greg, out-of-style clothes, which went to Goodwill.

Dorothy Willoughby moved ahead quickly and got our house listed and on the market about a week before Labor Day. Labor Day weekend was our annual "Club Greg" party for family and friends at his house, and Sam and I were ready for a break from all our downsizing and packing. A relaxing, long weekend with family was just what we needed. While we were in Dallas, things quickly started moving ahead on both houses. First we got a call from Jeff confirming that the owners wanted to close on the sale of their house in early September. The next day, Dorothy called us and said she had shown the house to a couple that were very interested, and she thought they might make an offer. Two days later, Dorothy called again to tell us she had a strong cash offer on the house with no conditions, and she thought we should accept it. Sam and I were stunned. In a little less than thirty days, we had bought a house in Punta Gorda and were about to sell our house in Little Rock. Dorothy had warned us she had houses for sale on the market for over six months with practically no traffic, and now we had a solid offer on our house in only eight days. As some of my friends and family said, it was beginning to look like this move was meant to be. After we got back to Little Rock, we met with Dorothy and she informed us that the buyers wanted to close by the end of September. For the second time in the last two weeks, I thought to myself, "Wow, that was quick!"

Frequently in this process, I didn't know if we could accomplish everything we needed to do in order to move in such a short time, but we were making very good progress. I kept reminding myself of something Jane Roark said to me: "You have to cross the moat in order to get to the castle."

There were many things we knew we would miss about Little Rock, including our lovely home and neighbors, many friends, the athletic club's facilities, working with Carla and Anne, and of course my beloved Razorbacks. However, we were also excited about living in Punta Gorda and cruising around Charlotte Harbor. In the last week of August, I wrote the following in my journal:

> Sam and I believe we need a new life together, and I have been pleased with the reaction of most of my good friends to our news. It would be easier in a lot of ways to stay in a familiar place with people we know. However, we only have a limited number of years left, so why not expand our horizons and live in a place where we feel like we are on vacation. And I think we will have plenty of visitors to our new home in Punta Gorda.

It was unfortunate that we didn't have more time to say a proper good-bye to our many friends. However, we agreed to be out of our house before the end of September, and our house in Punta Gorda was going to be empty in the next couple of weeks. We were able to have a going away dinner for our therapists and a few friends at our house before leaving, and we had some individual dinners with others. But time was creeping up on us, and we couldn't see everyone we wanted to. September seemed like a blur with multiple projects, including working with two real estate agents helping us close on houses in Little Rock and Punta Gorda; working with a moving company, which never goes as well as one hopes; cutting off phone, cable, electricity, gas, etc., while setting up all those services in Punta Gorda; getting both cars serviced before the trip; and continuing our efforts to downsize by getting rid of more and more stuff.

The movers were scheduled to be at the house on Monday, September 20, 2010, to pack everything except what we were taking in the car, then load the truck and leave on Tuesday. Packing everything was a laborious project. They obviously didn't have enough people on hand to get it done in a timely manner, and it took close to twelve hours for them to finish. Then, on Tuesday, it took almost as long to pack the truck with all our stuff plus Sam's Toyota convertible. It was after nine o'clock that night when we finally left to drive to Memphis in our SUV. We stopped on the other side of Memphis at about one o'clock in the morning and collapsed in our hotel room. We planned to go out of our way on the trip to visit Apalachicola one last time and stayed on the beach again over at St. George Island. I had some wonderful memories of Apalachicola with Joe Whitesell, and I wanted to go there just once more. The schedule was for the movers to arrive in a week, so we had some time and wanted to enjoy the trip south after all we had been through over the last thirty days.

The day before we were scheduled to meet the movers in Punta Gorda, they called and said they were running behind and would be a couple of days late. Since we had a house but no furniture, we decided to drop off all the stuff we had packed in the car and go on to Captiva Island for a couple of days on the beach. Captiva is connected to Sanibel, and we thought it would be fun to explore it. Jeff Cardillo was busy the afternoon we arrived at our new house, so he had his wife Ellen bring the house keys; and she helped us unload all the stuff we didn't want to ship with the movers, which completely filled our SUV from the front seats to the back end. I don't know what we would have done without Jeff and Ellen. The movers finally arrived a few days later, and we had boxes all over the house and more in the garage. Unfortunately, on our first day of unpacking, I fell and cracked my wrist. Consequently, we got introduced to the local emergency room. Damn, after three years of being careful not to hurt myself, I fell and cracked my wrist in our new home. This meant the burden of unpacking all our stuff was on Sam, as I was using a walker again to get around the house.

Fortunately, Tom and Connie came over more than once and were an enormous help to Sam, putting up many of our paintings and much of our décor (actually, 90 percent of that stuff was Sam's, as my décor consisted of some family pictures along with old sailing and triathlon trophies). In the meantime, we had workers in the house almost every day on multiple projects including: installing an accessible commode with a handrail; patching the wall in the commode area; adding a handrail to the shower in the master bathroom; replacing fixtures for the bathroom sinks and the kitchen sink; scheduling the furniture store to deliver a new mattress for the master bedroom along with the furniture for the living room and kitchen area; hanging Sam's antique chandelier and setting up her grandfather clock; plus a dozen other things which needed to be done. Doing all this was tiring, and I was very little help, but the weather was gorgeous, and when it was all done, we knew it was worth it.

Reflections

After things finally settled down, I had some time to reflect on all we had done. Yes, leaving Little Rock was bittersweet. I loved so many things about the city, and if I hadn't been paralyzed, I probably would have spent the rest of my life there. I don't believe in such things as fate, luck, or destiny. I can accept that bad things do happen to good people. You never know what is waiting around the next corner. One false move or a single wrong turn can have life-changing results. I can't allow myself to go back and rethink or second-guess myself about the decision to have an epidural injection to relieve the incredible debilitating pain I was experiencing. There was no question that the doctor made a terrible mistake. Our expert witness who had done this procedure for many years said that based on his review of the fluoroscopes of the procedure, it was obvious the doctor should have aborted the procedure. But he didn't. It was also obvious to some experts who read the before and after

MRIs of my lower spine that I would not walk again. However, there was one doctor who gave me some small hope of recovery, and that was critical. At one time or another, all of us will be dealt a bad hand. Some hands will be worse than others. The question is, what will we do with the cards we are given? What counts is whether and how we will fight our way back. There is no rewind in life. I was fortunate to have a loving wife and family, along with many good friends to help me. I was fortunate to have been taught that I could accomplish amazing things if I worked hard enough. I was fortunate to find the right doctors, therapists, and trainers to help me. I was fortunate to believe that when the student is ready, the teacher will appear. However, it may take a couple of missteps first before you find the right teacher.

I wish I could end this book with me walking away without braces, wheelchair, canes, or a walker. Now that would be a real miracle! However, miracles are extremely rare in the case of spinal column injuries. Frankly, as more than one of my therapists would tell you, the fact I could even stand and walk with canes was a true miracle. Maybe it is. I don't know about that, but I do know you can't do this by yourself. It took a village led by my wife Sam, along with my son Greg, my dear friend Mickey, my sister Dr. Debbie, and numerous friends and therapists to heal Randy Oates. I also know that waking up every morning and telling myself, "The Healing Begins Today," was the only way I could have accomplished as much as I did.

Epilogue

I will celebrate my seventy-first birthday this October, and I still wear braces on both legs and walk with a cane in each hand. Fortunately, I am continuing to achieve some improvement, but I believe I will spend the rest of my life with canes and some support for my legs. Even so, I am continuing to gain more mobility with better posture and good balance, and I can walk as far as I need to on a reasonably flat surface. I work with a personal trainer twice a week and a craniosacral therapist, Laurie Teisinger, once a week. She studied under the same doctor as Anne Miskin and has been an excellent source of both physical and mental support. When I had to replace my braces in 2011, we were lucky to find a first-rate orthotic resource in Ft. Myers. Pete DiPaolo at Hanger Prosthetics & Orthotics had me walk up and down their hallway and do several sit-to-stands to assess my issues. He then did a great job of creating a lightweight brace that was made from a mold of my right leg below the knee. My left leg has become stronger, and I have good control of the left ankle; consequently, I am now able to use an off-the-shelf ankle-and-foot orthotic on that leg. The best news is that my bladder has developed more sensitivity, and I am having very few accidents, but it appears I will continue to need to catheterize myself for the foreseeable future.

The biggest reason for my continuing improvement with walking is directly related to our new home in Punta Gorda, Florida. I expected to continue to use my wheelchair to get around the house, as I did in

Little Rock. Sam and my therapists had tried to get me to spend less time in the wheelchair, but it was such an easy way to get around that I was reluctant to give it up. That all changed as soon as we moved into our house in Punta Gorda. The previous owners had made several improvements to the house, including putting in new carpet with a very thick pad underneath. While the carpet is nice for those who can walk around barefoot, it was so soft that it was hard for me to get around in my wheelchair. As a result, the wheelchair ended up sitting in our office, and I found myself learning to walk around the house and spending much more time on my feet. Now the only time I use the wheelchair is when we go to watch the local minor league baseball team, the Charlotte Stone Crabs. The wheelchair makes it quicker and easier for me to get to the bathrooms at the ballpark, much as it did in Little Rock. Sam was right; I needed to quit depending on the chair. As a result, after only a month in our new home, my walking and sit-to-stand started improving.

Surprisingly, in spite of my age and physical condition, I am continuing to make slow but steady progress. I have even been able to take some trips with Sam on small ships in Europe, the Mediterranean, and the South Pacific; and I have found I can get around quite well in a variety of situations. With more sensation in my bladder, it's easier to manage my bladder issues when traveling, and of course I carry a fanny pack with all my bathroom supplies everywhere we go.

We have found excellent medical resources here in Charlotte County, in spite of the fact that we live in a place with a much smaller population than Little Rock. Our new family doctor has been very empathetic regarding my situation and has referred us to several other specialists who have provided excellent care. My urologist has been particularly supportive and had me change to a new type of catheter tube, which is significantly better than the ones I had used for the previous three years.

Our move to the southwestern coast of Florida turned out to be a wonderful thing for us in many ways. Little Rock will always be very special to me, but living in a tropical climate, with a beautiful house on a canal with a boat, has been wonderful. Within a couple of days after the moving van left, while the garage still had many boxes waiting to be unpacked, one of our new neighbors, Bob Dorman, walked over while I was in the garage. He introduced himself, gave me a copy of the Punta Gorda Isles Civic Association magazine, and told us we should join the association, which offers all kinds of activities. There are multiple boating clubs in the civic association, and Bob said, "When you get a boat, you need to join the Seafarers." Bob is a past commodore of the Seafarers, a group that has regular monthly social events, along with cruises to many interesting islands, restaurants, and marinas around Charlotte Harbor. He said this would be a great way to learn our way around the area and expand our horizons on the water. Note that Bob said, "_When_ you get a boat," not "_If_ you get a boat." He automatically assumed that anyone who bought a house on a canal was of course going to have a boat—and in our case, he was right.

Meeting Bob and Toni Dorman and joining the Seafarers quickly introduced us to many new people who are now friends, and as a result we quickly developed a very active social life. Also, due to Bob volunteering me for a board position, I am now in my second full year as the Seafarers' communications director, a role that has allowed me to get to know more of the members and become more involved in the club.

Part of the reason our social life is so active here is that the majority of our friends are retired; so social outings aren't restricted to getting together on the weekends. Instead, there is always something going on, regardless of what day it is. People here like to joke that "Punta Gorda Happy Hour" starts around four thirty in the afternoon, which is when many of our social events start, and "Punta Gorda Midnight" is around nine thirty in the evening, when people start going home.

Yes, we enjoy the warm and sunny climate, new friends, great neighbors, our house, and our boat, *Sam-a-Ran*. I love exploring Charlotte Harbor on our boat, and when I am at the helm, everything seems normal, as if I am no longer a paraplegic. I put my canes behind the captain's chair, and with plenty of handholds on the boat, I can get around just fine. Of course I need a hand getting onto a dock, but I have managed amazingly well. Being at the helm of our boat is a very special time for me. In addition to *Sam-a-Ran*, I believe one of the things we enjoy the most is the relaxed and laid-back lifestyle here in Punta Gorda. About three months after moving down here, I took off my watch and put it in a drawer by the bed. I'm pretty sure it's still there, but I can't remember the last time I used it.

While I suffered greatly with continuing bouts of depression, especially in the first couple of years following my paralysis, my psychological health and overall outlook have improved significantly over the last four years. I made a conscious decision that making the move to the gulf coast of Florida would be a good opportunity to have a new start in life. Also, writing this book has been a positive activity for me. Initially it was difficult to write about the injury, but it was also cathartic in many ways to look back and see where I was seven years ago, and then reflect on where I am today. The mental aspect of the recovery process is critically important, and I have found the more positive my mental attitude the better I am able to make progress with my recovery. Also, time tends to heal many wounds. I have learned to live with my limitations and take pleasure in the many things I am able to do, which seven years ago seemed impossible.

The move to Florida has definitely been therapeutic for both of us. I love sitting out on our lanai or at our kitchen table, where I wrote most of this book, and looking out at the lush vegetation, the canal, and our boat waiting for us on the lift next to our dock. Sam and I continue to enjoy our new life here in our little bit of paradise. We enjoy it so much that we find it hard to leave to visit family and friends. As Mickey Freeman said to me on the phone recently, "You have taken a tragic mistake and used it as a catalyst to start a new life in a beautiful place." Yes, Sam and I are very lucky people. As we frequently say to each other, "We have taken lemons and turned them into lemonade."

Randy Oates, Living easy in Punta Gorda
August 2014

About the Author

R andy Oates grew up in Little Rock, Arkansas, with parents who were very active and involved in the community. His father was a well-known physician and his mother was very active in politics and multiple volunteer organizations and was elected to the Arkansas House of Representatives in 1957. Oates is one of five members of his family who are graduates of the University of Arkansas, where his mother was a legendary cheerleader; and the family still has season tickets for Razorback football games. His grandfather on his mother's side, Harry Long of Arkansas City, Kansas, was his most important role model growing up. This was a man who dropped out of high school to help support his family and without any formal education became the town's pharmacist and later it's mayor. Long had a great sense of humor, was very outgoing, and treated everyone from the farmer in overalls to the local bank president with dignity and respect, which young Oates never forgot.

Oates education and career was in marketing and advertising, primarily for the financial industry. He loved his work and particularly enjoyed the creative aspect of the business. He considers his last position as the marketing director for Bank of the Ozarks to be one of the most rewarding and successful jobs of his career.

As a young man he started racing sailboats at the Grande Maumelle Sailing Club in Little Rock and served in various positions including treasurer and commodore of the club. He raced two-man sailboats for over 20 years and collected multiple regatta trophies. However, he considers his finest sailing accomplishment to have crewed with Max Mehlburger on his Swan 38, *Pirate*, which won the Marion to Bermuda ocean race. Oates also was an avid runner, cyclist and started racing triathlons in his fifties. He became a contender in his age group and the year he turned sixty was an Honorable Mention on USA Triathlon's All American team.

Oates is now a recovering paraplegic as a result of a common medical procedure gone tragically wrong two months before his sixty-fourth birthday. This book, *The Healing Begins Today*, is a true story based on the three journals he faithfully kept about his recovery following his injury. As he vividly demonstrates in the book, it can be extremely difficult at times to hang onto even the smallest window of hope, but the tenacity of the human spirit can be a wonderful thing. His mother and grandfather never gave up on anything and neither did he.